IMAGES
of America

MINGO COUNTY

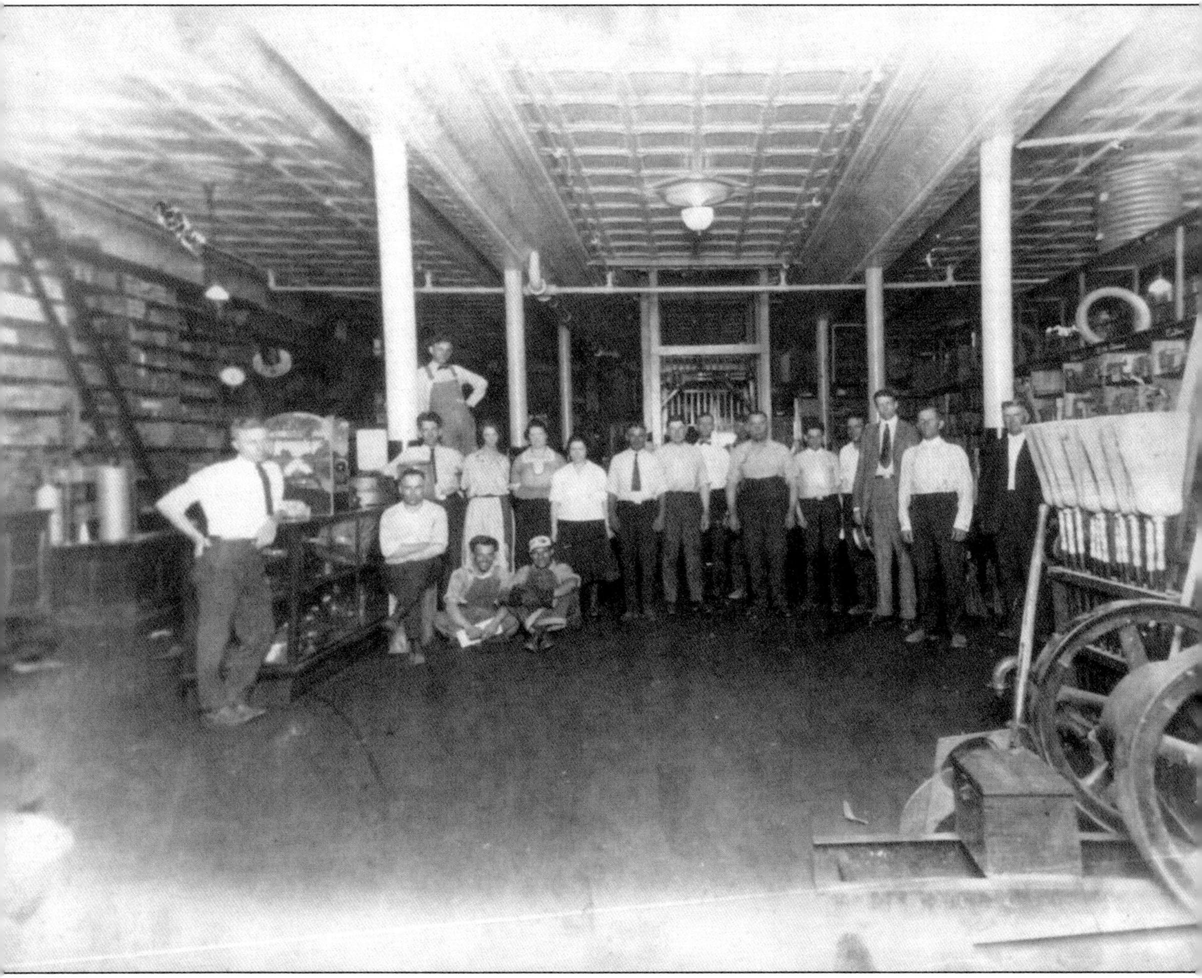

Pictured here is the Persinger Hardware & Supply Company in Williamson in 1923. From left to right are Howard M. Persinger Sr.; office staff Sid Smith, Hector Hancock, unidentified, Clyde Shockley (rear left) and a Mr. Vest, his two sisters, Mr. and Mrs. Fred Smith, O.E. Hogan's brother, M.G. Waskey, unidentified, Moses T. Persinger, Mr. Koontz, unidentified, Mr. Quisenberry, unidentified, and Mr. Hurst. Howard M. Persinger came to Williamson at the age of 16 to work at the Persinger Hardware & Supply Company. (Courtesy of Jeanne and Howard Persinger.)

On the Cover: This photograph of the Hatfield family was taken around 1897 at the family home on Beech Creek in Mingo County, West Virginia. Please see page 114 for more information. (Courtesy of Lahoma Lee Farley Schuller.)

IMAGES
of America

MINGO COUNTY

Andrew Chafin

ARCADIA
PUBLISHING

ISBN 978-1-4671-2097-5

Published by Arcadia Publishing
Charleston, South Carolina

Printed in the United States of America

Library of Congress Control Number: 2013945015

For all general information, please contact Arcadia Publishing:
Telephone 843-853-2070
Fax 843-853-0044
E-mail sales@arcadiapublishing.com
For customer service and orders:
Toll-Free 1-888-313-2665

Visit us on the Internet at www.arcadiapublishing.com

This book is dedicated to Charlotte Hope Oliver Sanders, who chronicled the life and times of Mingo County's inhabitants for 68 years.

Contents

ACKNOWLEDGMENTS

Every effort has been made to provide accurate information. Much of the information regarding the photographs was based on information provided by those contributing the photographs and stories which had been passed down from family member to family member, so minor discrepancies may exist. Every attempt was made to obtain a variety of pictures from as many contributors as possible. The long and varied history of Mingo County and the many changes that have occurred since its beginning made it impossible to include all that has occurred. This book is intended to be a "backward glance" of life the way it was.

I wish to thank the many Mingo Countians who generously came forth with their photographs and stories depicting the county's past. I hope this book justifies the faith they had in me and reflects life in Mingo County in the earlier years in a meaningful manner.

I want to thank Patty J. Nichols for typing, editing, and arranging this book and the many others who gave both their time and their photographs and shared their special stories and recollections that made this book possible. In no particular order, I would like to thank the following folks for their kind assistance: William Woodward; Kay Vance; Dimple Tiller Allara; Lahoma Lee Farley Schuller; Hester Kinder Keatley; Clarence and Sue Hatfield; Hazel M. Chafin; Leleah Matney; Jennifer Ooten; Williamson Public Library employees director Joseph Scarberry and Sarah Sexton; Eddie Nenni; Norville Estep; Ty Chafin; Margaret Chafin; Jack McGuire; William Terry Sanders; James W. Sanders; Nona Sanders; Leif Sanders; Beverly and Frank Horton; Rebecca Hoskins Goodwin; West Virginia State Archives; Joshua Byers and the folks at the *Williamson Daily News*; Natalie Young, executive director of the Tug Valley Chamber of Commerce; Marvin Vernatter PE, CPA; and my brother, Sen. H. Truman Chafin.

Finally, a special thanks to the folks at Arcadia Publishing, especially Rebekah Collinsworth, who believed in this project and that there should be an Images of America: *Mingo County* book to chronicle the history of our county. Thanks for your support.

INTRODUCTION

Mingo County, the youngest county in West Virginia, was formed in 1895 from parts of Logan County. The county, named in honor of the Mingo Indian tribe, the earliest known settlers of the region, borders five counties in West Virginia, two in Kentucky, and one in Virginia. The county has a population of about 27,000.

The founding of the county occurred after a moonshiner claimed that the Logan County Court, which had found him guilty, did not have jurisdiction over his case because his moonshine still was located in Lincoln County. A land survey revealed that the moonshiner was correct. The state legislature then determined that Logan County was too large for the adequate administration of justice and formed Mingo County.

In the 1800s, the famous Hatfield-McCoy Feud, which actually started during the Civil War, expanded throughout southwestern West Virginia and eastern Kentucky. Both the Hatfields and McCoys supported the South, but Asa McCoy served in the Union Army. After his release from the army, he was killed and the McCoys blamed the Hatfields. When the two families went to court over the ownership of a razorback hog, a Kentucky jury awarded the hog to the Hatfields. Soon after the trial, a Hatfield who was one of the trial's witnesses was found shot to death.

During an election day in Kentucky in August 1862, three McCoy boys stabbed and shot Ellison Hatfield, brother of Hatfield leader Anderson "Devil Anse" Hatfield. Devil Anse and his posse captured the McCoy boys, and warned that if Ellison died, the McCoy boys would be executed. Ellison died two days later and the McCoys were taken down on the banks of the Tug River and shot to death. The feud boiled over.

The county seat, in Williamson, was incorporated in 1892 and named after Wallace J. Williamson, who owned all the land where Williamson now stands. Other towns in the county would later include Matewan, Delbarton, Kermit, Gilbert, and more than 20 unincorporated communities.

In May 1920, the Matewan Massacre became national news when Matewan chief of police "Smilin'" Sid Hatfield and his group of union miners had a shootout with the Baldwin-Felts detectives who had come to town to evict striking coal miners from houses owned by the coal operators. The battle resulted in the deaths of seven detectives and four townspeople, including Matewan mayor Cabell Testerman. Police Chief Hatfield married the mayor's widow two weeks later. Never in American history has a gunfight on the streets changed so many lives. The shootout led to the greatest confrontation in history between the government and the labor movement in Logan County.

In 1934, circuit judge B.F. Howard, in appealing for an orderly election in Williamson, referred to the county as the "Hell Hole of Creation."

Today, the residents of Mingo County live peacefully beside the Tug Fork River, protected by multimillion-dollar floodwalls after decades of floods of historical proportions. All is well, even the Hatfields and the McCoys are now friends.

One

Family, Friends, and Neighbors

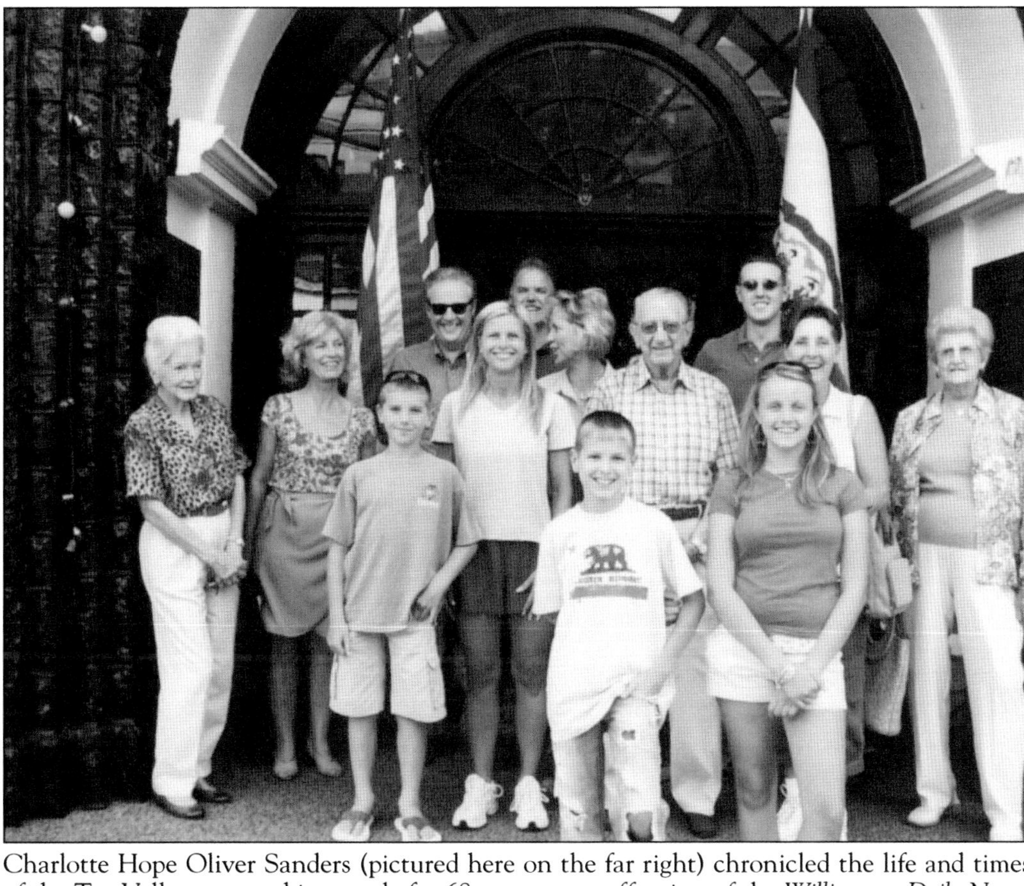

Charlotte Hope Oliver Sanders (pictured here on the far right) chronicled the life and times of the Tug Valley area and its people for 68 years as a staff writer of the *Williamson Daily News*. Charlotte was an inspiration to may young Tug Valley writers and freely gave her suggestions, assistance, and support to many, including the author of this book. She was an award-winning journalist and was acknowledged by the West Virginia Senate for outstanding achievements in the field of journalism. (Courtesy of Jamie H. Weaver.)

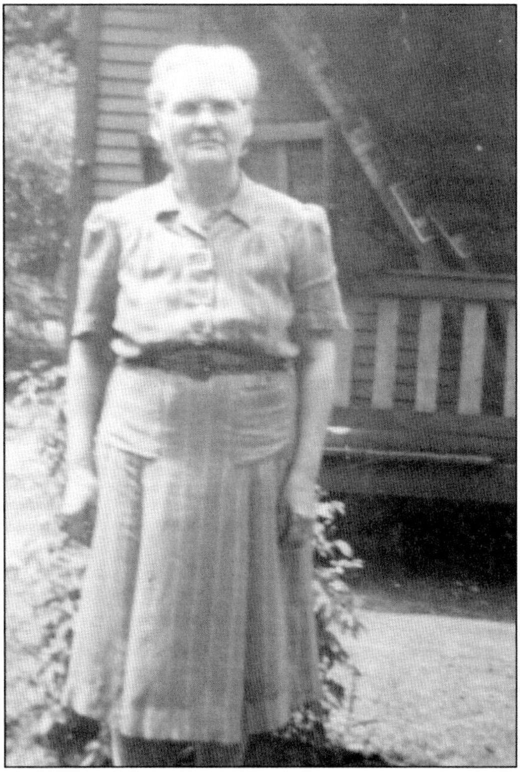

Sarah Elizabeth Dooley Woodward is pictured outside her home in Red Jacket, West Virginia, in the 1950s. Sarah was a strong woman with a great love for her family. (Courtesy of William Woodward.)

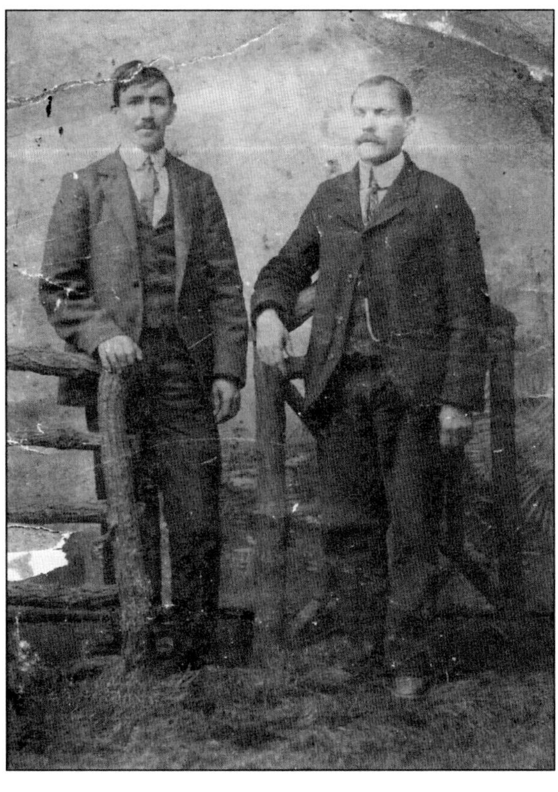

This late-1890s image taken in Red Jacket, West Virginia, shows William Woodward Sr., left, and Thomas Dooley, who was William Woodward's maternal grandfather. Since it could take up to 15 minutes to produce a picture negative, folks were told to be perfectly still while the negative processing took place. (Courtesy of William Woodward.)

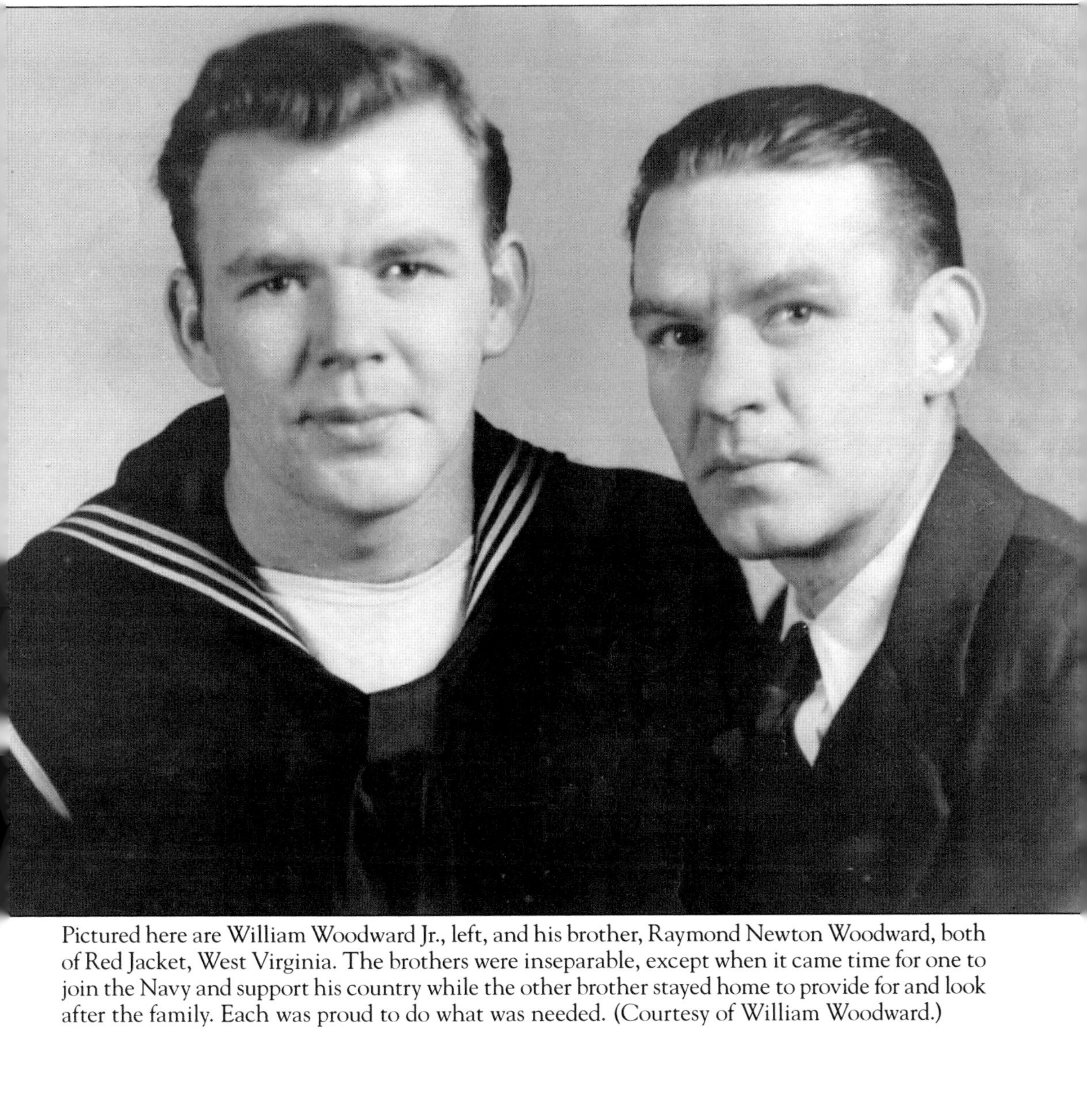

Pictured here are William Woodward Jr., left, and his brother, Raymond Newton Woodward, both of Red Jacket, West Virginia. The brothers were inseparable, except when it came time for one to join the Navy and support his country while the other brother stayed home to provide for and look after the family. Each was proud to do what was needed. (Courtesy of William Woodward.)

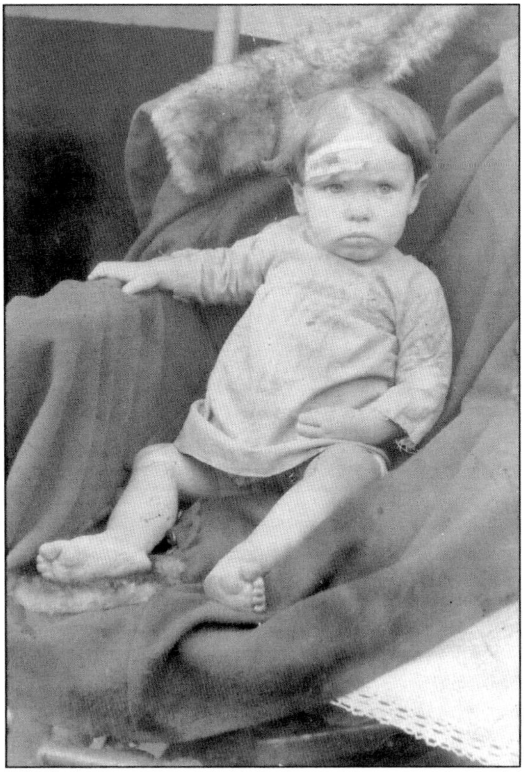

The baby pictured here is Alice Richardson. Her mother was Mattie Richardson of Red Jacket, West Virginia. This picture taken in the early 1920s and shows little Alice with a bandage on her head. It is not known what brought about her injury, but she did have a full recovery. She was lovingly known in her family as little Alice. (Courtesy of William Woodward.)

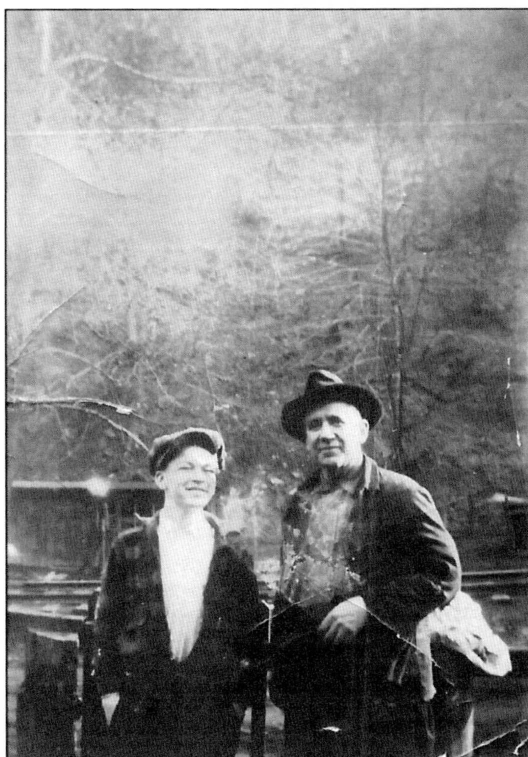

Pictured here are Raymond Woodward, left, and Daniel Woodward. These folks lived in Red Jacket, West Virginia, and were known and respected as a hardworking and reverent family. (Courtesy of William Woodward.)

This photograph was taken in Red Jacket, West Virginia, in the 1920s. Houses of the day had large porches where families socialized and relaxed, as time and weather permitted. In those days, it would have been unheard of to build a home without a large porch. (Courtesy of William Woodward.)

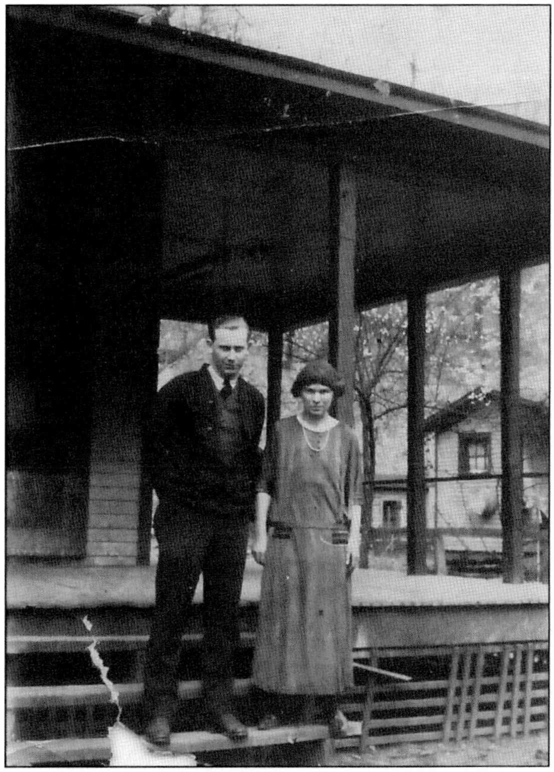

This lovely summer porch scene is at the home of Mrs. Cummins in Red Jacket in the 1940s. The children are Bill Cummins, left, and his sister Rebecca Cummins. The rich and lush soil of Mingo County was ideal for growing plants and vegetables. The cool mountain breezes encouraged the growth of the ferns and ivy. The summers were enjoyed and the times moved at a slow and peaceful pace. (Courtesy of William Woodward.)

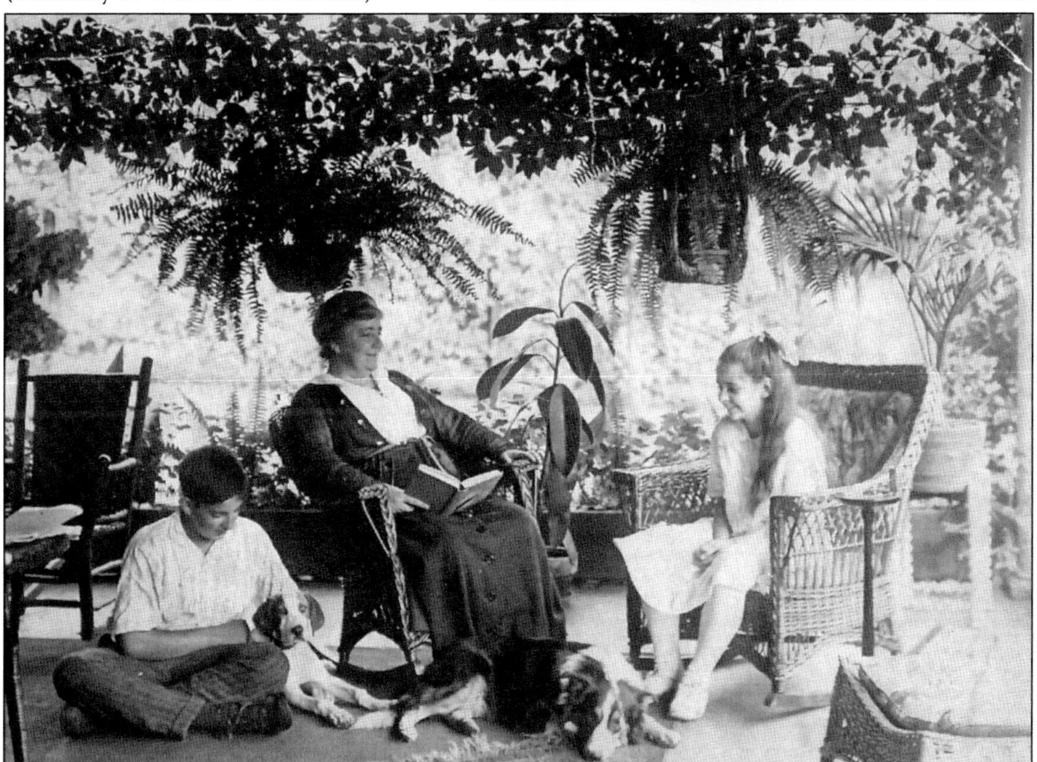

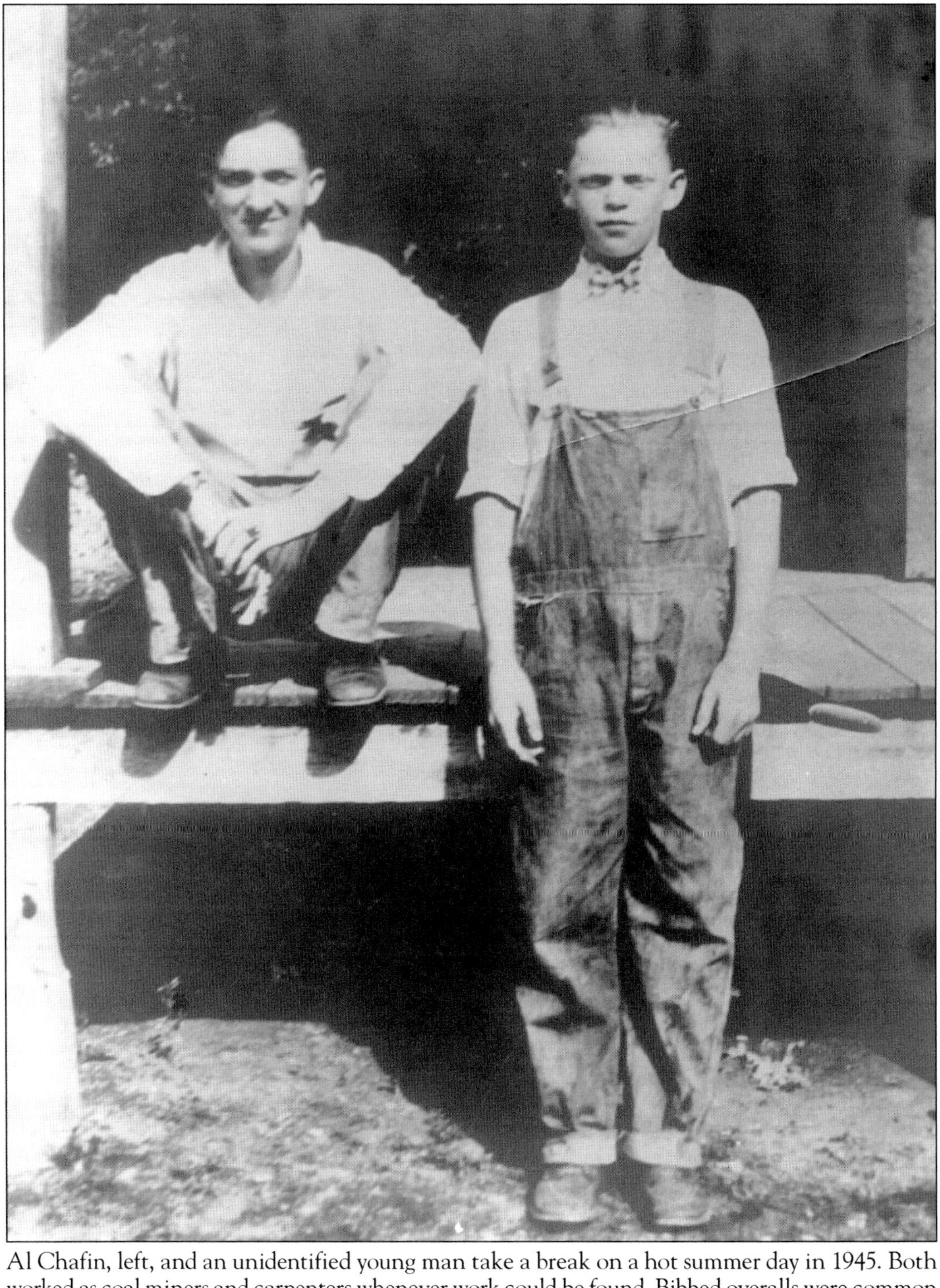

Al Chafin, left, and an unidentified young man take a break on a hot summer day in 1945. Both worked as coal miners and carpenters whenever work could be found. Bibbed overalls were common for miners and farmers during this time period. (Courtesy of Hazel M. Chafin.)

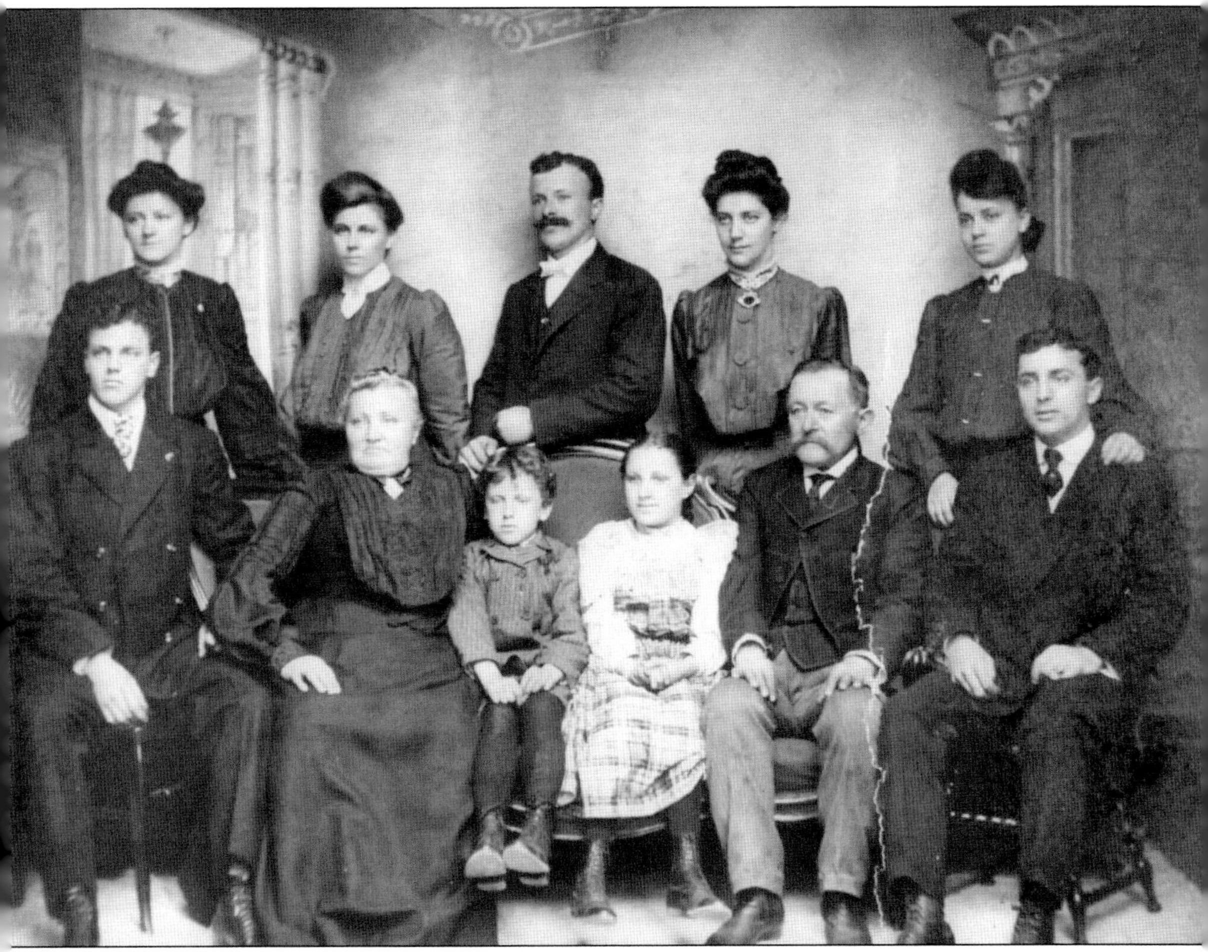

Members of the Allara family are pictured here. Frank M. Allara's grandparents are seated on the sofa with his aunt and uncles. Peter Matoon Allara (Frank Allara's father) is standing with his four sisters behind the sofa. The others are brothers and sisters; Allara's mother and father are seated on the sofa. (Courtesy of Dimple Tiller Allara.)

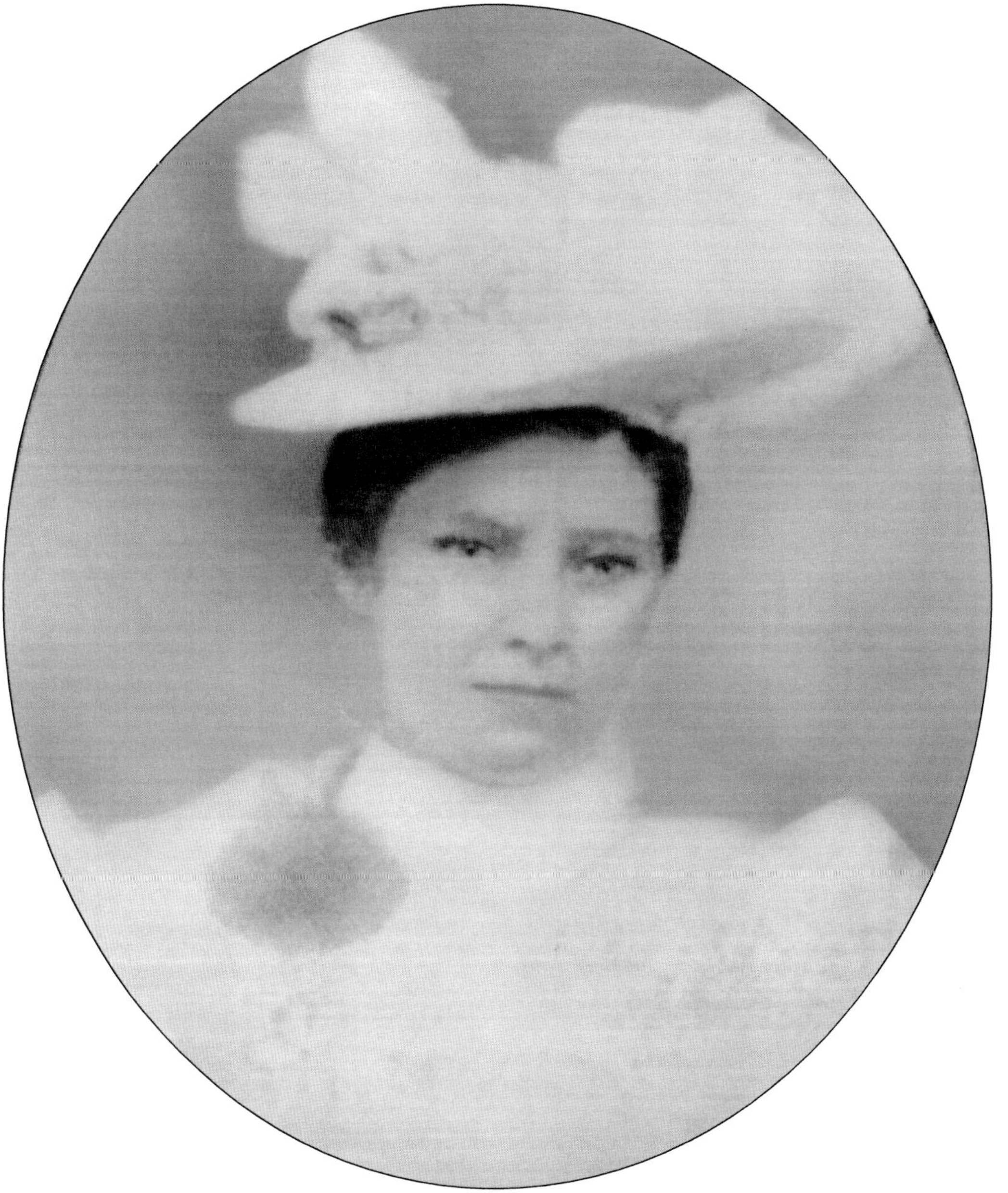

Mary Maynard Farley, pictured here, was born in 1879 and passed away in 1911. She was the mother of Robert, Bruce, William, Rush, Sally, Nancy, and Lula Rush and was the grandmother of Lahoma (contributor of this photograph).This portrait was taken in 1907. Mary was a schoolteacher and was riding in a horse-drawn wagon with her husband on the way to a teacher's meeting when a gust of wind blew her hat into the creek. Her husband, James A. Farley (Jim), stopped on the way to the meeting and bought her the lovely hat that she wears in this photograph. (Courtesy of Lahoma Lee Farley Schuller.)

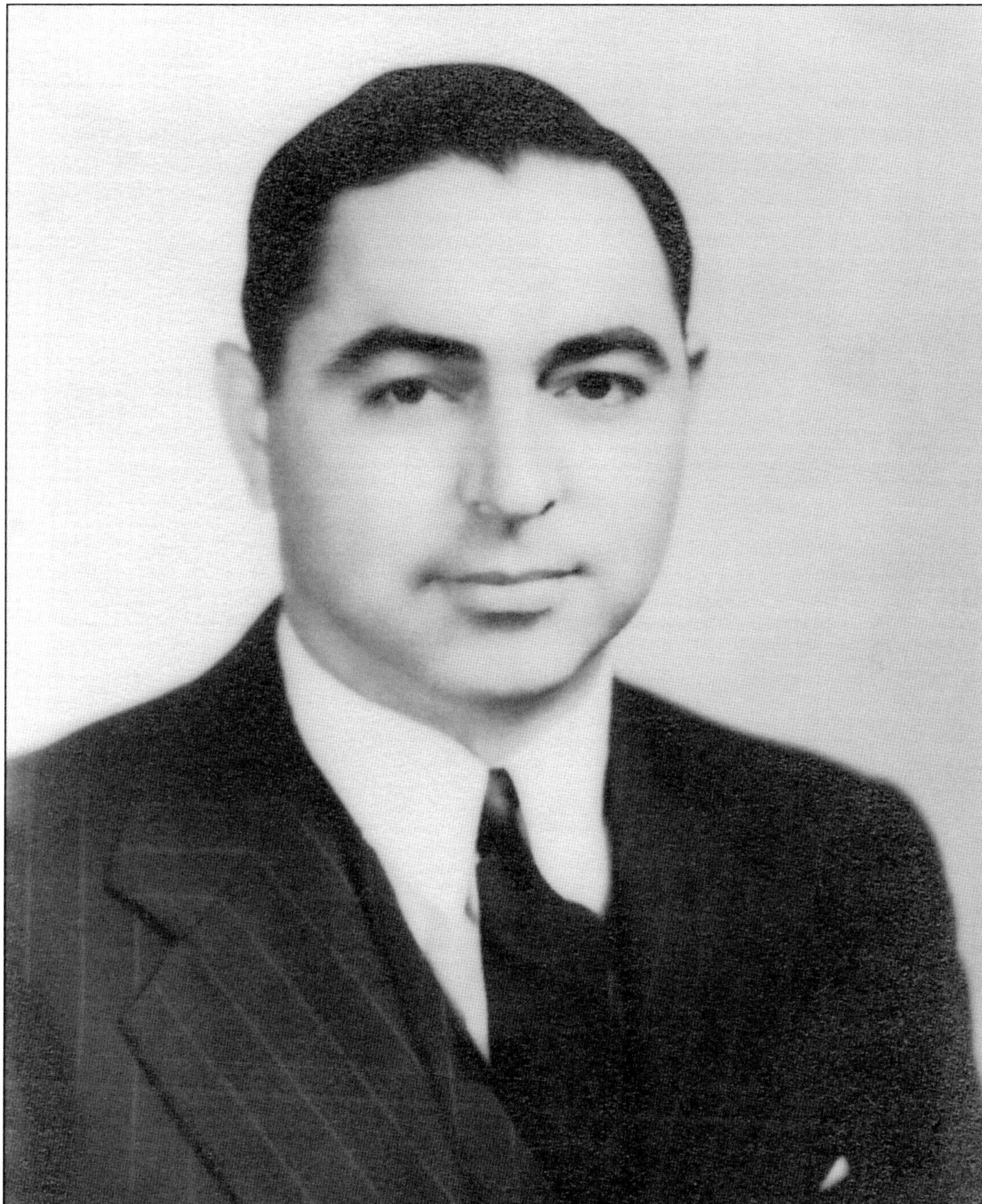

Pictured here is James Robert "Bob" Farley, DDS. In addition to being the local dentist, Farley was a civic leader, democratic politician, sportsman, mayor of Delbarton, president of the board of education, and a member of the county court for Mingo County. He was a member of the Baptist faith. (Courtesy of Lehoma Lee Farley Schuller.)

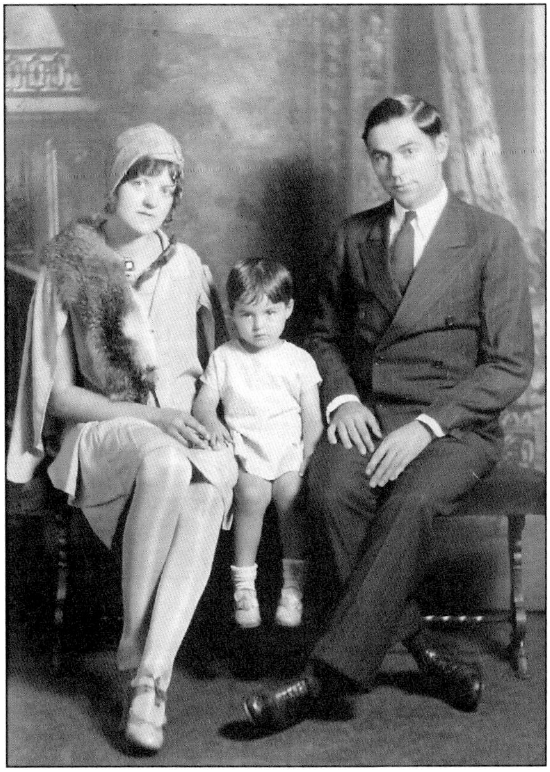

In this 1930 photograph, James Robert "Bob" Farley, DDS, is pictured with his lovely wife, Gladys, and their daughter, Lahoma. Lahoma's father felt that it was important to document life in the form of professional photographs, so during the course of her life she sat for photographs at regular intervals. (Courtesy of Lahoma Lee Farley Schuller.)

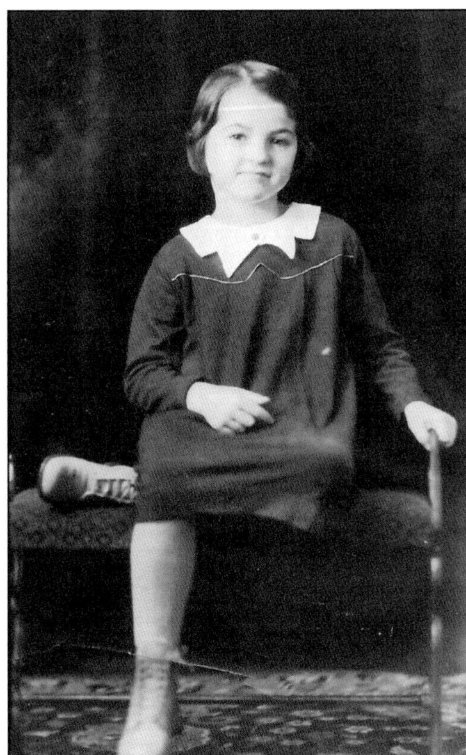

James Robert "Bob" Farley, DDS, liked to have pictures taken of his family on a regular basis. Little Lahoma Lee Farley was seven years old and remembers the long stockings she wore on the day her father had this picture made. (Courtesy of Lahoma Lee Farley Schuller.)

This 1930s photograph shows, from left to right, Katherine Isaac and her friend, Loretta, posing with Katherine's father, Charles Isaac. Note the automobile in the background. Few people were able to afford these automobiles in the late 1930s. (Courtesy of Hazel M. Chafin.)

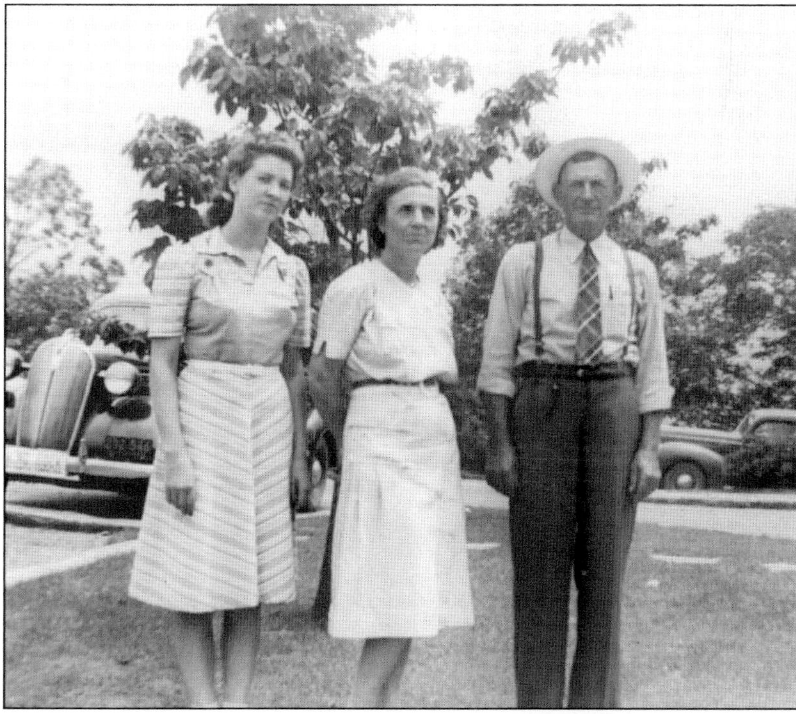

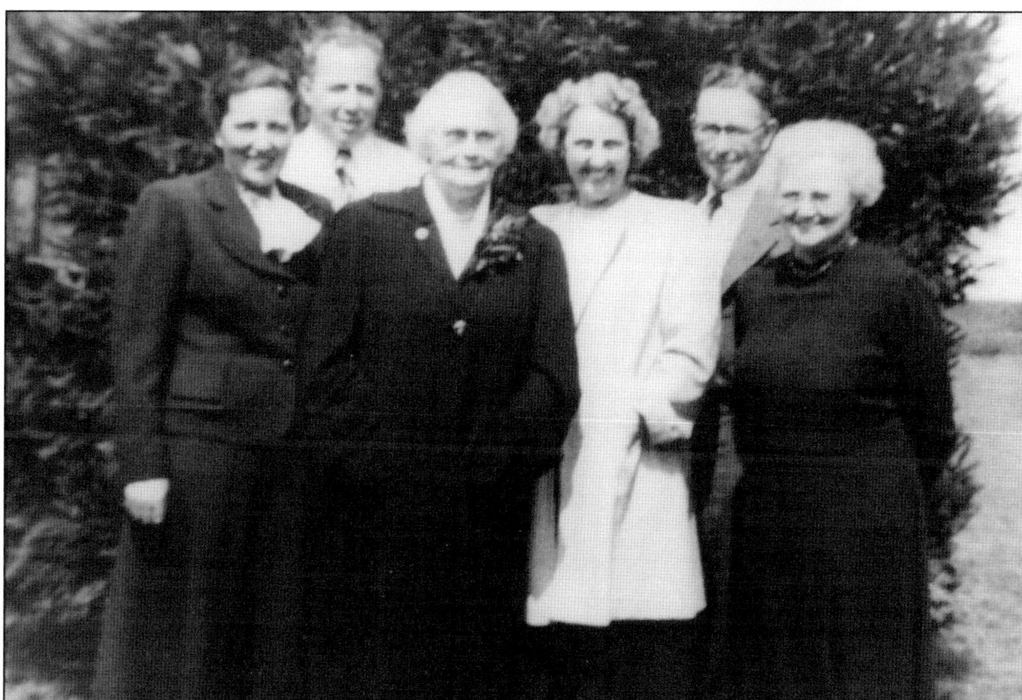

Jenny Allara is pictured with her children. From left to right are Josephine Hope, Frank M. Allara, Marie Brown, Jack Allara, and Elizabeth Ross. One child, a baby boy, had died and was buried at Fort Gay in Louisa, Kentucky. This photograph was taken in the 1940s in Matewan. (Courtesy of Dimple Tiller Allara.)

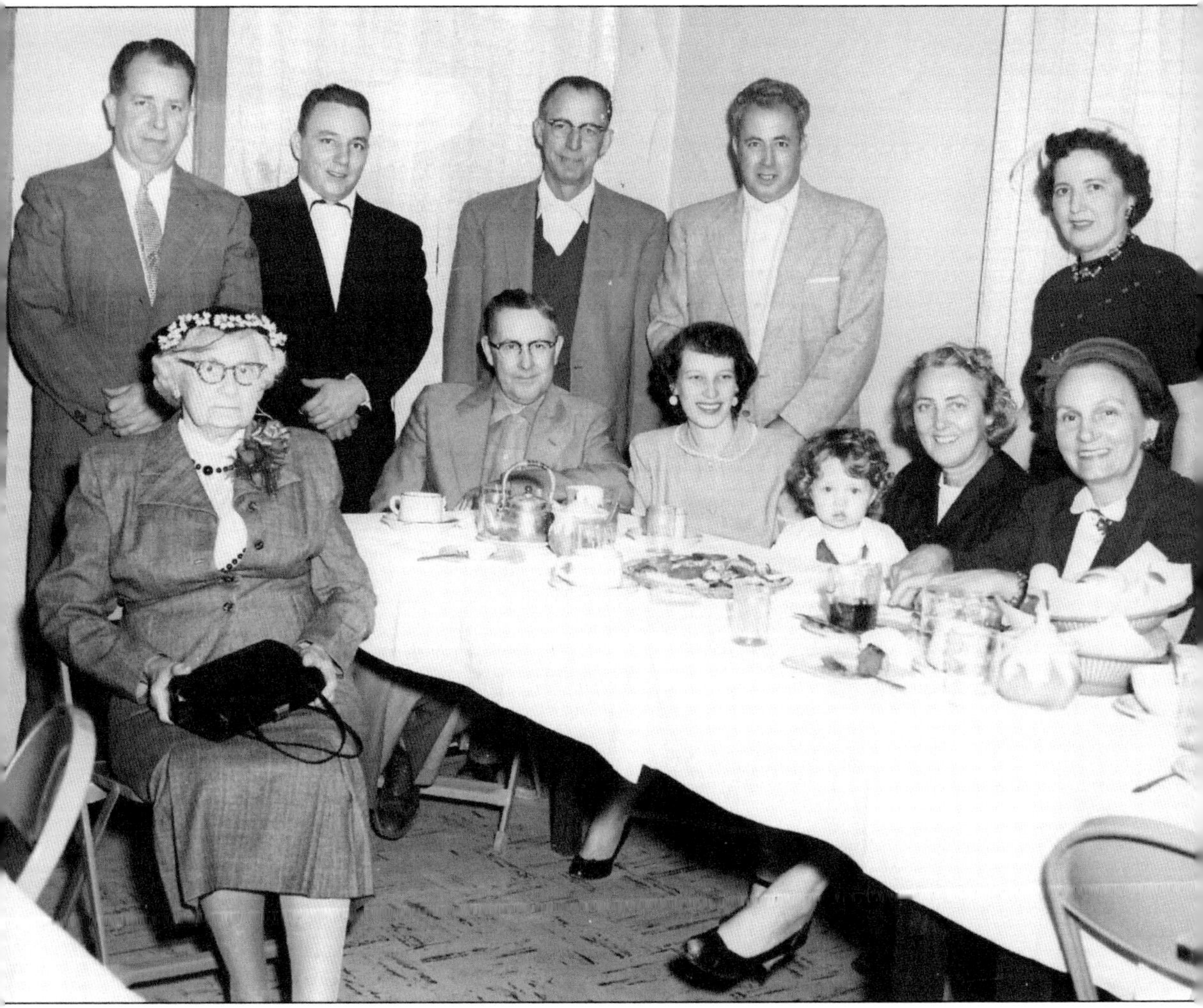

The Allaras, having ancestry from Italy, had a strong sense of family. Here they are pictured at a celebration, perhaps honoring Jenny Allara, the lovely lady seated in front of the table. Shown from left to right are (first row) Jack Allara, Ernestine Price, Anna Marie Finley, Marie Brown, and Mattie Ruth Allara; (second row) Terry Hope, Victor Allara, E.E. Brown, Frank M. Allara, Marie Brown, and Josephine Hope. (Courtesy of Dimple Tiller Allara.)

This family portrait was taken around 1910. The woman standing with the lovely hat is Emma Buskirk McCoy, the mother of the children in the picture. Emma's family came from Amsterdam, Holland, after the Revolutionary War. The father is Sailor McCoy. The children are, from left to right, Mattie, William, Nollis (seated on father's lap), Sally, and Nellie, seated in front. (Courtesy of Dimple Tiller Allara.)

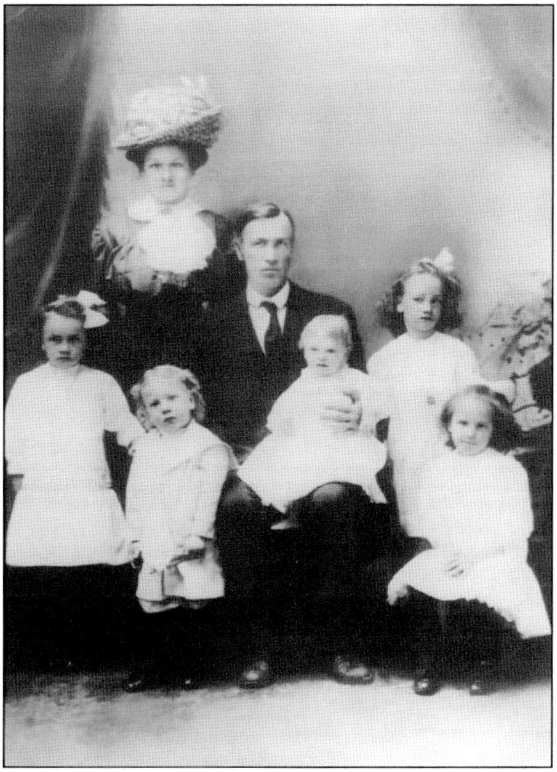

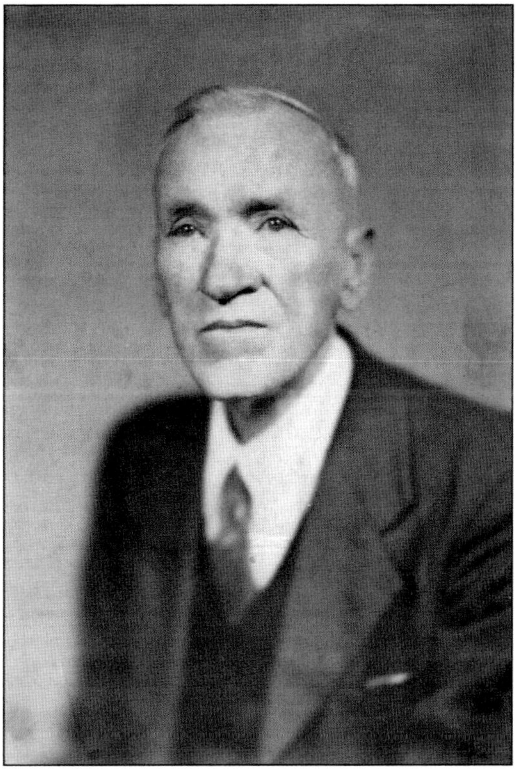

This photograph is of Sailor McCoy in later years. The development and processing of photographs took as long as 15 minutes, during which time folks were told to sit very still. Often, this led to the seriousness in the expressions of those photographed, although here McCoy has an ever-so-slight look of happiness in his eyes. (Courtesy of Dimple Tiller Allara.)

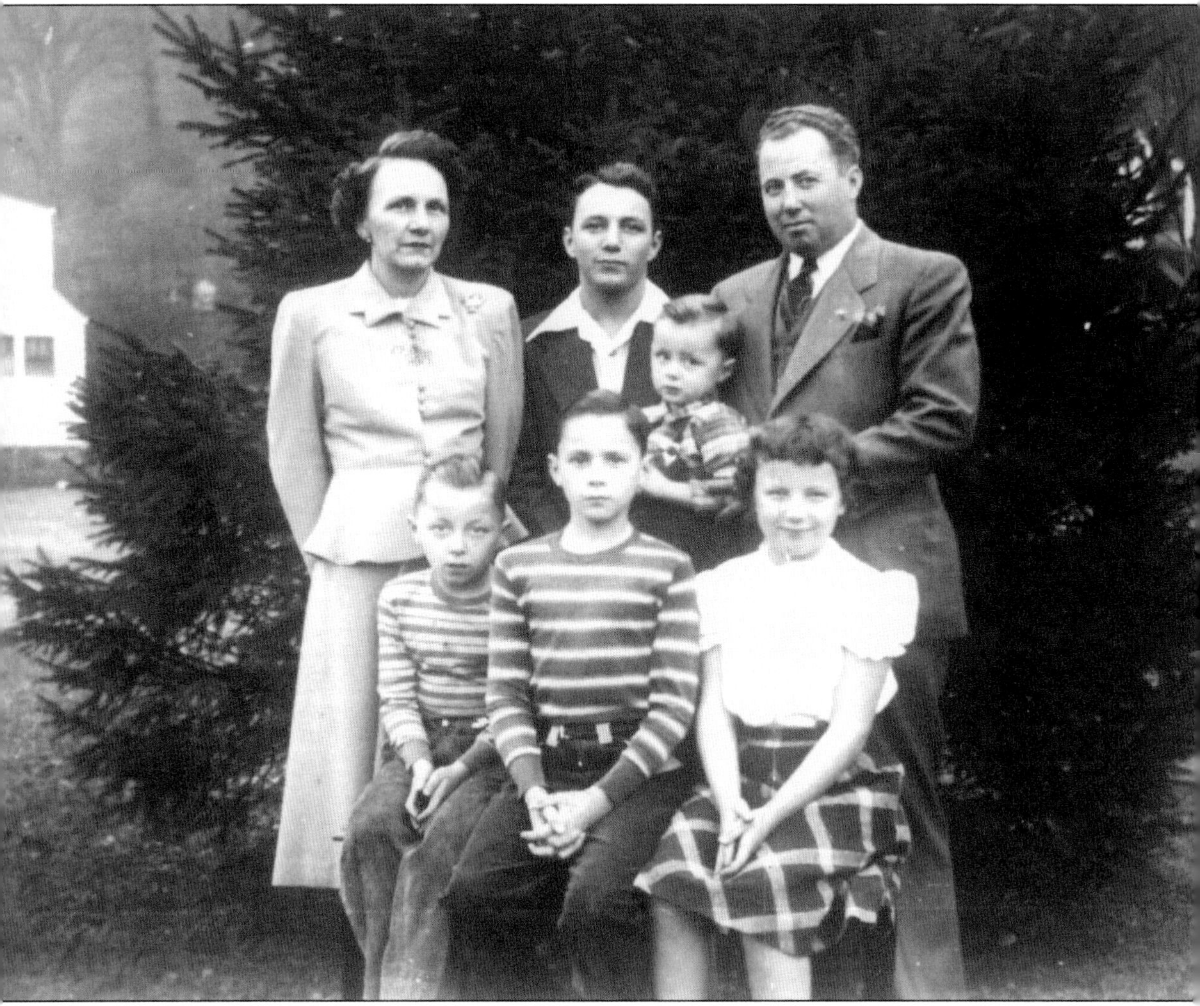

From left to right in this family portrait are (first row) Frank Winford Allara, Robert Keith Allara (baby boy), and Jacqueline Jo Allara; (second row) Mattie Ruth McCoy Allara, Victor G. Allara, Frank M. Allara, and William Morris Allara. (Courtesy of Dimple Tiller Allara.)

Mattie Ruth McCoy Allara, wife of Frank Marion Allara, was born on September 13, 1904. Mattie was a schoolteacher, and her father, Sailor McCoy, sent her to Greenbrier Girls' School in preparation for her work as a teacher. (Courtesy of Dimple Tiller Allara.)

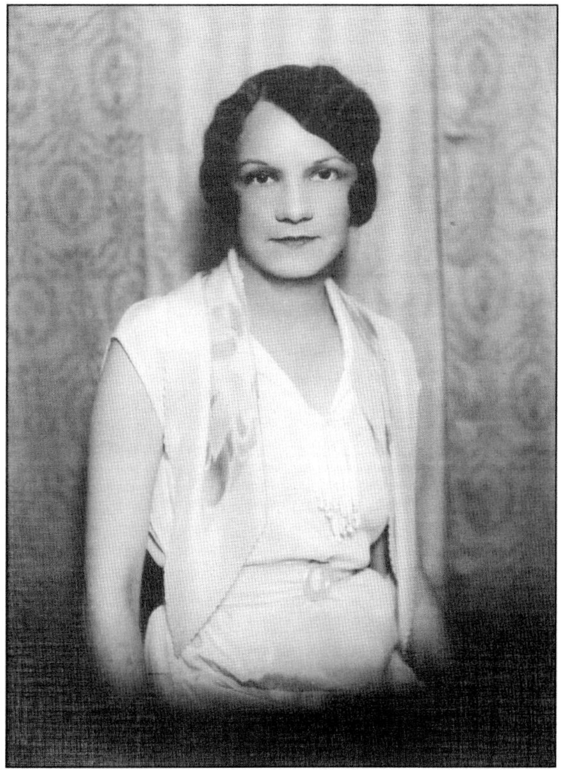

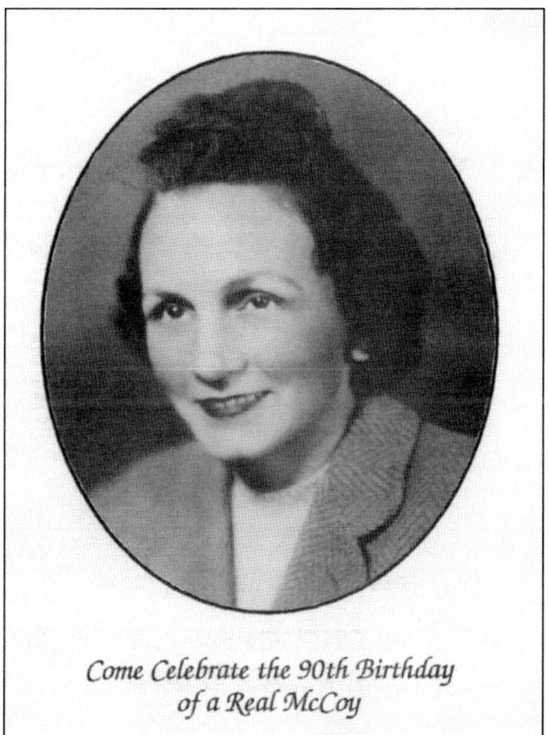

This is an invitation for the 90th birthday of Mattie Ruth McCoy, wife of Frank M. Allara. "Buck" Harless of Gilbert, West Virginia, hosted this 90th birthday party with many friends and family joining in the celebration. Mattie lived to be 93 years of age and passed away on June 22, 1997. (Courtesy of Dimple Tiller Allara.)

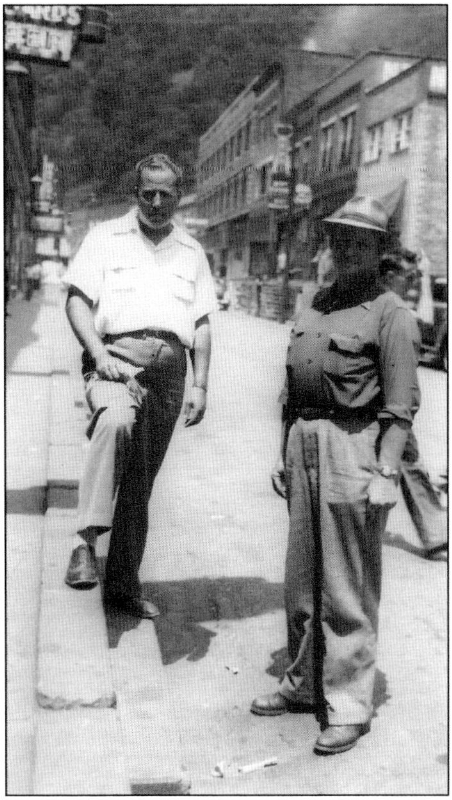

In the warm summer days of June 1949, two friends stop to chat and share the time of day. On the left is Frank Allara; the man on the right is friend and neighbor Tom Maynard. (Courtesy of Dimple Tiller Allara.)

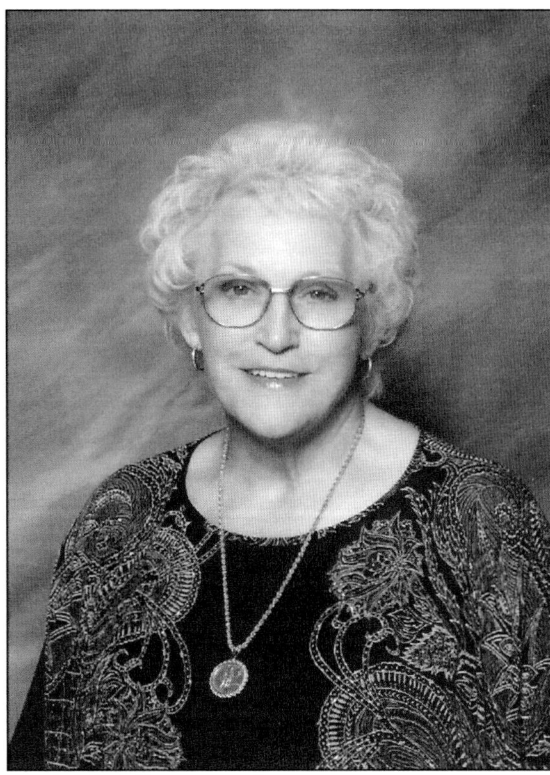

Pictured here is Dimple Fay Tiller Allara. Her parents were Mose and Elizabeth Tiller. Dimple was married to Victor G. Allara Sr. on November 17, 1956. She and her husband had two children, Victor Glenn Allara Jr. and Emily Virginia Allara. Emily Virginia was named for a sister of her father who had passed away at an early age. Dimple continues to live in Mingo County and is very active in participating in and supporting Mingo County. She has touched the lives of many and continues to do so. (Courtesy of Dimple Tiller Allara.)

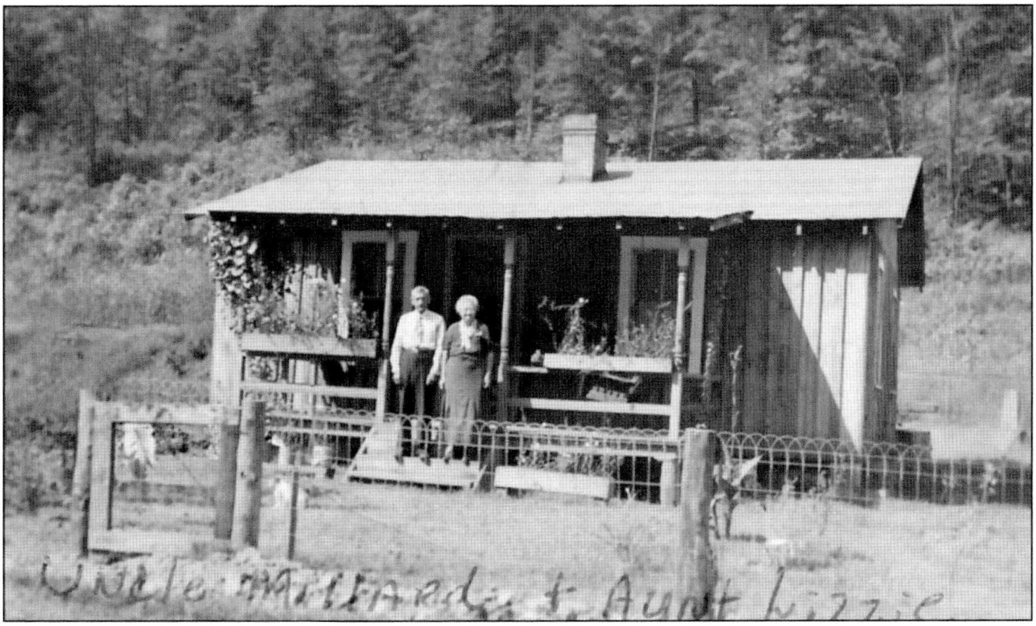

This is the home of Millard and Lizzie Kinder. When Millard's half-brother and his wife were unable to take care of their son, who was suffering from tuberculosis, his Uncle Millard went and got the child, Raymond, and raised him. Other half-brothers and sisters of Uncle Millard were Theodore, Omi, Estil Kinder, Andy Kinder, Christina "Teenie" Kinder, and Lawrence Kinder. (Courtesy of Hester Kinder Keatley.)

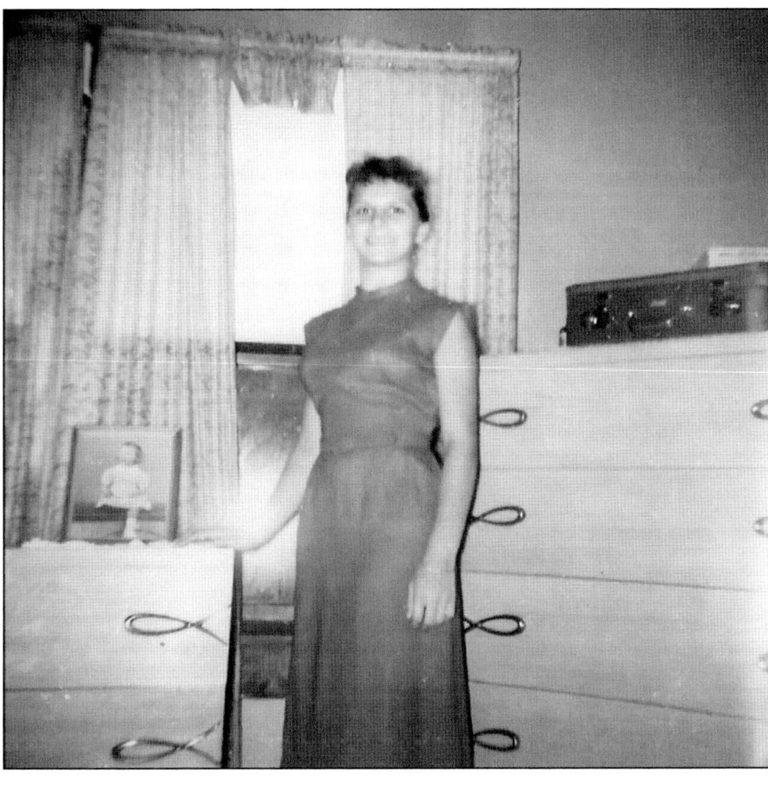

Pictured here is Hester Kinder. This was the first dress that Hester ever made. Her mother had made all of their clothes in the past and was considered by many to be a very good seamstress. (Courtesy of Hester Kinder Keatley.)

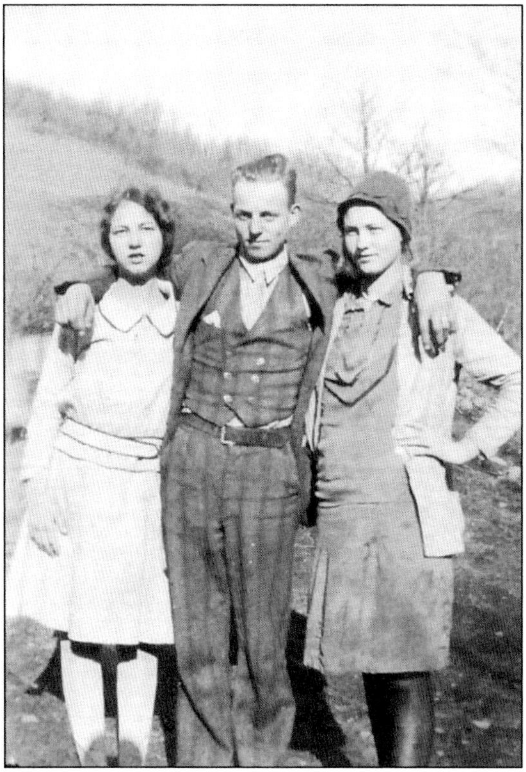

This trio displayed the 1920s dress fashion in grand style. The rip-roaring 1920s inspired thousands to dress for the times, and Mingo County was no exception. Common features of the 1920s were beads, sequins, lace fringes, chiffon, satin, and flowers, all shiny and shimmering. Pictured here from left to right are Jane Chafin, Tom Chafin, and Biddie Chafin. (Courtesy of Clarence and Sue Hatfield.)

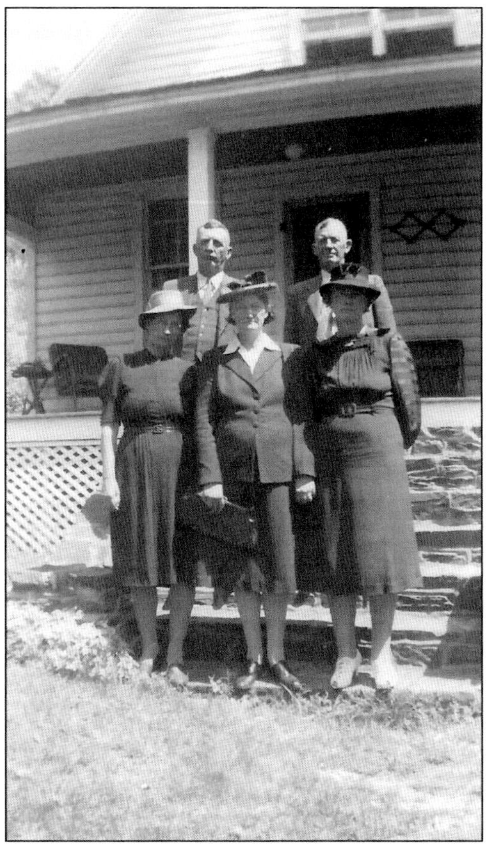

Pictured here from left to right are (first row) Bessie, Mary, and Mattie Isaac; (second row) Ben and Charlie Isaac. This picture taken in the late 1940s in Matewan shows the stylish dress of the day. (Courtesy of Hazel M. Chafin.)

Posing sweetly for a picture here are Althea Reed and the children, from left to right, Debbie, Jerry, and Cindy Reed. This photograph was taken in New Town. Althea was the beloved aunt of Clarence Hatfield. (Courtesy of Clarence and Sue Hatfield.)

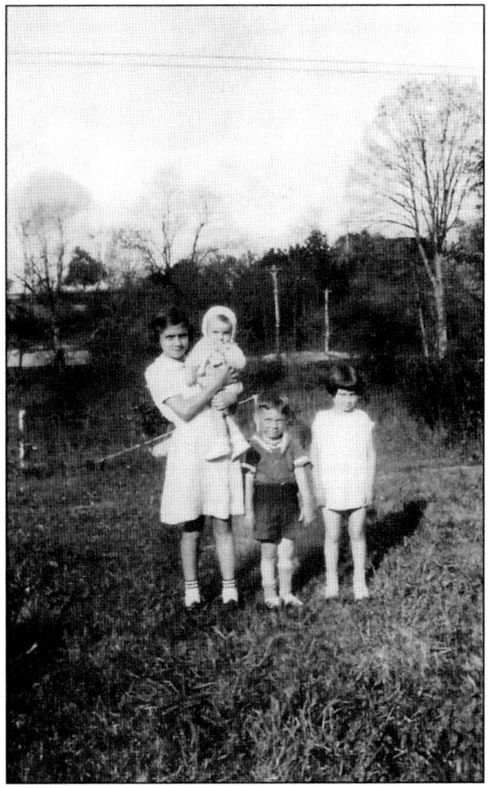

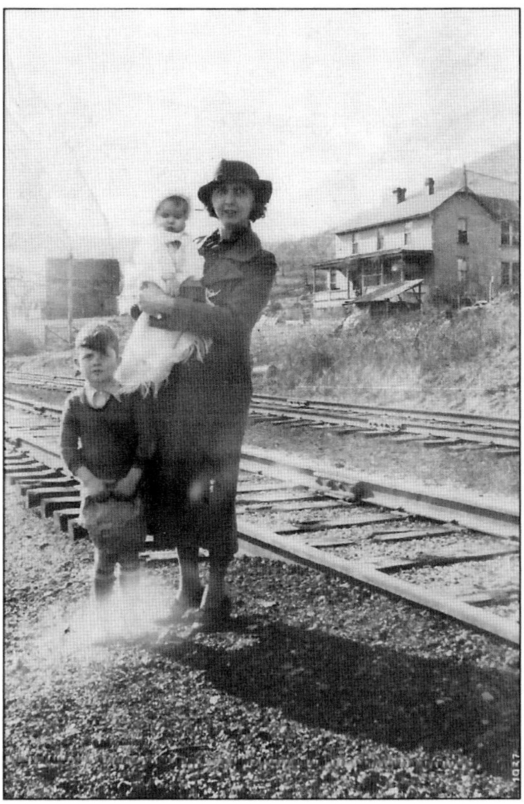

Pictured from left to right are C.D., Glenna (the baby), and Nannie Stump. Train travel was often the means for traveling long distances and brought with it the pleasure of anticipated arrivals or the sadness of departure. (Courtesy of Clarence and Sue Hatfield.)

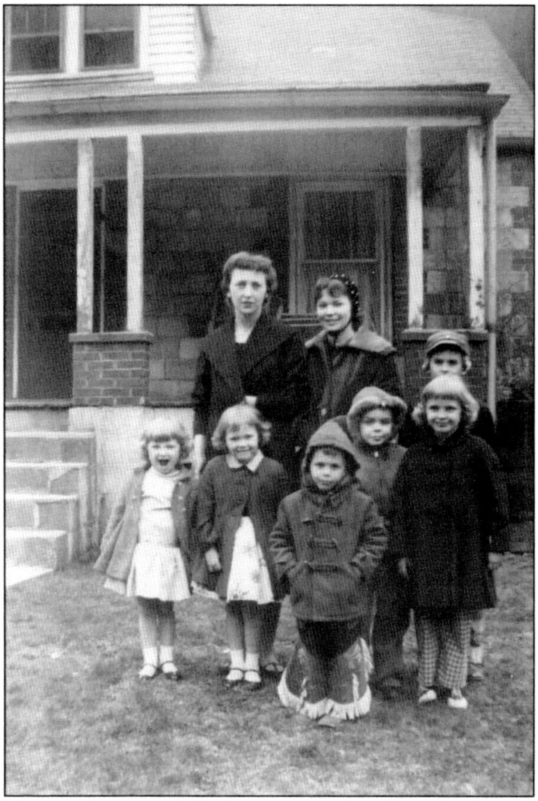

Jackie Isaac and Jeanne Chafin pose behind a group of neighborhood children in this early-1950s photograph that was taken in front of the Tom C. Chafin house at New Town. The children are, from left to right, Diane Isaac, Irma Lou Isaac, Truman Chafin, Chris LaPorte, and Vickie Ann Isaac. Behind Vickie Ann is Sam LaPorte. (Courtesy of Hazel M. Chafin.)

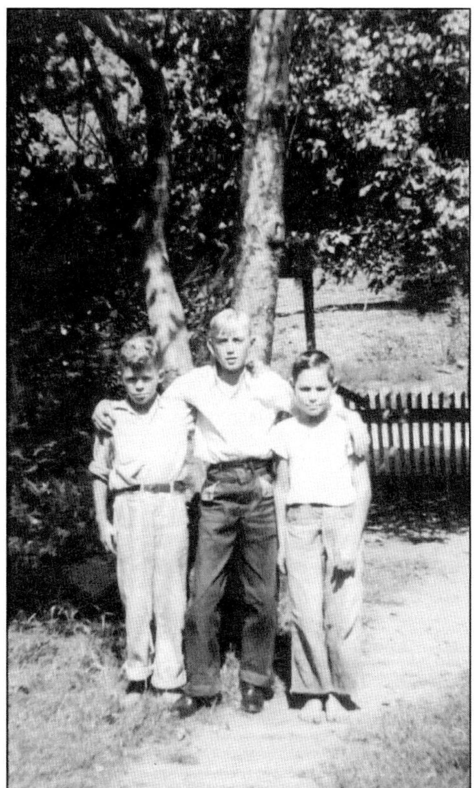

This 1930s photograph was taken at Meader, a small, unincorporated Mingo County community. From left to right are Jack Isaac, Darrell Kinder, and a friend, ? Harmon. Jack later entered the US Navy, and Darrell moved to Detroit, Michigan. (Courtesy of Hazel M. Chafin.)

Jacqueline Smith of New Town poses for this late-1940s photograph. Jacqueline married Ray Isaac, and the couple had several children, including Rocky, Phillip, Vickie Ann, Irma Lou, and Candice. The family moved to the Washington, DC, area in the 1950s. (Courtesy of Hazel M. Chafin.)

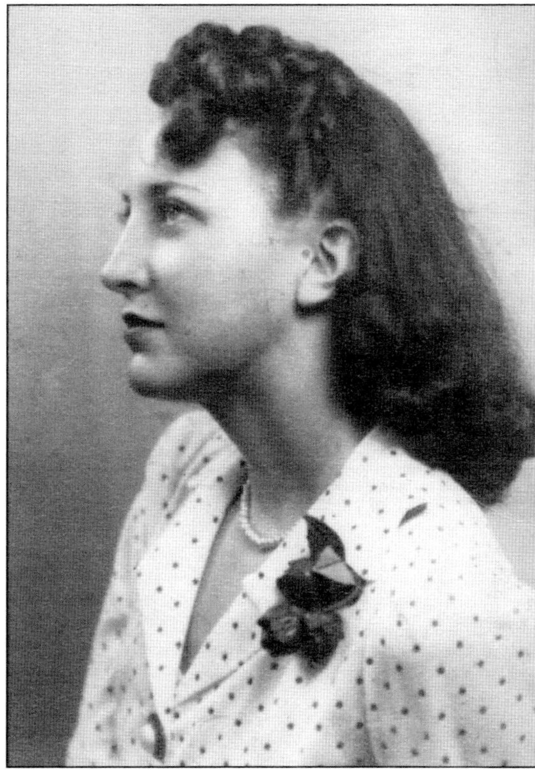

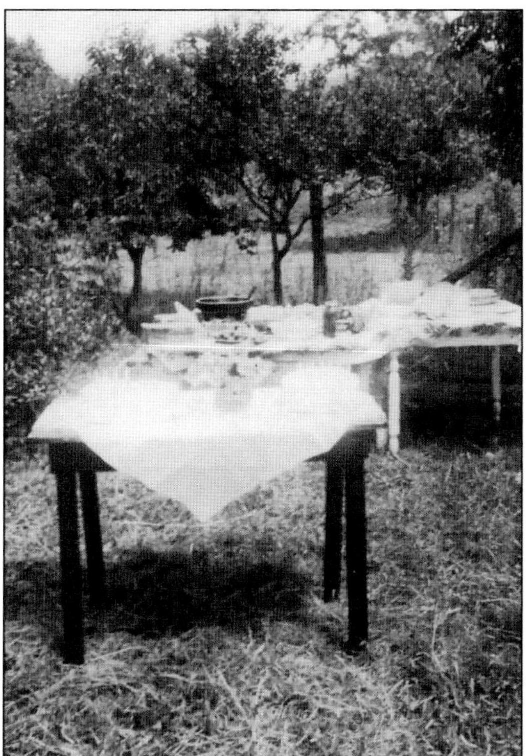

On the Fourth of July at the home of Howard and Josie King, the tables are laden with a bounty of food for the summer celebration. (Courtesy of Clarence and Sue Hatfield.)

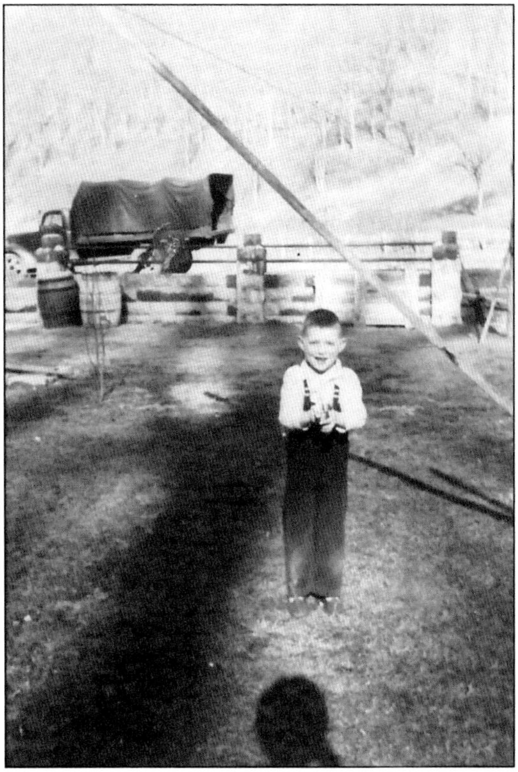

Young Wetzel Hatfield poses in the yard of his father, Dutch Hatfield, in New Town. In the background is the old Red Jacket Coal Company truck. The miners bought their supplies at the company store. Script was provided by the mines as a form of payment for the work performed by the miners. Often, the script was insufficient to pay the monthly bills. (Courtesy of Clarence and Sue Hatfield.)

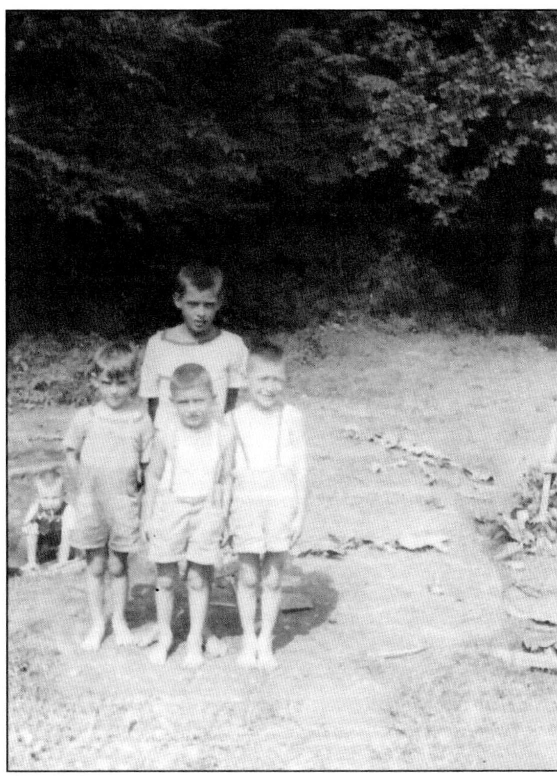

This is an early-1940s photograph of, from left to right, Joe Hatfield, Clarence Hatfield, and Wetzel Hatfield. In the back is Eugene Hatfield and on the far left on the ground is Tom Hatfield. This image was taken in the backyard of Dutch Hatfield, a prominent member of the Hatfield family. (Courtesy of Clarence and Sue Hatfield.)

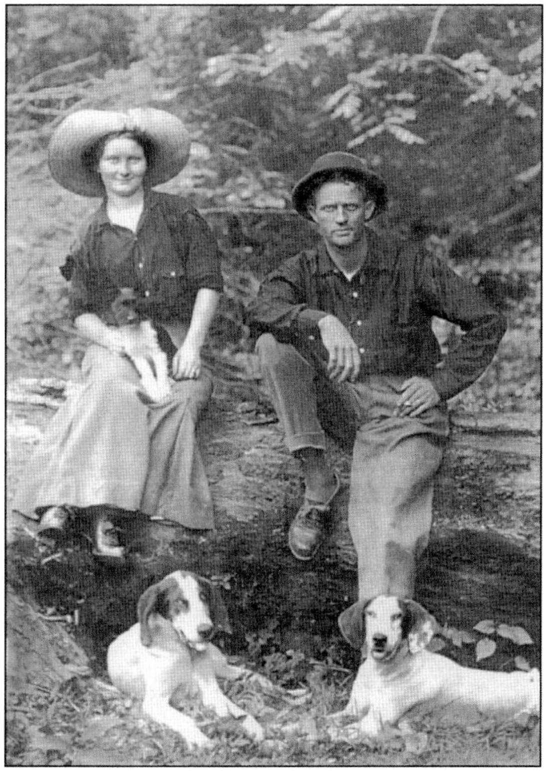

India Chambers Hoskins and John Wesley Hoskins are pictured with their canine companions. John had served for a period of time as the chief of police in Matewan. John and India had three daughters: Nina, Hope, and Joan. At the age of 35, John Hoskins was found dead in the Mitchell Branch mine of the Red Jacket Consolidated Coal & Coke Company in 1919. The cause of death was given as a heart attack, since no violence or injury was apparent. (Courtesy of Rebecca Hoskins Goodwin.)

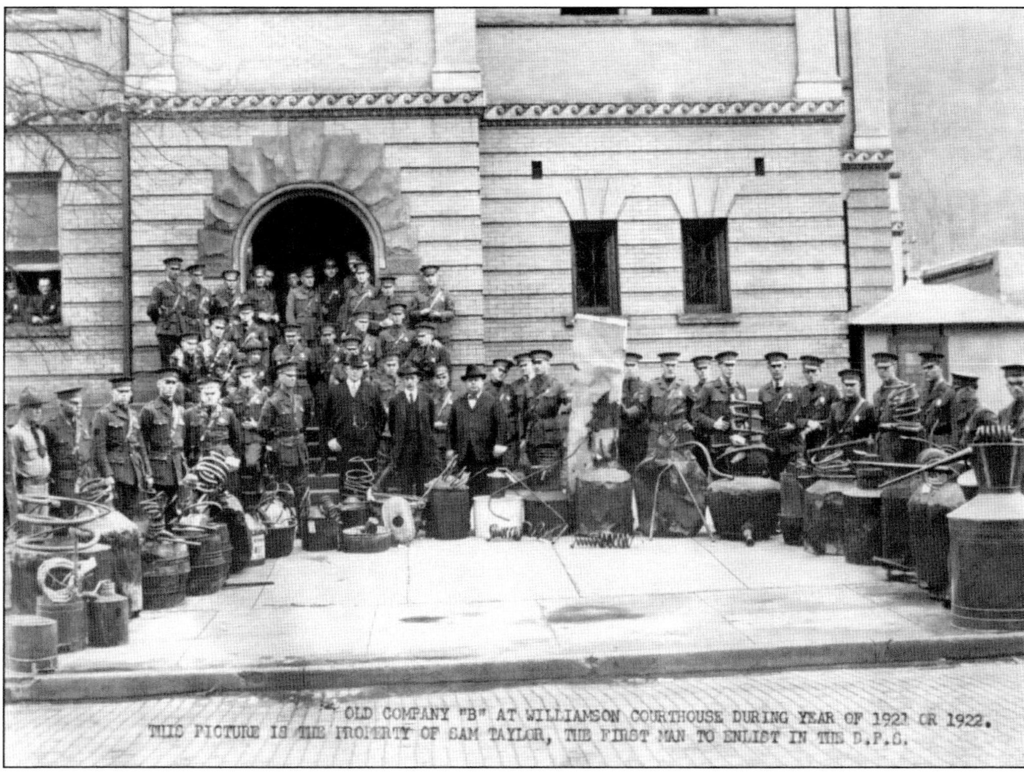

Old Company B poses in front of the Mingo County Courthouse in Williamson in 1921 or 1922. The display of moonshine stills captured by Company B includes quite a variety of apparatus. Moonshining was regarded by mountaineers as their birthright and contributed largely to their economic survival. (Courtesy of West Virginia State Archives, West Virginia State Police Collection.)

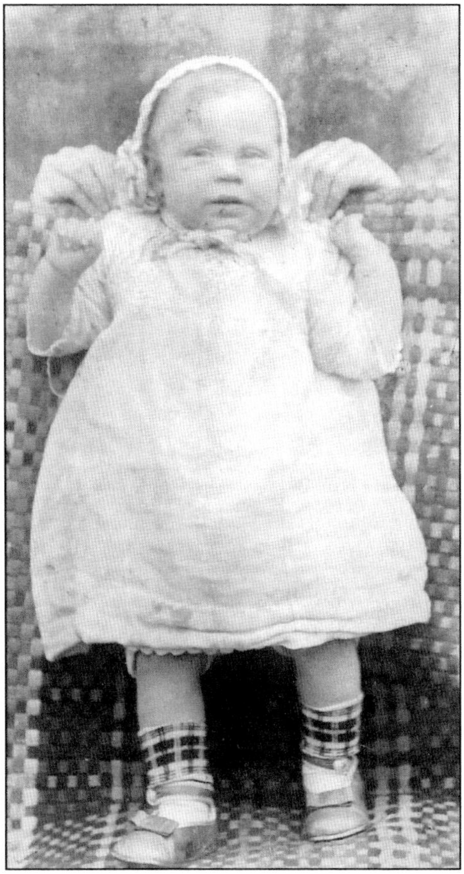

The infant pictured here is Hazel Marie Isaac Chafin, who was born in 1918 to Charles and Georgia Chafin. Hazel went on to marry Tom C. Chafin, and the couple had five children. Their children were Andrew, Don, Truman, Georgia, and Jeanne. After her children were grown, Hazel took up painting and created great images of early Appalachian life. As of the printing of this book, Hazel recently celebrated her 96th birthday. (Courtesy of Georgia C. Griffith.)

This 1930s photograph shows Georgia Chafin Isaac with the first three of her five children. The children pictured here are, from left to right, Tommy, Hazel, and Ray. Katherine and Jack were born after this photograph was taken. Georgia was married to Charles Isaac. (Courtesy of Hazel M. Chafin.)

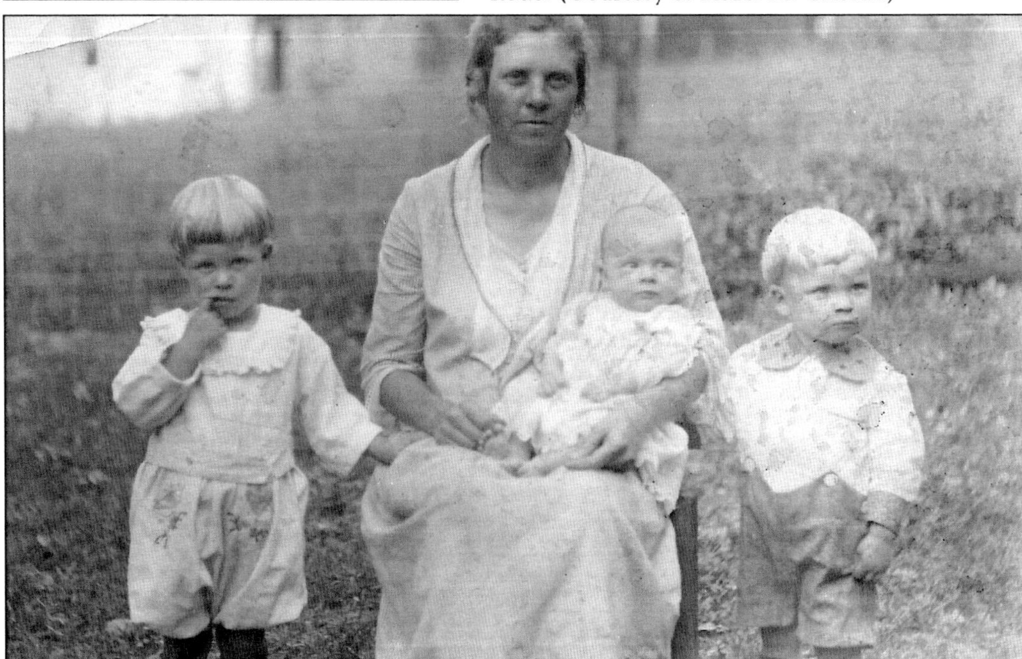

This photograph shows Katherine Isaac, left, and Ella Chafin of New Town. These two young ladies were great friends. (Courtesy of Hazel M. Chafin.)

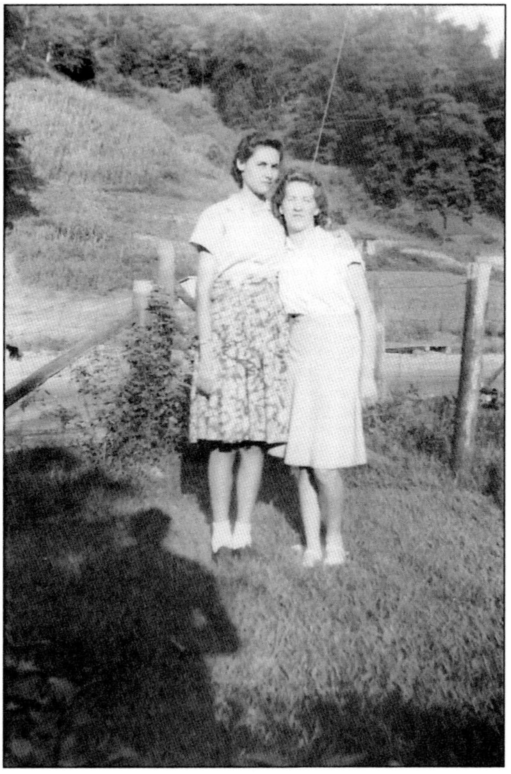

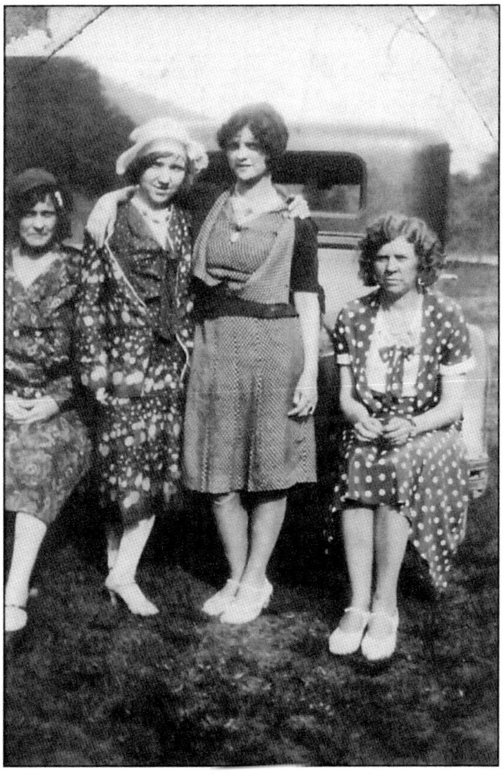

This 1928 photograph reflects the glamour of Mingo County residents all dressed up in their Sunday best. From left to right are Maude Chafin, Inez Chafin, Virginia Chafin, and Georgia Isaac in their 1920s finery. (Courtesy of Hazel M. Chafin.)

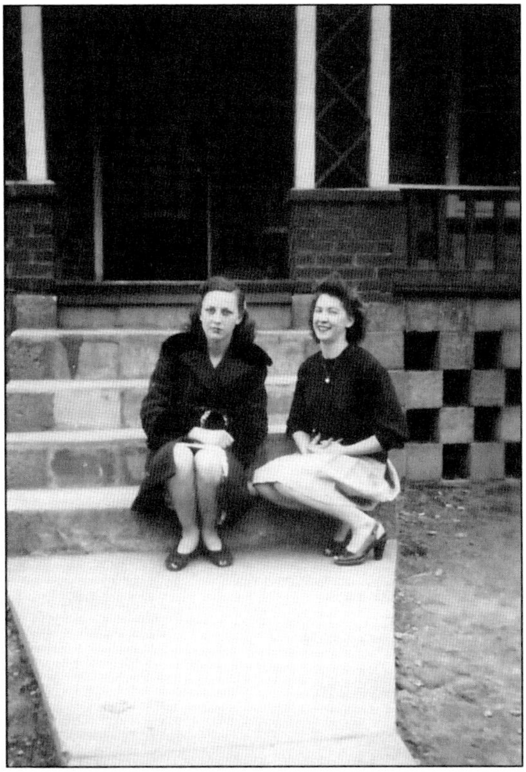

This late-1940s photograph shows Jackie Smith, left, and Katherine Isaac. Jackie married Ray Isaac and Katherine married Joe LaPorte. Ray Isaac, upon discharge from the Navy, opened a popular night club in New Town called the Spinning Wheel. Katherine moved to Elizabethton, Tennessee, where she and her husband, Joe, had four sons. (Courtesy of Hazel M. Chafin.)

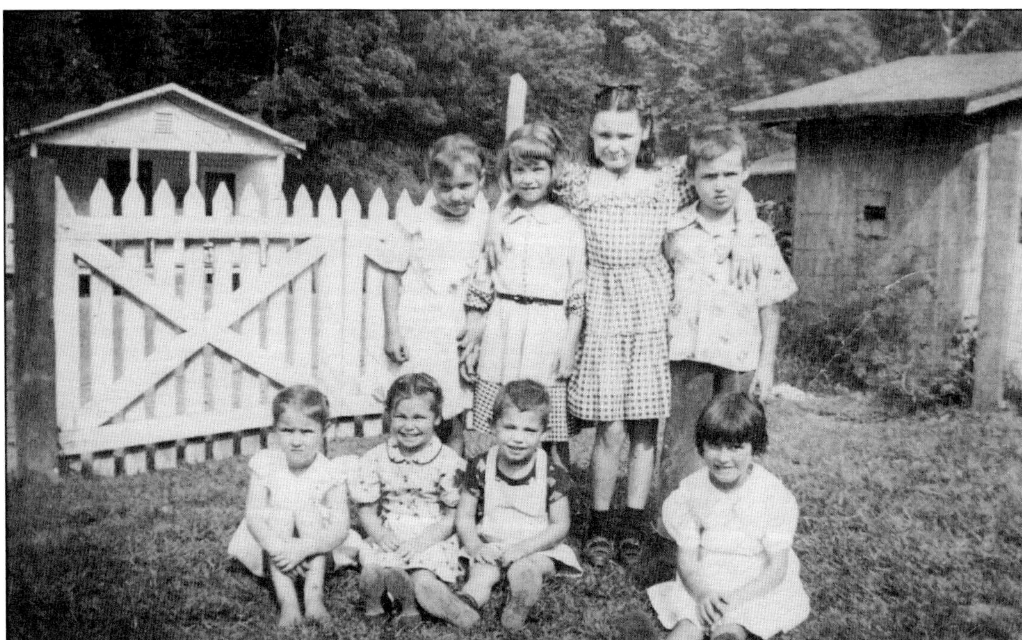

A group of first cousins stop long enough from their game of hide-and-seek for this late-1940s photograph at New Town. From left to right are (first row) Lou Chafin, Jeanne Chafin, Truman Chafin, and an unidentified girl; (second row) Mary Lou Chafin, Georgia Ann Chafin, Anita McGuire, and Tommy Roger Steele. (Courtesy of Hazel M. Chafin.)

It must have been a holiday or a special occasion to get these three men all dressed up. From left to right are Tommy Isaac, the son of Charles Isaac (who is standing next to his son); Clyde Mars; and Lon Chafin. This photograph was taken in the 1930s. (Courtesy of Hazel M. Chafin.)

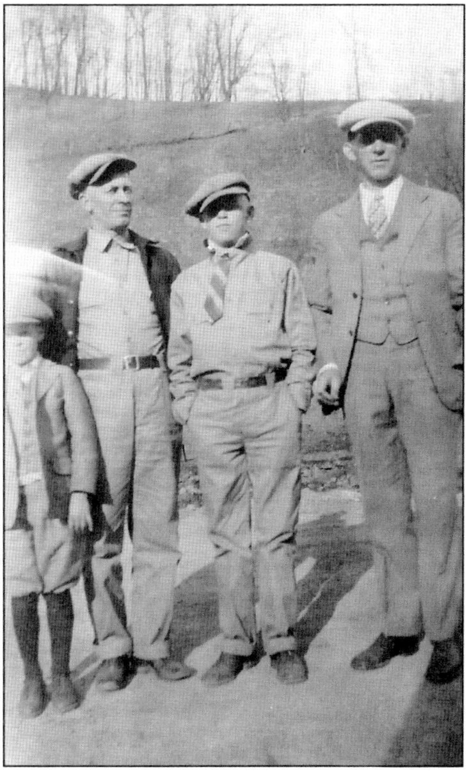

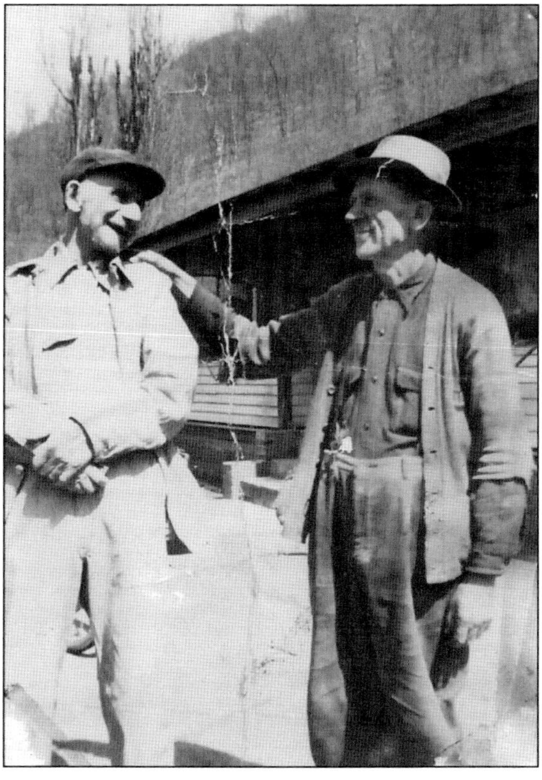

Pictured on the left is Floyd Hatfield, son of Kirk and Agatha Hatfield. The person on the right is Thomas Jefferson Chafin, brother of Georgia Chafin. Thomas was the father of a large family. Floyd was always a kind and cheerful soul, as this early-1930s image reflects. (Courtesy of Hazel M. Chafin.)

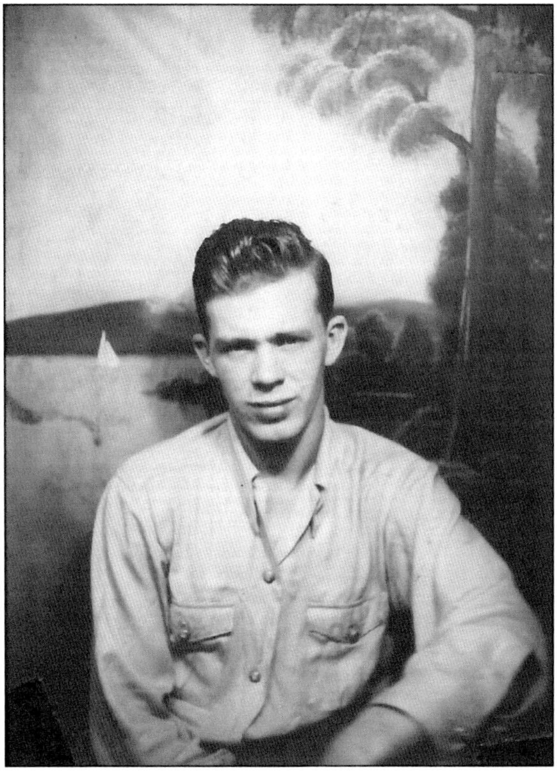

This 1941 photograph of Raymond Alfred Isaac was taken before he entered the US Navy during World War II. Raymond was the son of Charles and Georgia Isaac, one of five children. After getting out of the Navy, he married Jackie Smith and they moved to Washington, DC, where he worked for the US General Services Administration. (Courtesy of Hazel M. Chafin.)

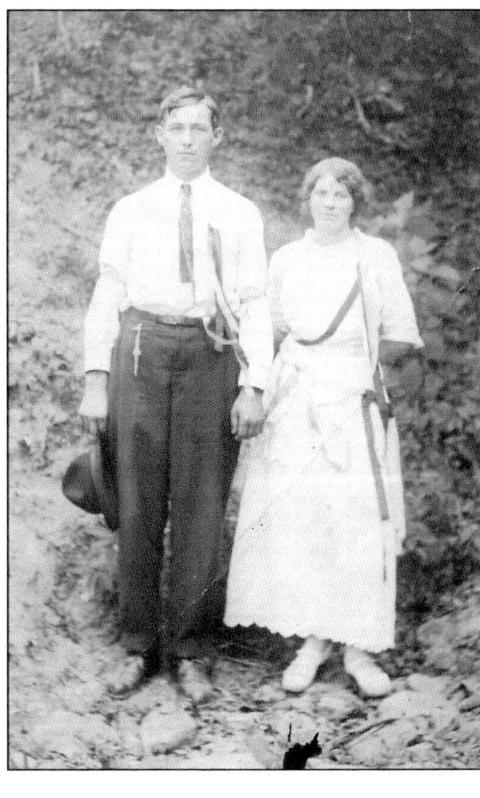

Pictured here are Harry Baisden, left, and Georgia Chafin. Note the steep and rocky terrain, which was abundant in the mountains of Mingo County. (Courtesy of Hazel M. Chafin.)

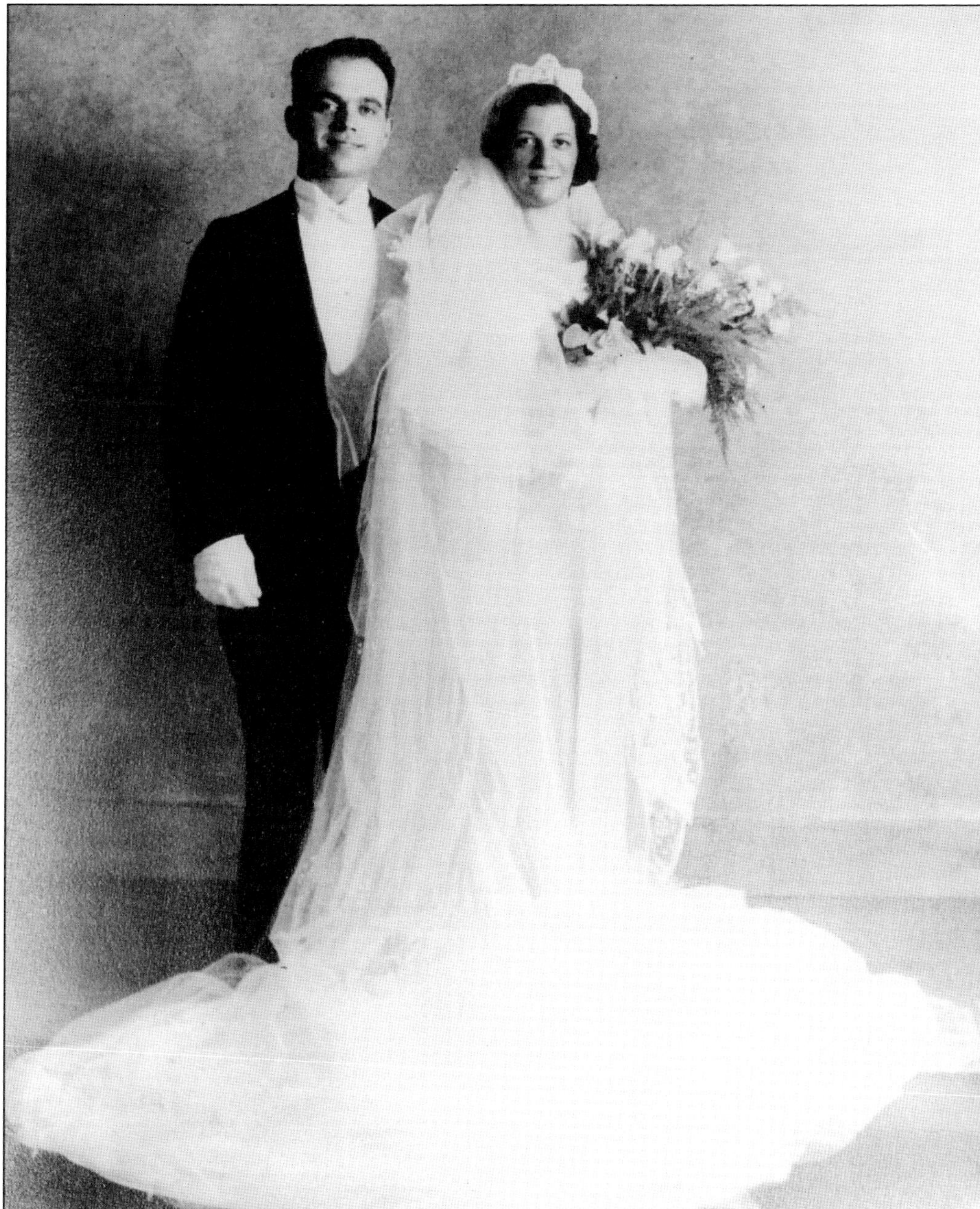

Attilio Nenni and his lovely bride, Nellie Gentile, pose for their wedding photograph in 1937. In 1909, Attilio Nenni opened a shoe shop in Matewan. In 1919, the shop became a store that sold men's and women's fashions. The store became one of the leading clothing merchandisers in Mingo County. Both the Nenni family and the Gentile family had emigrated from Italy. Attilio and Nellie had two children, Eddie and Jerinell. (Courtesy of Eddie Nenni.)

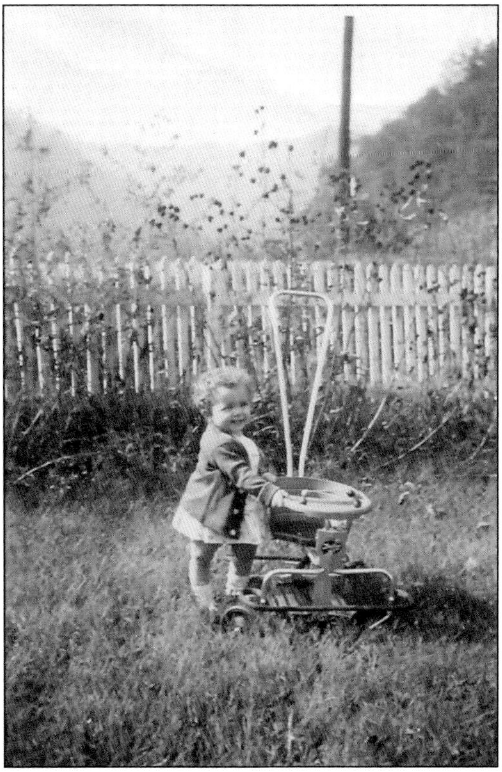

This photograph shows Jerinell Nenni attempting to push her own stroller with no one in it, or maybe she was just getting ready for an outing with her family. The Nenni children had loving parents, Attilio and Nellie Nenni, that were able to provide well for them. (Courtesy of Eddie Nenni.)

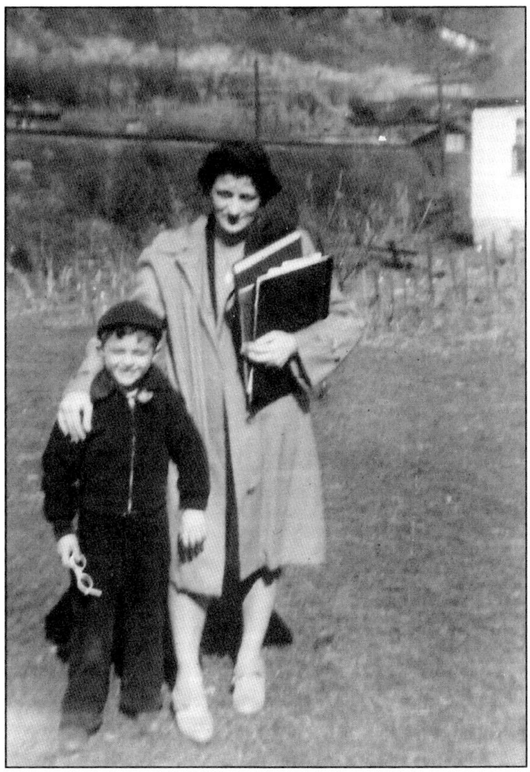

Eddie Nenni is pictured here with his mother, Nellie Nenni. Nellie is carrying some ledgers from the family business, a department store which, in addition to being a shoe shop and repair store, sold the latest fashions to the residents of Mingo County. Their store was located in the town of Matewan and is still there today. (Courtesy of Eddie Nenni.)

Hazel Chafin sits in the sand in front of her son-in-law Kelly Griffith in this 1960s photograph at Myrtle Beach, South Carolina. The Griffiths' Myrtle Beach condo was often a vacation spot for the family. This photograph was taken by Hazel's daughter, Gerogia Ann, wife of Kelly. (Courtesy of Hazel M. Chafin.)

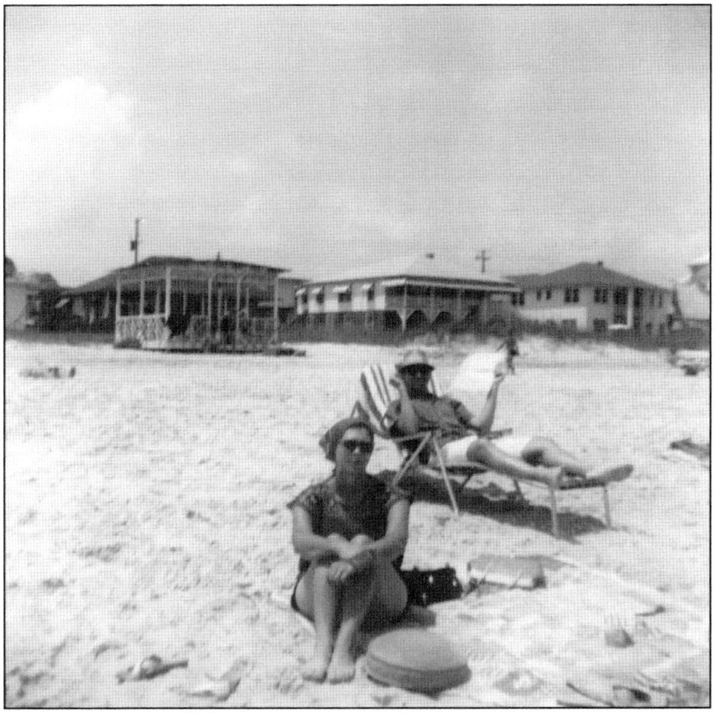

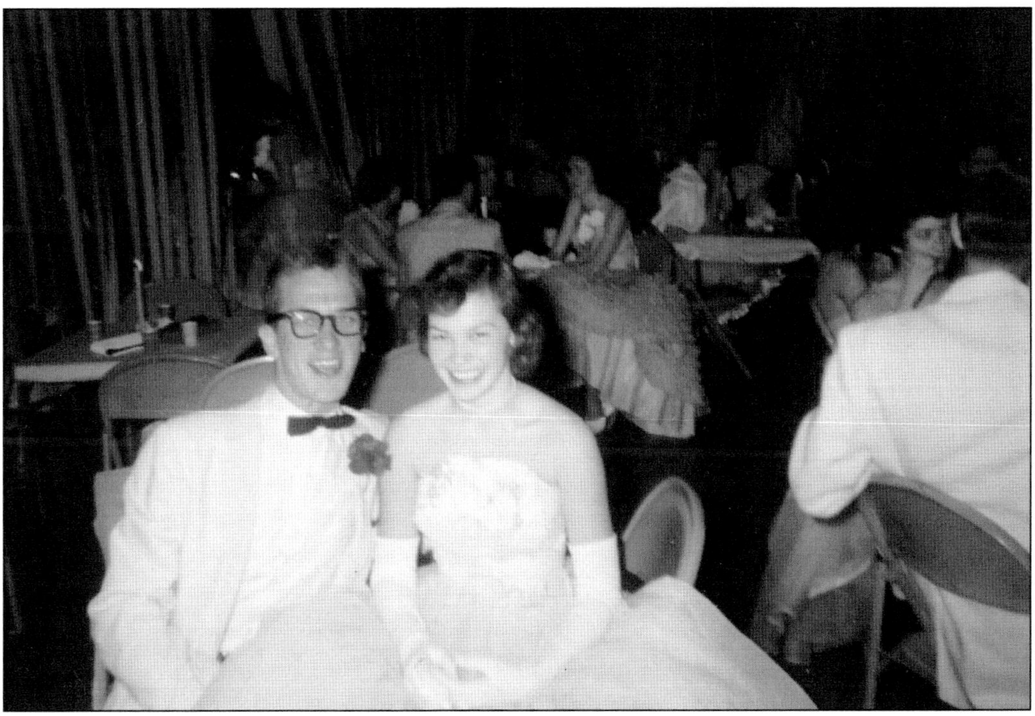

Proms and dances were popular in Mingo County during the 1950s. The young people learned all the newest dance moves and very much enjoyed the music of the day. This 1950s photograph shows Jeanne Chafin with her date at a prominent dance. Jeanne later married Howard Persinger, and they had three children: Moses, Holly Marie, and Courtney. (Courtesy of Hazel. M. Chafin.)

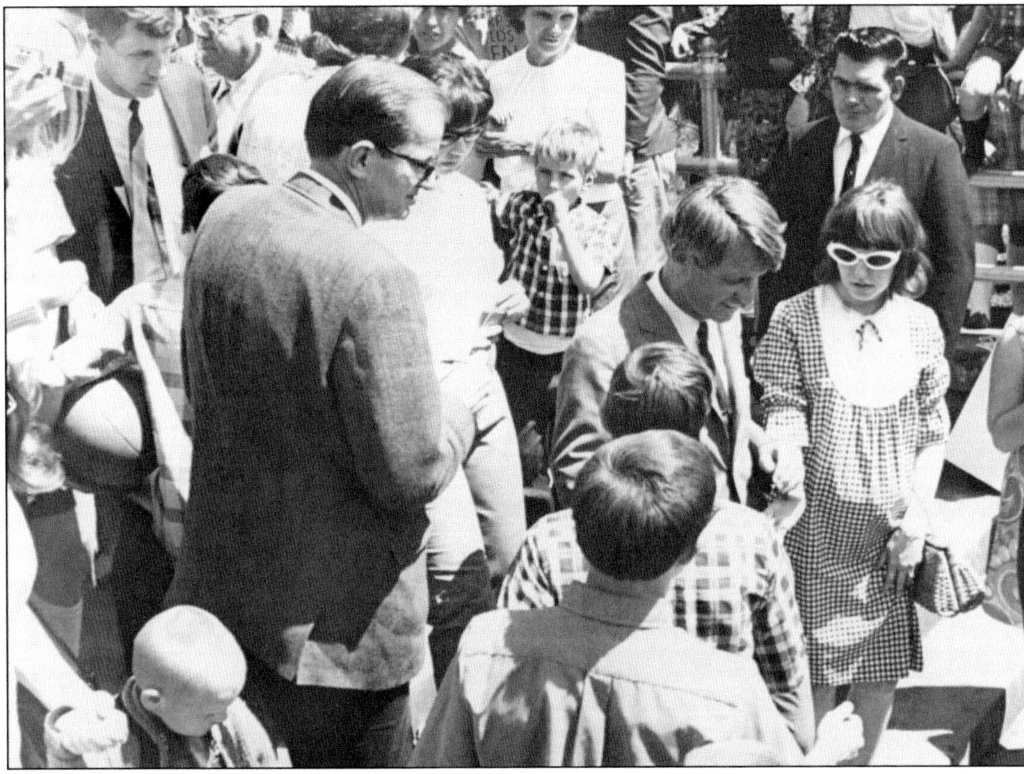

Robert F. Kennedy visits Mingo County during his 1968 presidential campaign. Herb Little of the Associated Press is standing in the left foreground. Kennedy was assassinated in June 1968 in Los Angeles at the Ambassador Hotel. (Courtesy of West Virginia State Archives, Herb Little Collection.)

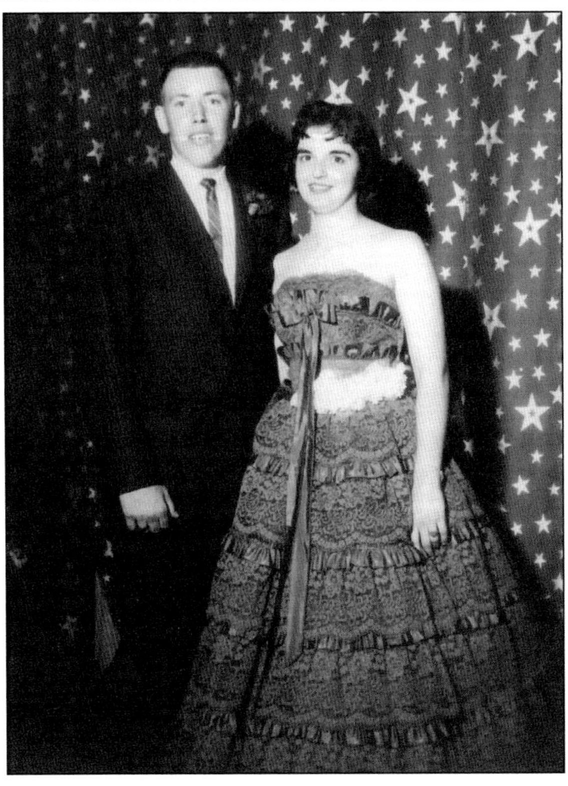

Kay Elkins, all grown up here, is pictured with Bobby Hamlin, her date for the Magnolia High School of Matewan prom in 1958. (Courtesy of Leleah Matney.)

Pictured here are two former Mingo County educators: Ralph Vinciguerra, left, and John Anderson. Ralph Vinciguerra was a teacher and principal at Red Jacket Junior High School in the 1950s. John Anderson was principal at Matewan High School in the 1950s and later became superintendent of Mingo County Schools. Both were known for being the favorites of students. (Courtesy of Dimple Tiller Allara.)

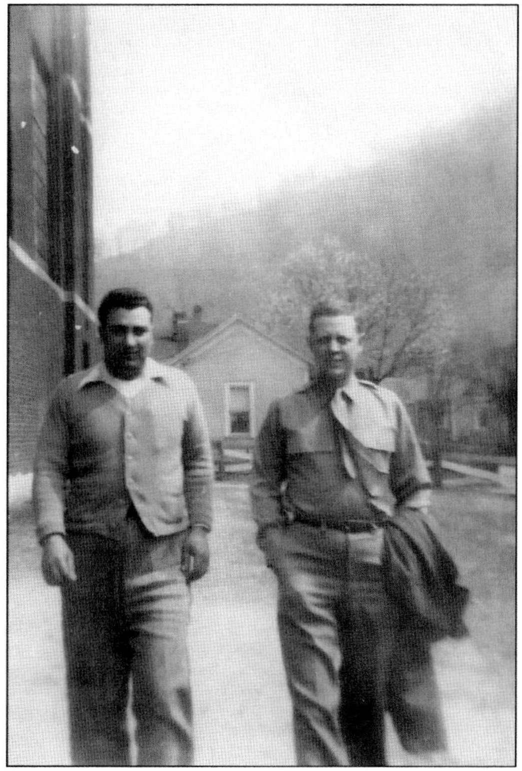

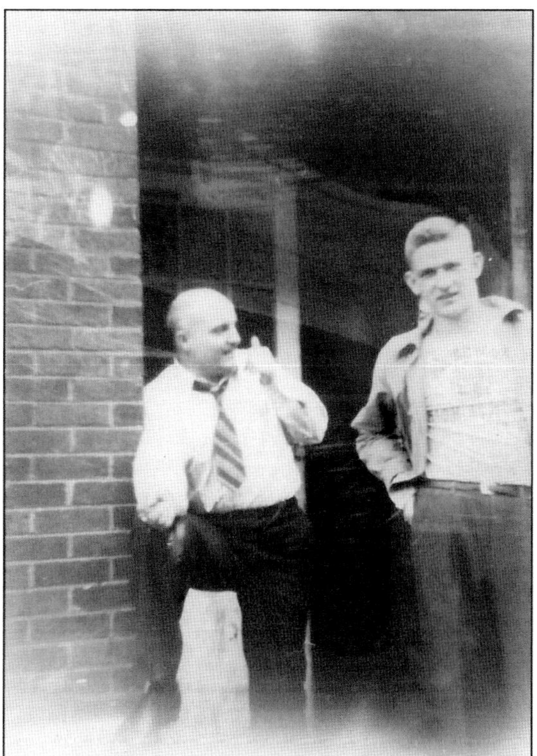

Pictured here in the late 1940s are Joe Hofstetter, left, and Hiram Keatley. Hofstetter was a longtime teacher at Matewan High School, and Keatley was the father of Jim Keatley, who starred in football at Matewan High School and Marshall University. He later served as coach of the Matewan High School football team. (Courtesy of Dimple Tiller Allara.)

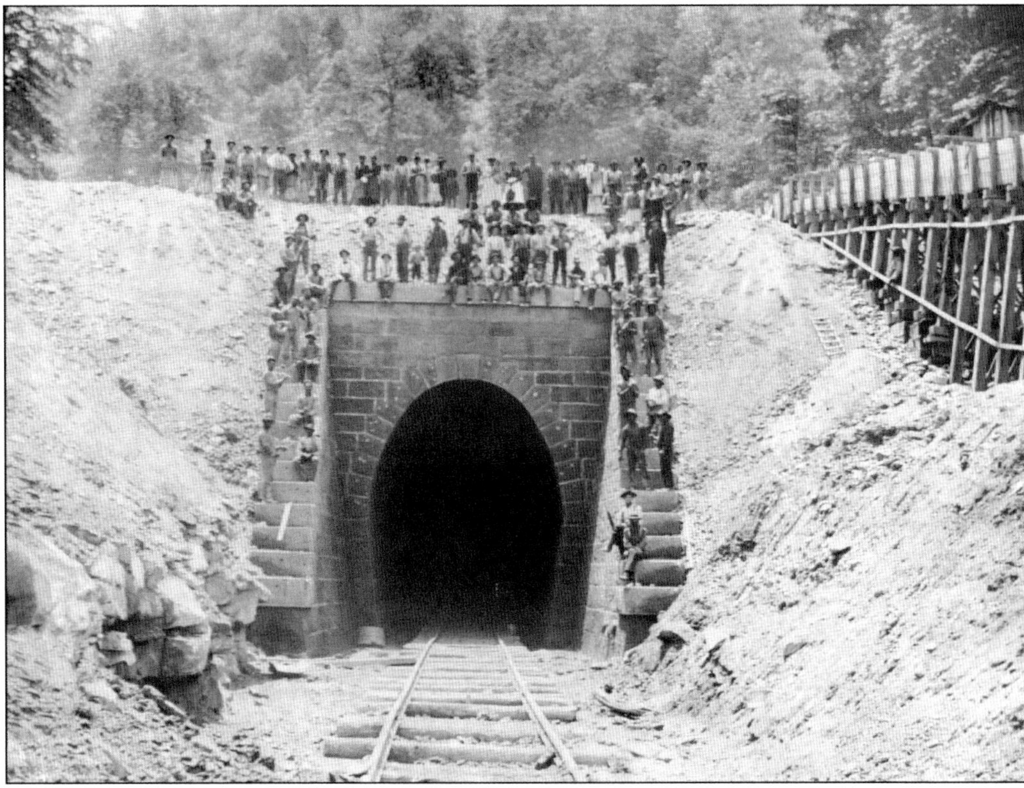

Workers and locals gather around the portal of the Dingess Tunnel in 1893. The tunnel was built by the Norfolk & Western Railroad (now Norfolk Southern) and was a main line between 1892 and 1904. Items were unloaded in Dingess from the railway to wagons, which then hauled the goods to nearby towns for delivery. In 1913, following the removal of the railroad rails, the tunnel was converted into a roadway. In 1960, the tunnel became a part of the West Virginia Department of Highways. The tunnel is almost a mile long and is only wide enough for one automobile, but the driver is able to see all the way through the tunnel. (Courtesy of West Virginia State Archives, Kenneth King Collection.)

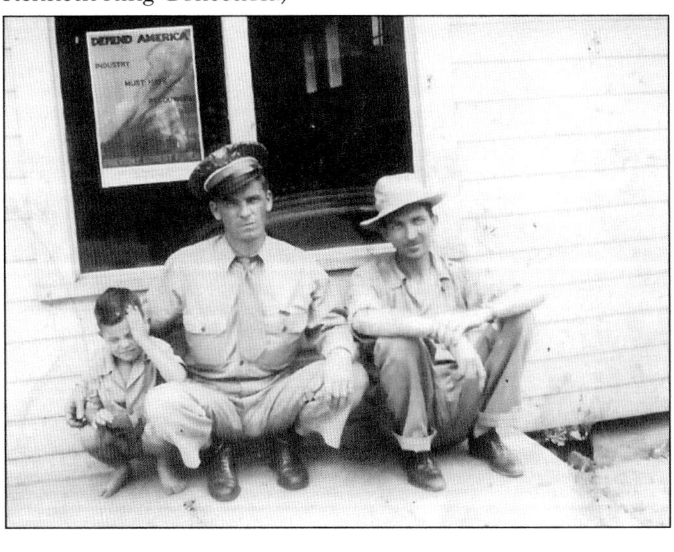

In the 1940s, folks often gathered at the Chafin grocery store to reminisce and talk about the weather. From left to right are Andrew Chafin, Tommy Isaac, and Allen Chafin. Tommy was on leave from the US Army and had to return to service at the end of World War II. (Courtesy of Andrew Chafin.)

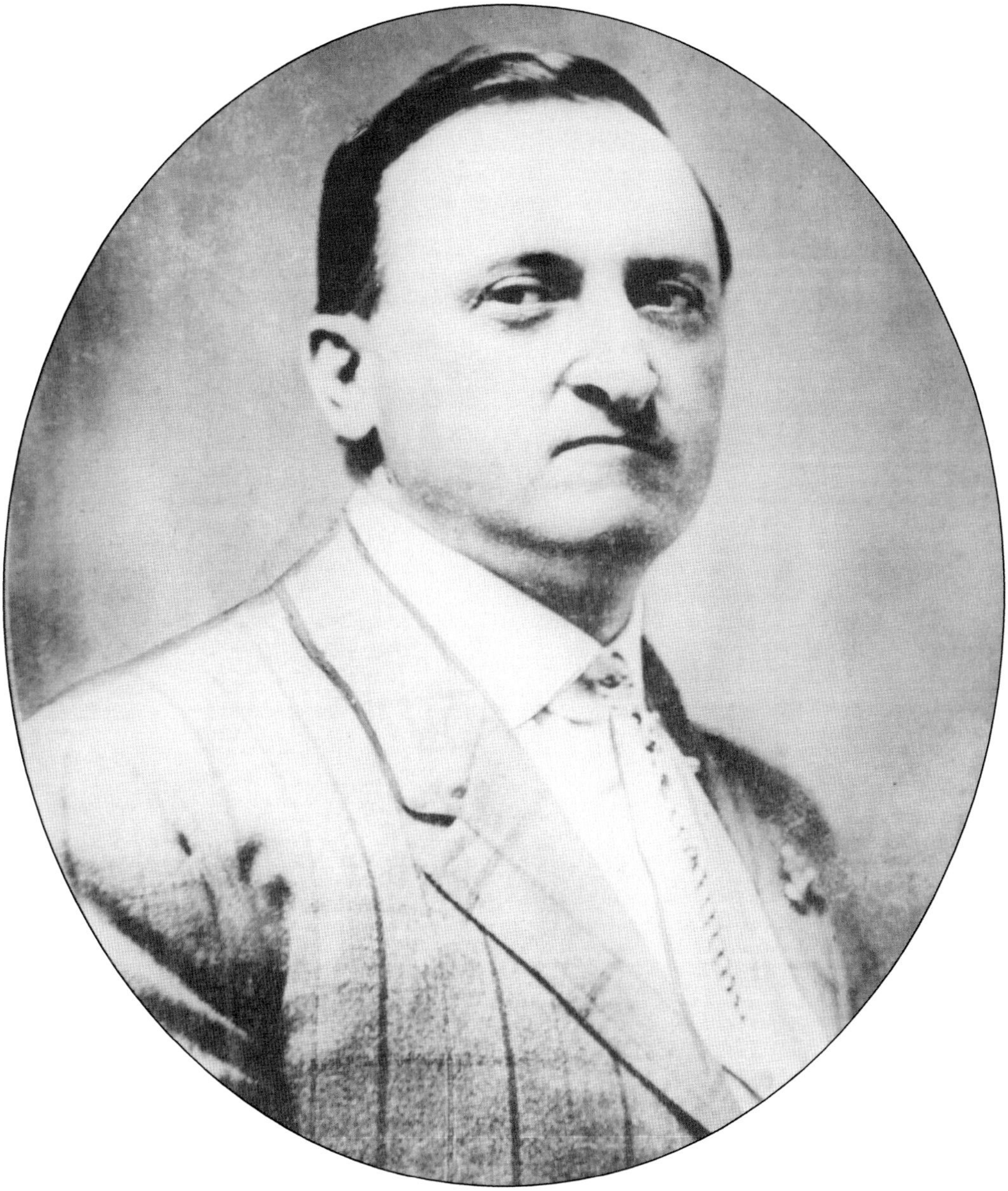

John B. Maynard, chief of police for Williamson, was shot and instantly killed by Constable Jesse Huffman in front of Strosnider's drugstore on July 29, 1919. As Chief Maynard reached out to take the arm of Huffman, perhaps to arrest him, Huffman shot Chief Maynard twice. Pierce B. Maynard, brother of Chief Maynard, was in the drugstore when he heard the shots and darted outside. Pierce then took the chief's pistol from its holster and proceeded after Huffman, who has gotten into his car to leave. As Pierce Maynard approached one side of the car, gun in hand, Bert Maynard, cousin of the chief, approached the other side of the car. The chief's son, Beverly Maynard, approached Pierce, preventing yet more tragedy. Chief Maynard was widely known and admired throughout the region. He was considered kind and accommodating in the exercise of his duty, but he feared no man. It is believed that the matter with Huffman was related to his behavior regarding a woman from the Kentucky side of the Tug River. (Courtesy of Rebecca Hoskins Goodwin.)

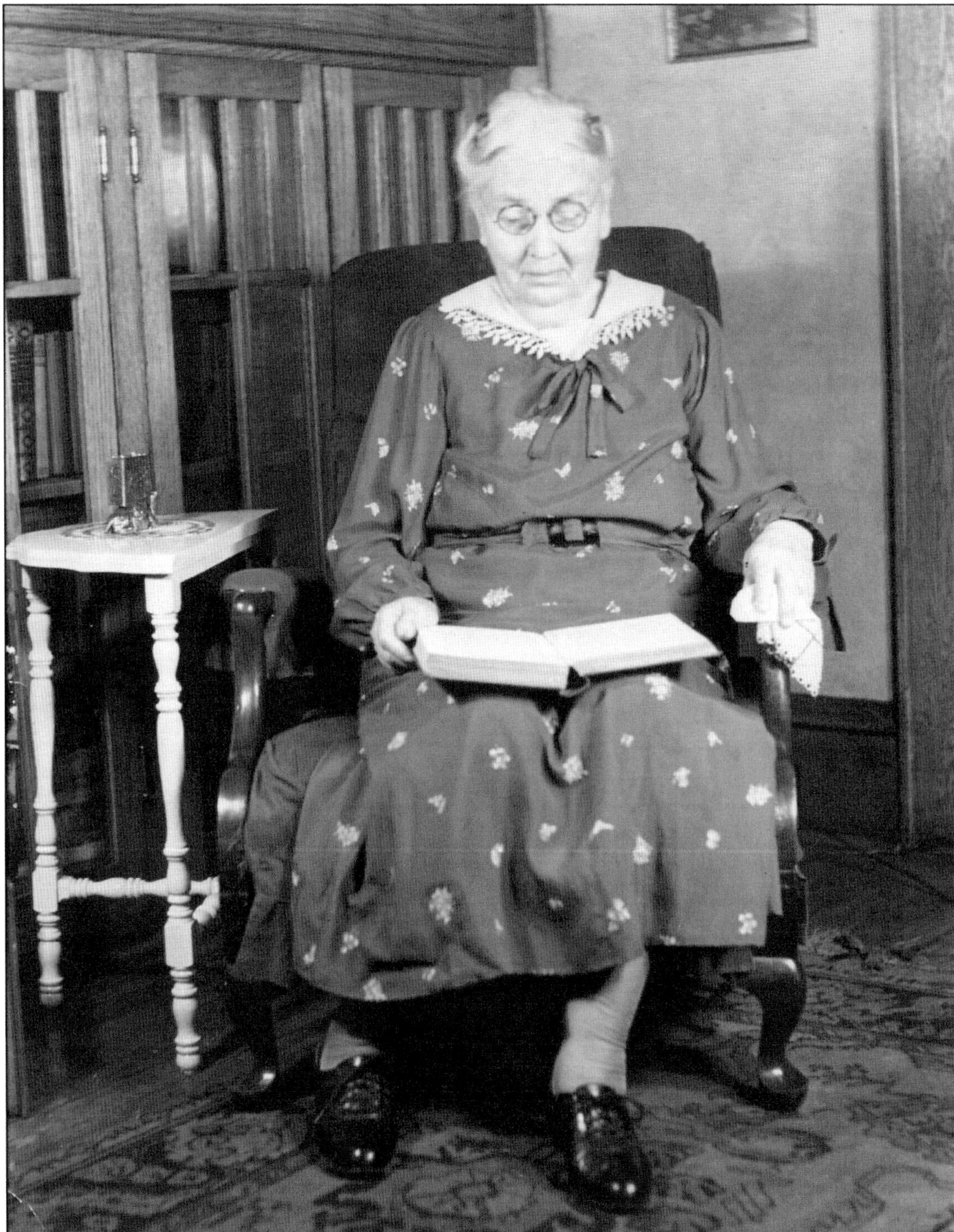

Rebecca Scott Williamson was born on December 25, 1857, and lived until September 2, 1942. Her father was James Thomas Scott, and her mother was Lavinia Stafford. She married G. William Williamson and was the loving mother of three sons: Simeon, Robert K., and John Freeland Williamson; and one daughter: Lida Gertrude Williamson. Here, she sits enjoying her bible. (Courtesy of Rebecca Hoskins Goodwin.)

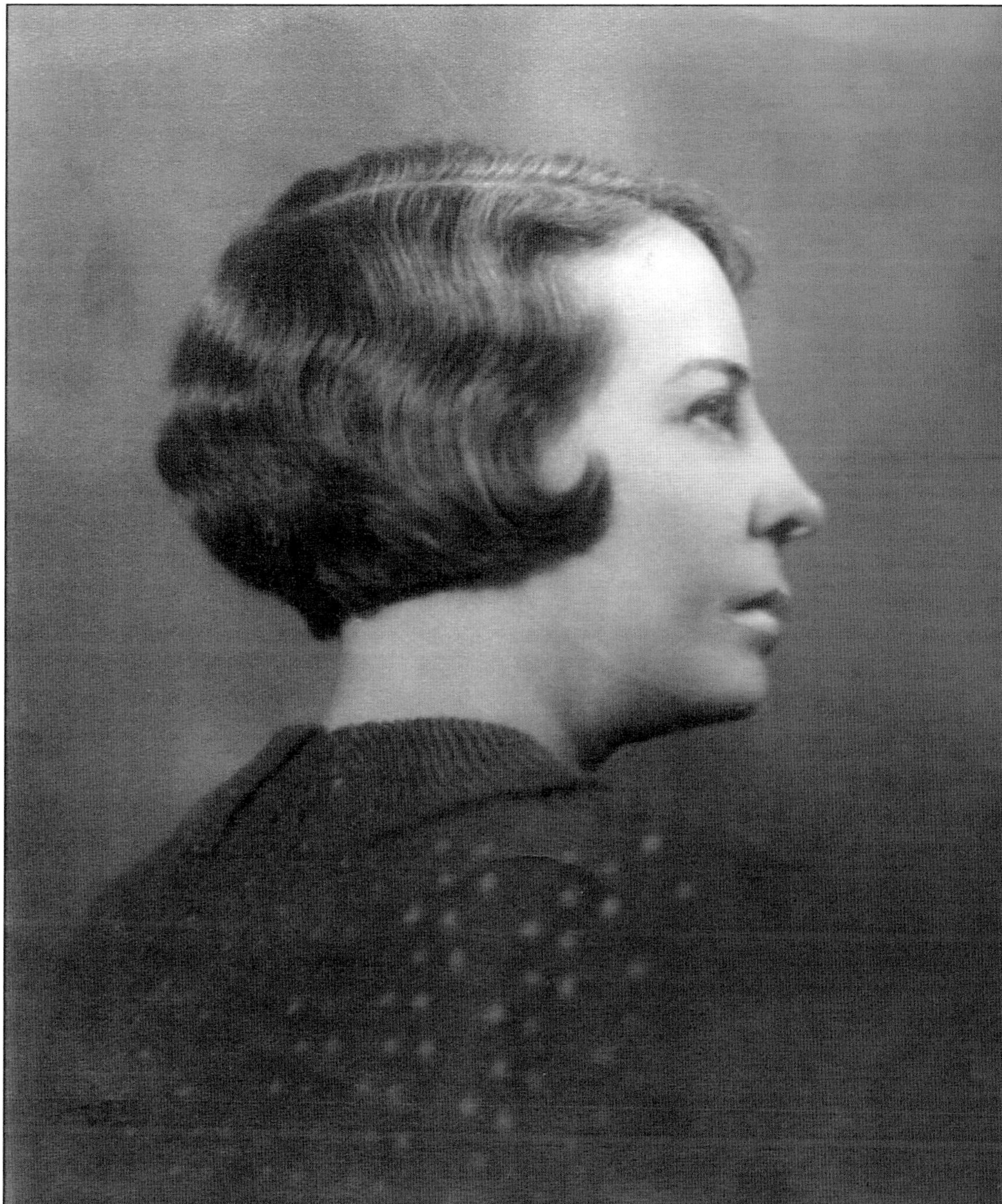

This lovely photograph of Lida Gertrude Williamson was taken in 1911. Born on September 6, 1895, she lived until August 14, 1980. Her father was G. William Williamson, and her mother was Rebecca Scott Williamson. On May 24, 1911, Lida spoke at the third-annual commencement of the Williamson High School, the largest graduating class to date, which was five students. At her valedictory speech, she successfully delivered her handwritten speech on the subject of women's suffrage in the United States. In 1913, she married Beverly Johnson Maynard, the son of John B. Maynard and Louisa Hatfield Maynard. (Courtesy of Rebecca Hoskins Goodwin.)

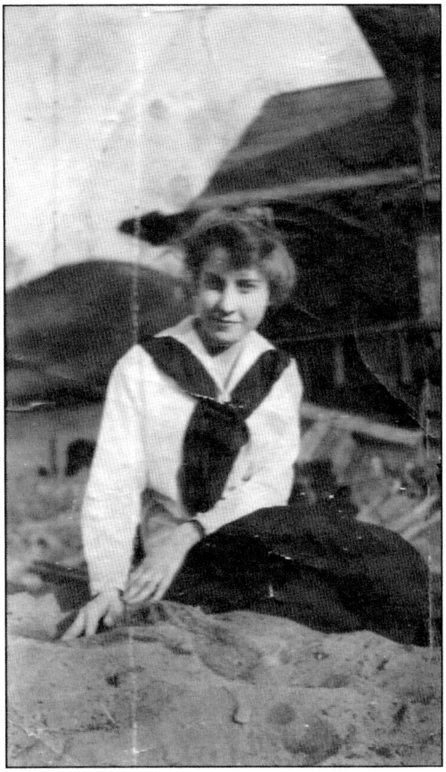

Lida Williamson Maynard is pictured at the beach in 1913, dressed in the latest beach fashion. (Courtesy of Rebecca Hoskins Goodwin.)

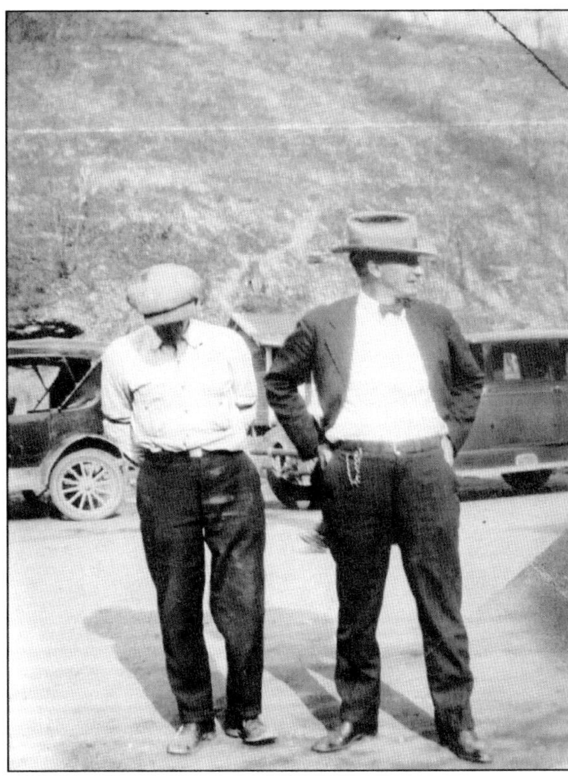

People gathered in the downtown communities of Mingo County. Folks came to town to transact their business, attend social gatherings, and get caught up on the news of the day as well as the happenings in the lives of family and friends. (Courtesy of Hazel M. Chafin.)

Pictured here is Myrna Louise Maynard Hoskins, the daughter of Lida Gertrude Williamson and Beverly Johnson Maynard. She was born on September 25, 1916 and lived until November 24, 1978. Here she is happily posing in her fancy little frock at about two years of age. (Courtesy of Rebecca Hoskins Goodwin.)

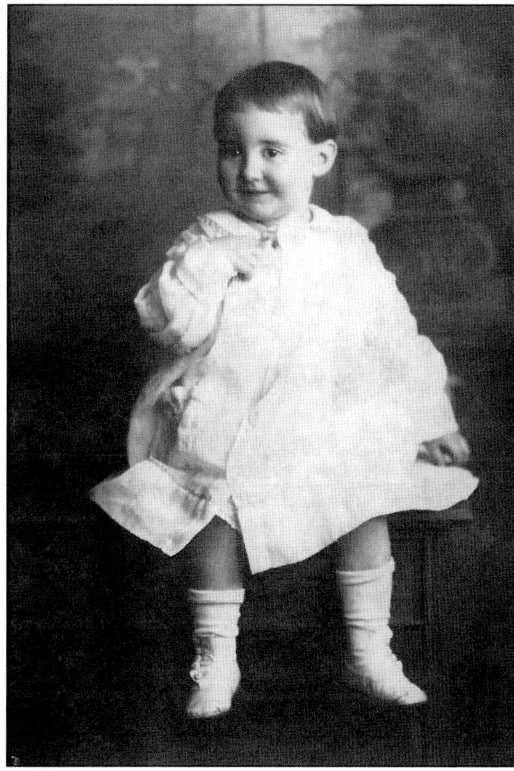

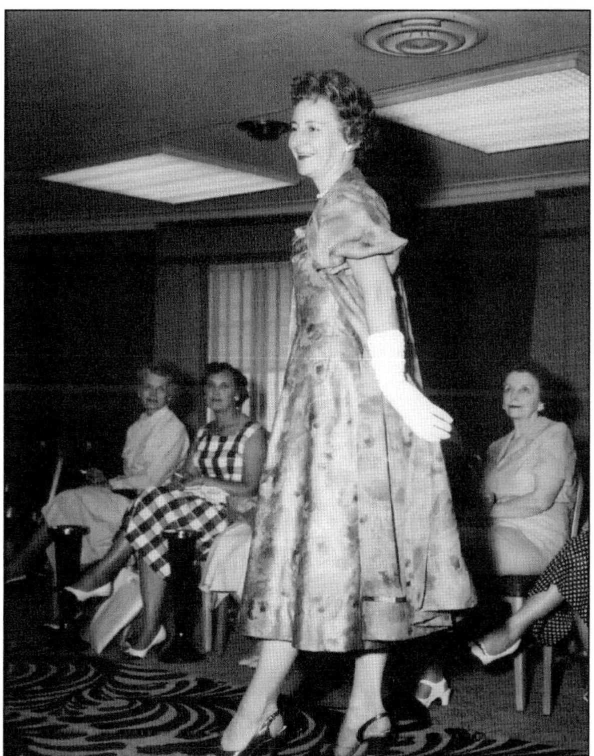

Myrna Louise Maynard Hoskins is pictured here exhibiting her incredible sense of style. Myrna spent the winter of her high school senior year in Miami, Florida. She was featured in newspaper photographs and in the social columns and was recognized for her sense of style as well as her outstanding abilities in horseback riding, swimming, ballroom dancing, and serious dance training. While there, she attended a catholic school and one of her classmates was Al Capone's son, Sonny. She graduated from Williamson High School in 1934, attended Virginia Intermont College, and also studied dance in New York City and Cincinnati, Ohio. On December 21, 1939 she married Herman Ray Hoskins, who was from Matewan, West Virginia, and had attended Concord College, where he was a star athlete; he later became a coach at Williamson High School. (Courtesy of Rebecca Hoskins Goodwin.)

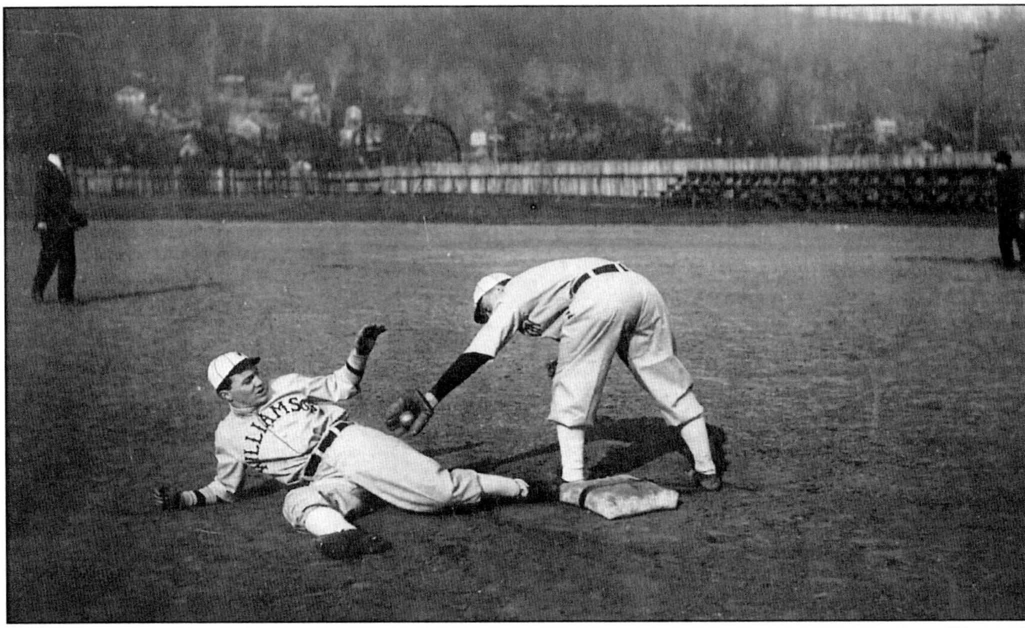

Beverly J. Maynard, born on September 25, 1893, passed away in his sleep on December 25, 1941, at 48 years of age. After graduating from Williamson High School, he attended Marshall College. He was believed to be one of the greatest pitchers in Marshall College's baseball history. Beverly Maynard shutout Notre Dame's baseball team 2-0 in a game that still stands out as Marshall's greatest upset victory. (Courtesy of Rebecca Hoskins Goodwin.)

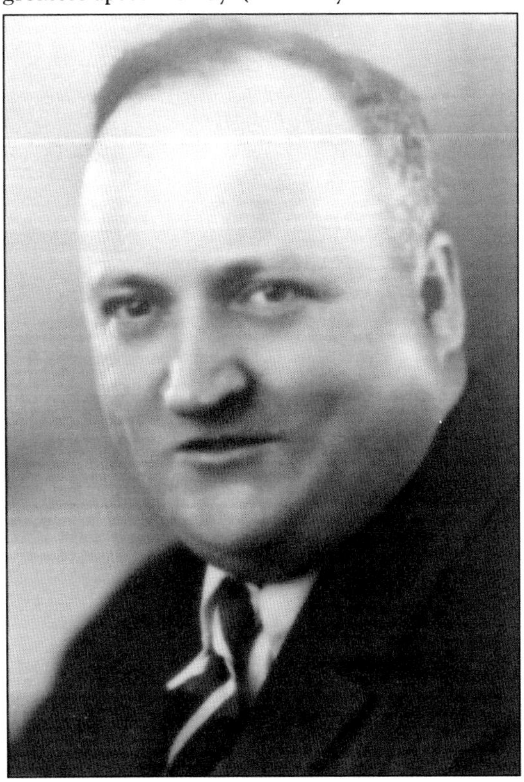

Pictured here is Beverly J. Maynard, who was known as the father of organized baseball in Williamson. He was known by friends as "Bev." He died at the age of 48 years as the result of an automobile accident six months prior, which had required him to spend five months in the hospital. He was loved and well known and was the son of the late John B. Maynard and Louise (Hatfield) Maynard. His father had died while serving as chief of police of Williamson, West Virginia. (Courtesy of Rebecca Hoskins Goodwin.)

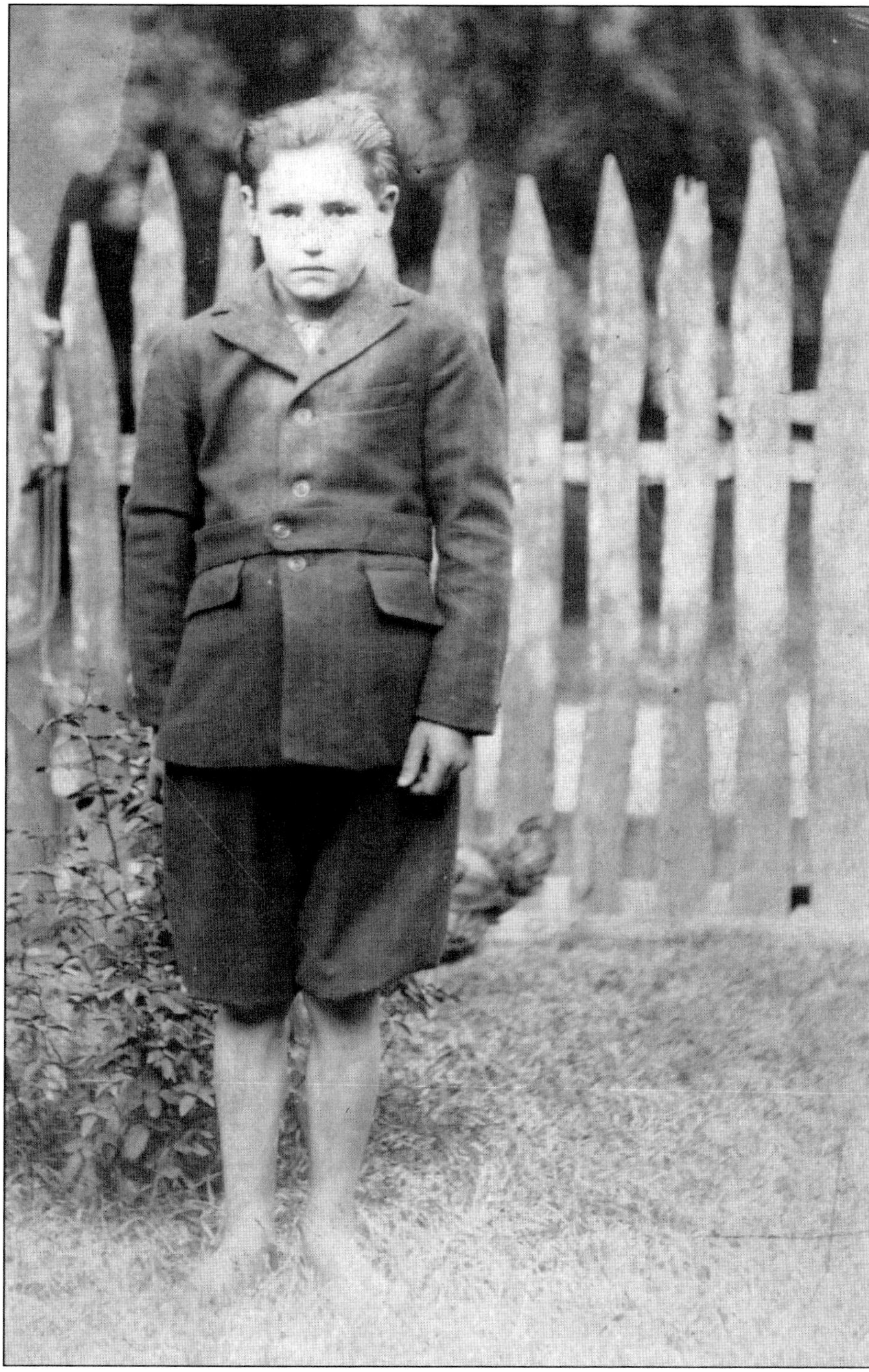

This early-1930s photograph of Tommy Roger Steele was taken in front of his home on Mate Creek. Tommy was the son of Perry and Biddie Steele and had a sister, Phyllis, and a brother, Alfred Lee. Tommy was killed at an early age in an automobile accident in the 1950s. (Courtesy of Hazel M. Chafin.)

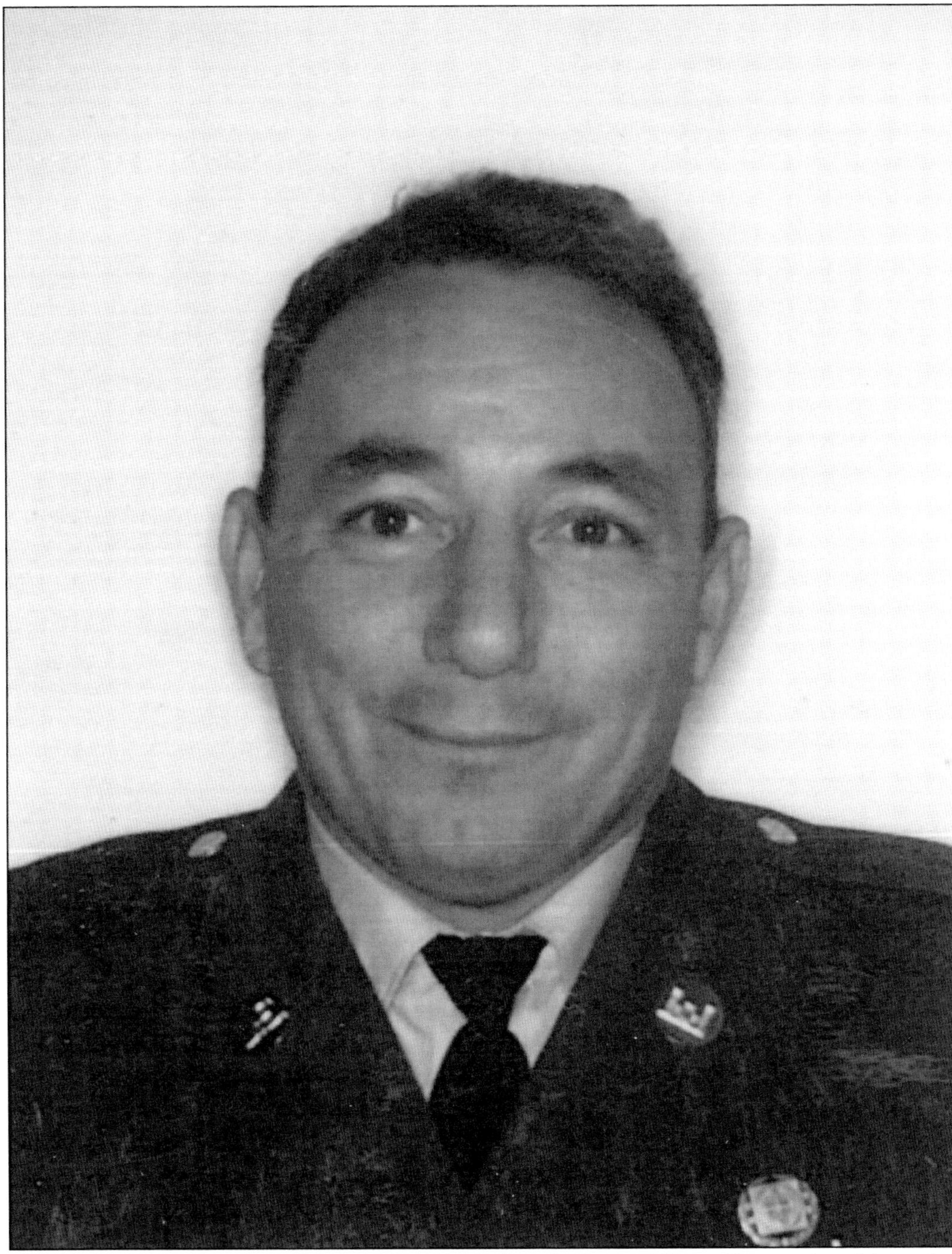

Pictured here is Victor G. Allara Sr., son of Frank and Mattie Allara. He was the oldest of six children. Victor was born on December 6, 1930, and lived until April 17, 1993. He was married to Dimple Tiller Allara, and they had two children. Victor retired from the US Army in 1979 after more than 20 years of working as an engineer in the United States Nuclear Power Program. After retirement, he opened up a movie theater and some other businesses. The last 13 years of his life he worked at nuclear power plants; he died on the job at VC Summer Station in Winnsboro, South Carolina. (Courtesy of Dimple Tiller Allara.)

For Vic

A jolly old man we came to know,
One on whom you could always count.
We'd work and laugh and work and leave,
Only to drag back in at sunrise's eve.
We called Vic sleepy and picked now and then,
But he'd just roll his eyes and give us a grin.
He'd sting you back, that was for sure,
He'd set you up; then slam the door.
But now we're filled with such disdain,
Because he was one of us, of ours, our chain.
It makes you question, it makes you think,
How can we be a chain, without this link?

From the Steam Generator Crew
V.C. Summer Station 1993

This poem was written for Victor G. Allara Sr. by his coworkers at the time of his retirement from the Army and the nuclear power plant program in 1979. (Courtesy of Dimple Tiller Allara.)

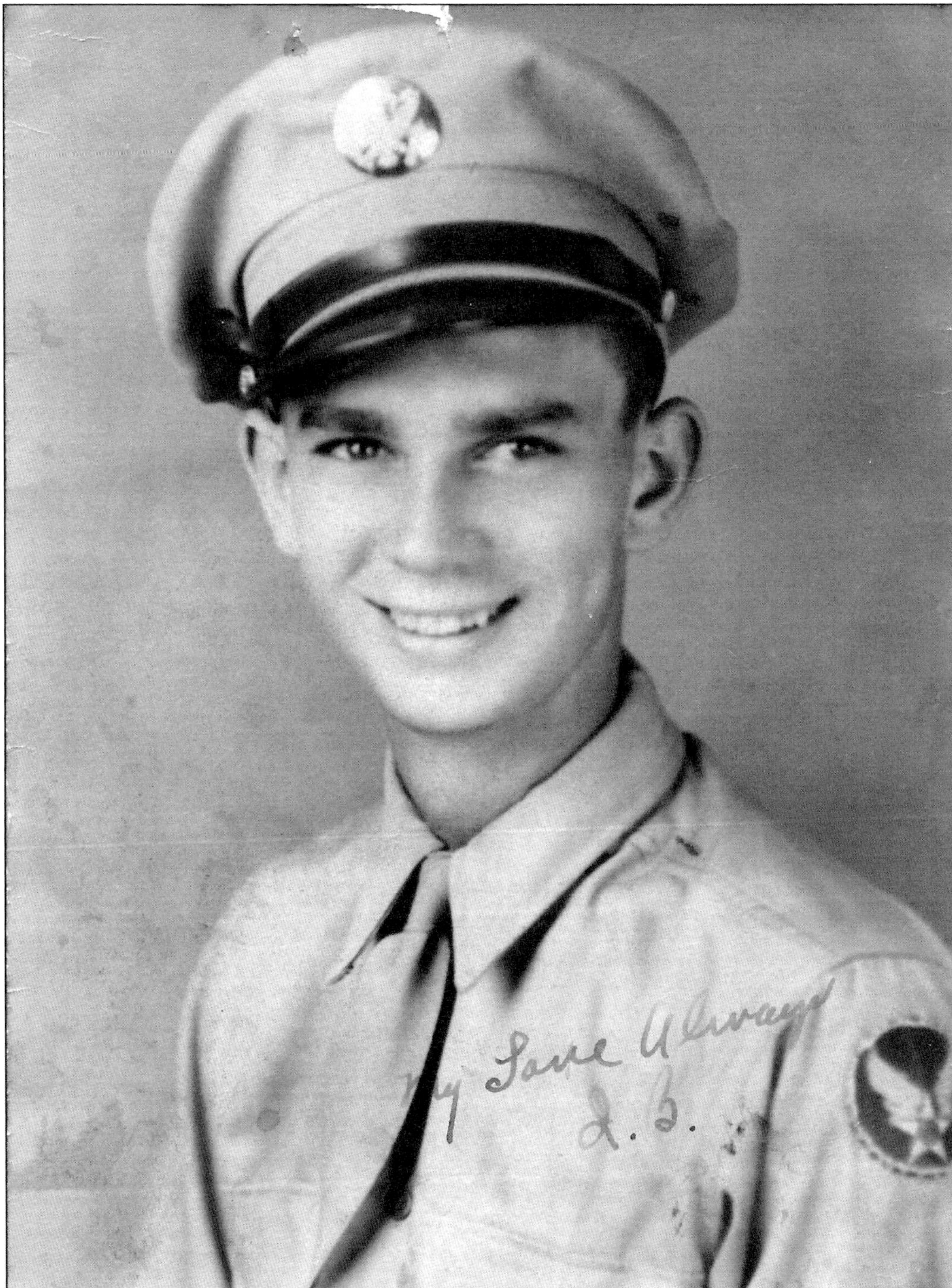

This photograph of I.B. Estep as a young airman in the US Air Force was taken in the 1940s. Estep was married to Ella Chafin and had two children, Norville and Lydia. He was born in North Matewan and, after his time in the Air Force, like many young Mingo countians, pursued a career in coal mining. He was loved and cherished, especially by his nieces and nephews. (Courtesy of Norville Estep.)

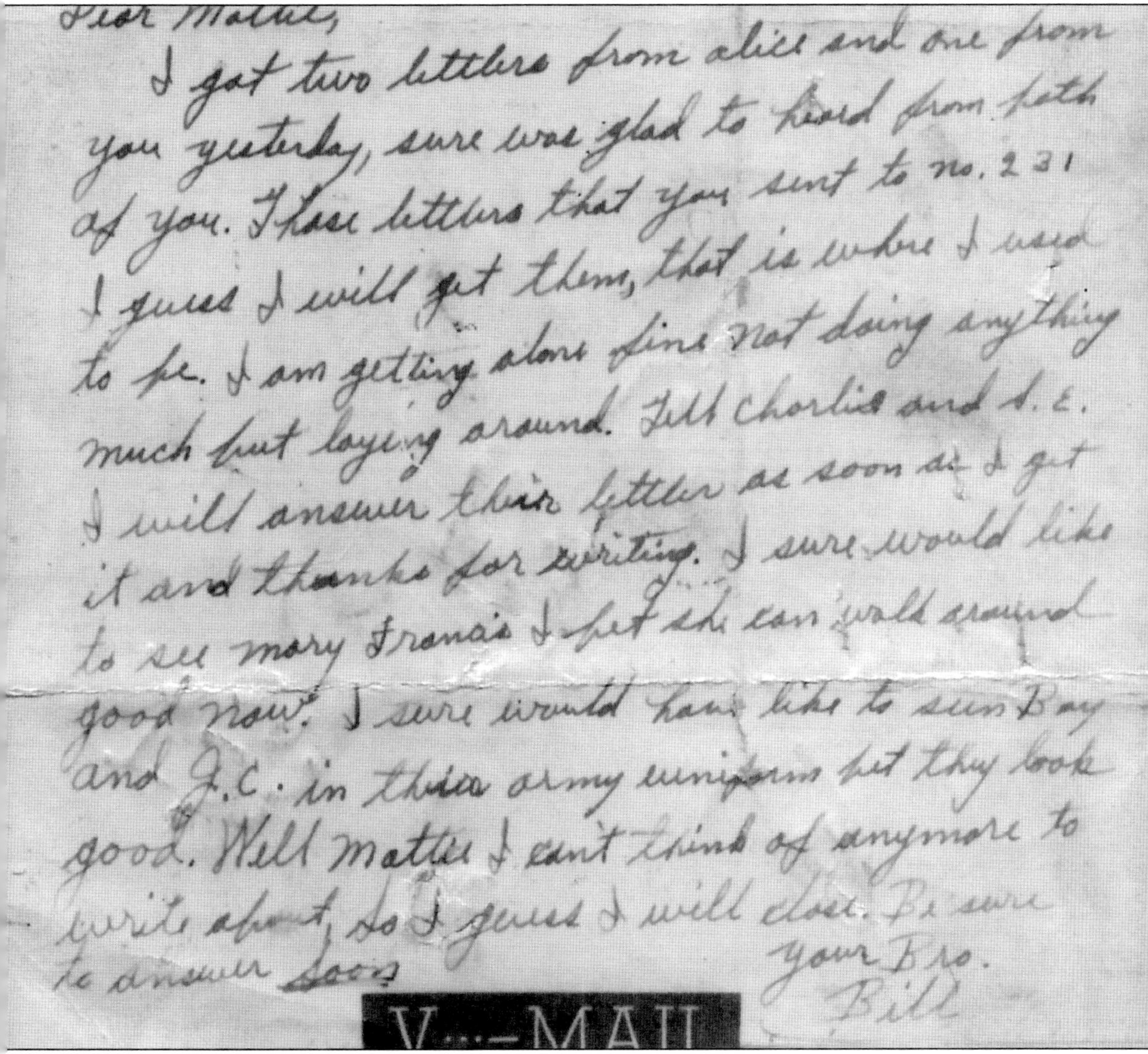

Dear Mother,
I got two letters from alice and one from
you yesterday, sure was glad to heard from both
of you. Those letters that you sent to no. 231
I guess I will get them, that is where I used
to be. I am getting along fine not doing anything
much but laying around. Tell Charlie and J. E.
I will answer their letter as soon as I get
it and thanks for writing. I sure would like
to see mary Francis I bet she can walk around
good now. I sure would have like to seen Bay
and J.C. in those army uniform bet they look
good. Well mother I can't think of anymore to
write about, so I guess I will close. Be sure
to answer soon
Your Bro.
Bill

V...-MAIL

William Woodward of Red Jacket in Mingo County sent this letter to his mother, who also lived in Red Jacket. The letter was delivered during World War II using V-Mail, short for Victory Mail, which was written on small sheets that would go through mail sensors before being photographed as thumbnail-sized images on microfilm. Upon arrival to the destination, the microfilm negative would be blown up to the original size and printed. Woodward provided a number of the images used in this book. (Courtesy of William Woodward.)

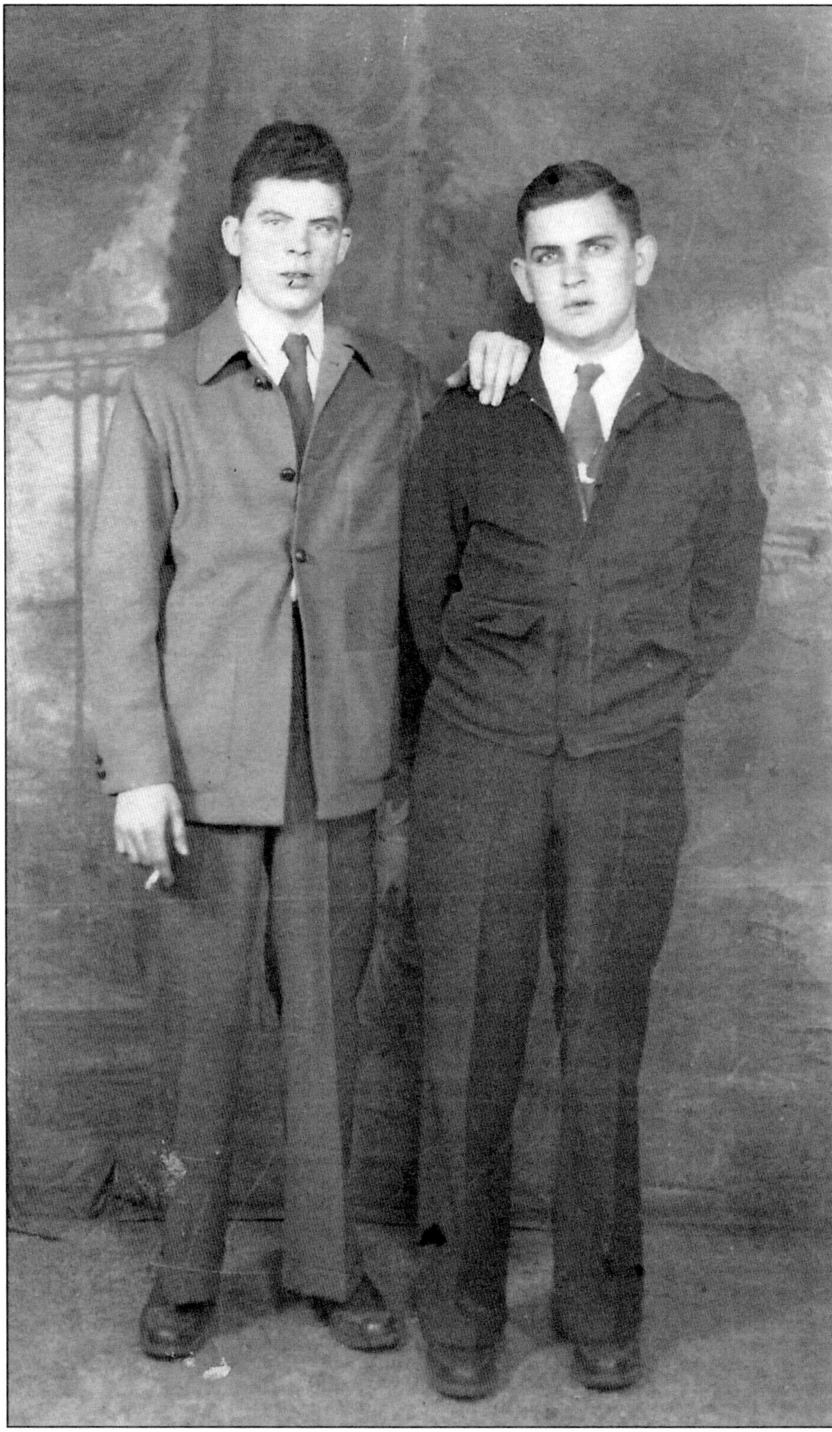

Jack Isaac and Thomas "Peaky" Chafin are pictured here in the 1940s before they enlisted in the US military. Jack was the son of Charles and Georgia Isaac and Peaky was the son of Tom and Maude Chafin. Both of them were well known as sharp dressers in the small, unincorporated Mingo County town of New Town. (Courtesy of Andrew Chafin.)

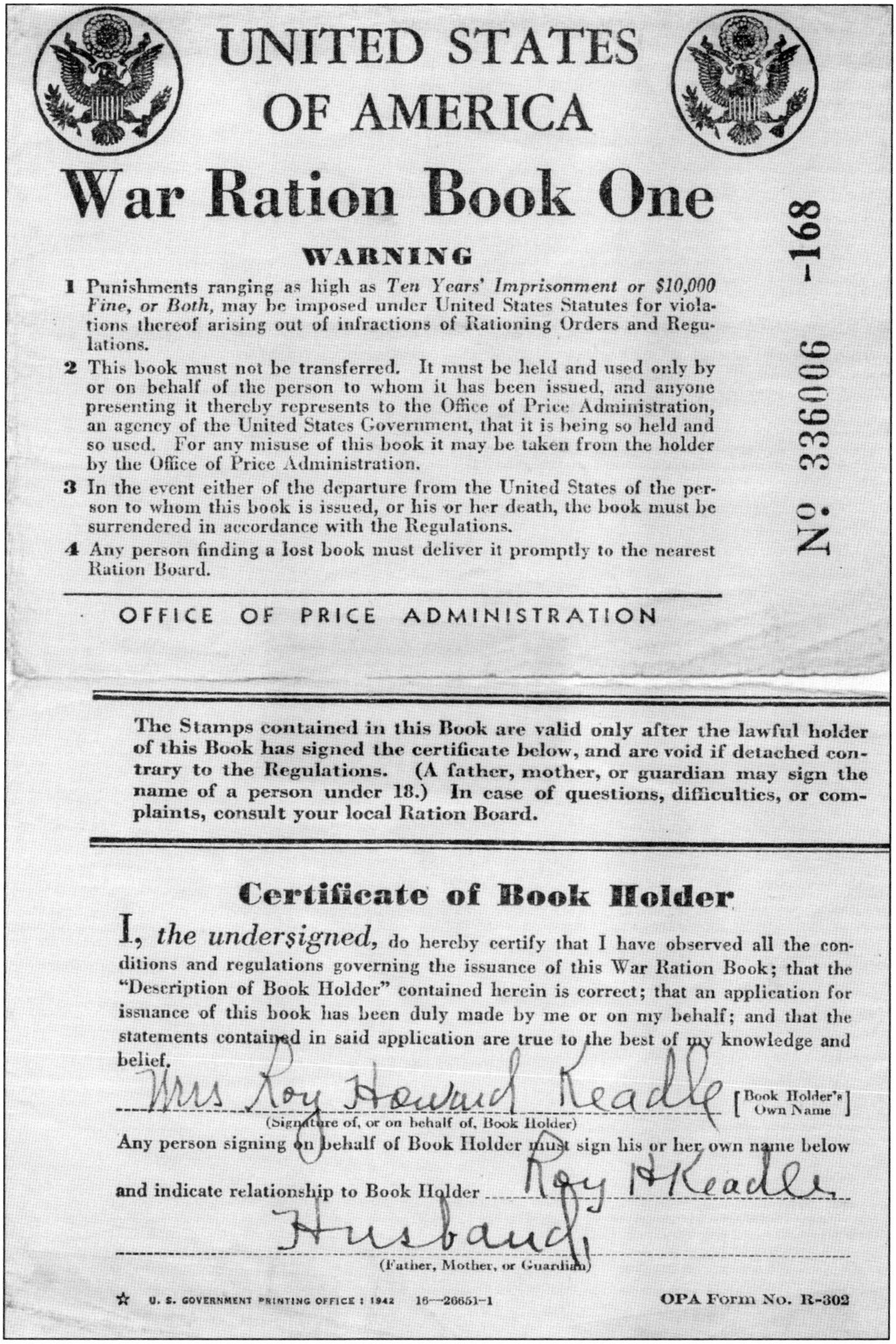

UNITED STATES OF AMERICA

War Ration Book One

No. 336006 -168

WARNING

1 Punishments ranging as high as *Ten Years' Imprisonment or $10,000 Fine, or Both,* may be imposed under United States Statutes for violations thereof arising out of infractions of Rationing Orders and Regulations.

2 This book must not be transferred. It must be held and used only by or on behalf of the person to whom it has been issued, and anyone presenting it thereby represents to the Office of Price Administration, an agency of the United States Government, that it is being so held and so used. For any misuse of this book it may be taken from the holder by the Office of Price Administration.

3 In the event either of the departure from the United States of the person to whom this book is issued, or his or her death, the book must be surrendered in accordance with the Regulations.

4 Any person finding a lost book must deliver it promptly to the nearest Ration Board.

OFFICE OF PRICE ADMINISTRATION

The Stamps contained in this Book are valid only after the lawful holder of this Book has signed the certificate below, and are void if detached contrary to the Regulations. (A father, mother, or guardian may sign the name of a person under 18.) In case of questions, difficulties, or complaints, consult your local Ration Board.

Certificate of Book Holder

I, *the undersigned,* do hereby certify that I have observed all the conditions and regulations governing the issuance of this War Ration Book; that the "Description of Book Holder" contained herein is correct; that an application for issuance of this book has been duly made by me or on my behalf; and that the statements contained in said application are true to the best of my knowledge and belief.

Mrs Roy Howard Keadle [Book Holder's Own Name]

(Signature of, or on behalf of, Book Holder)

Any person signing on behalf of Book Holder must sign his or her own name below and indicate relationship to Book Holder Roy H Keadle

Husband

(Father, Mother, or Guardian)

☆ U. S. GOVERNMENT PRINTING OFFICE : 1942 16—26651-1 OPA Form No. R-302

This copy of a war ration book helps to define a lifestyle required by the sacrificing families during wartime. War rations books and tokens were issued to American families during World War II and dictated how much gasoline, tires, sugar, meat, silk, shoes, nylon, and other items any one person could buy. Ration coins introduced in 1944 allowed retailers to give change back for food bought with ration stamps. (Courtesy of Williamson Public Library.)

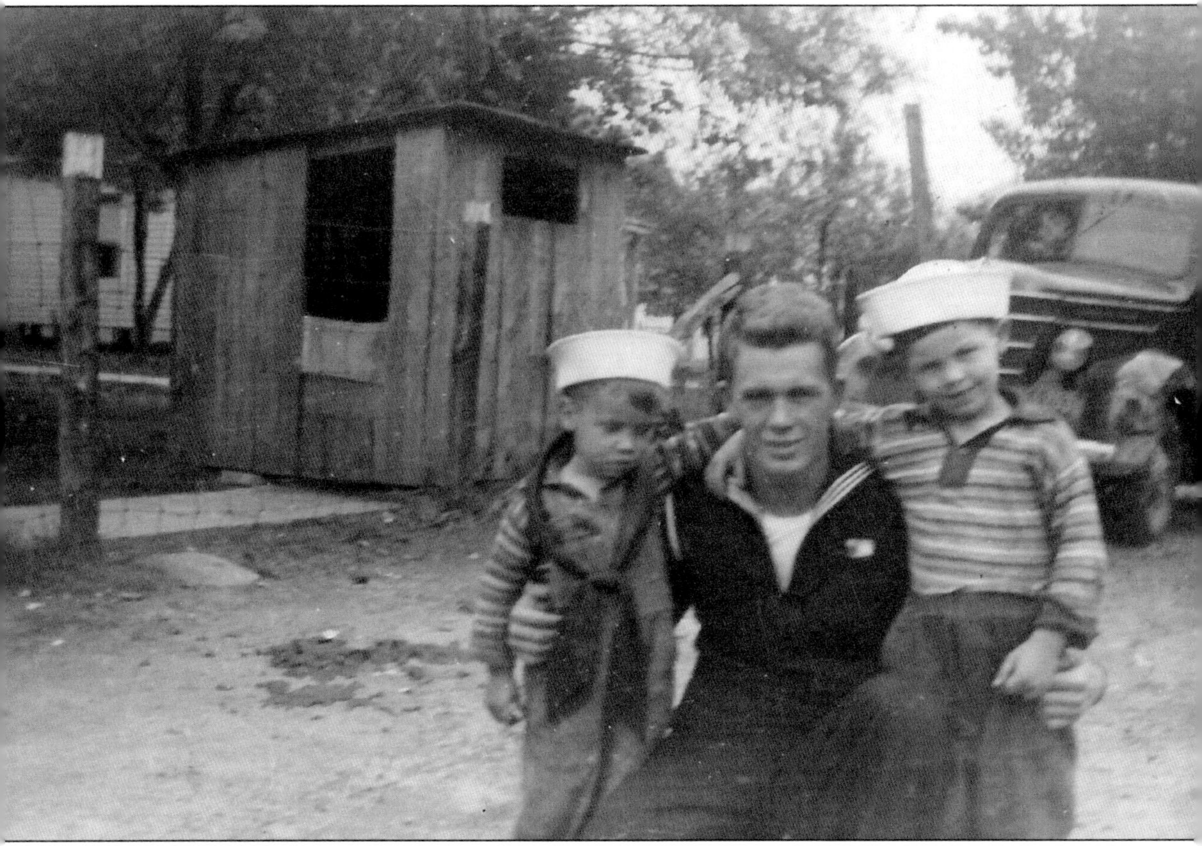

Donald Ray, left, and Andy Chafin, right, pose with their uncle Ray Isaac, who was on leave from the Navy in the 1940s. Note the coal house in the background and the unpaved street. Upon discharge from the Navy, Ray opened a popular night club in New Town called the Spinning Wheel. (Courtesy of Hazel M. Chafin.)

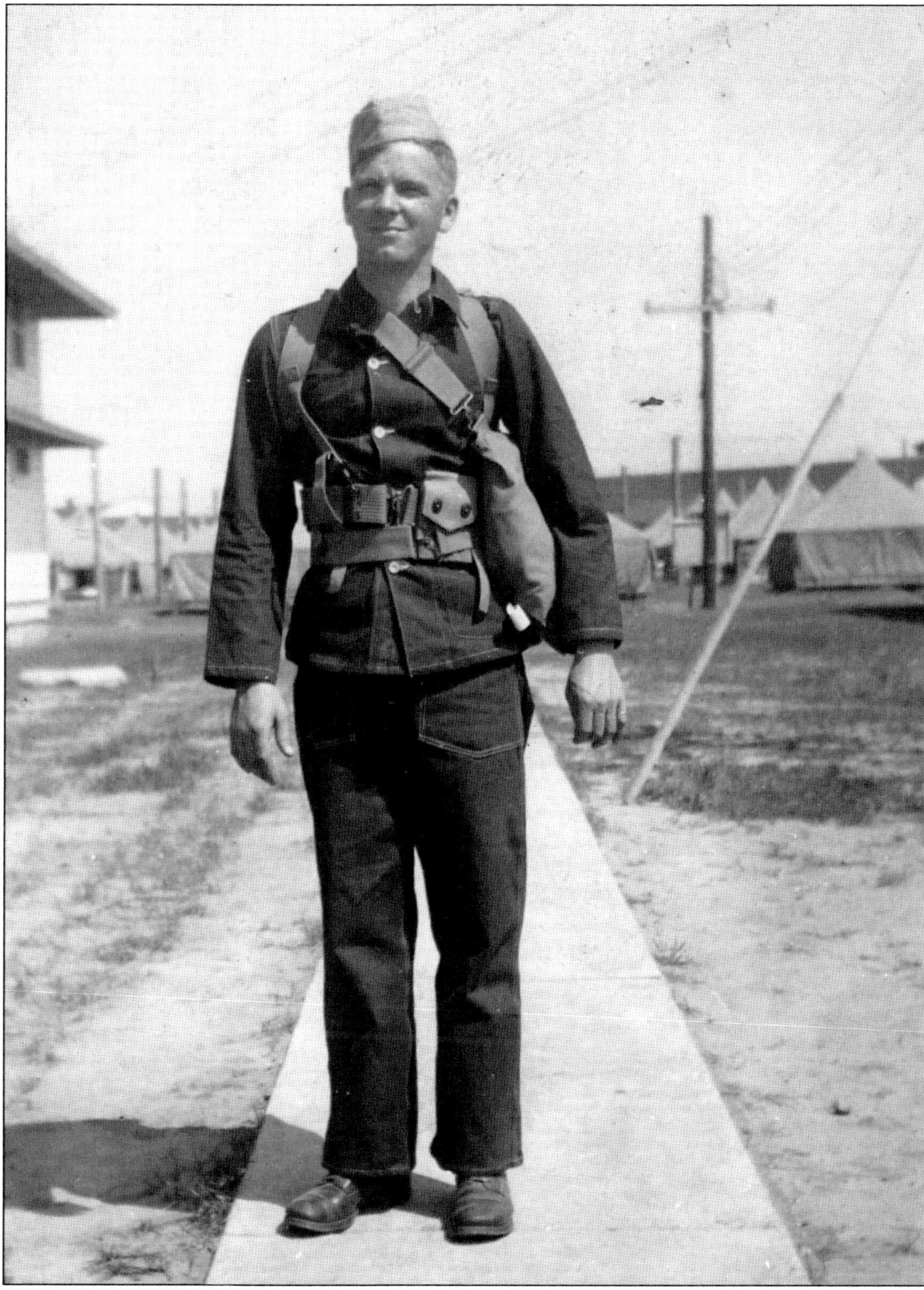

This 1940s photograph of Tommy Isaac was taken during World War II. After military duty, Tommy worked in the coal mines and later as a commercial bus driver for the Scott-Nichols Bus Company. Many Mingo County inhabitants worked in coal mining after military discharge. (Courtesy of Hazel M. Chafin.)

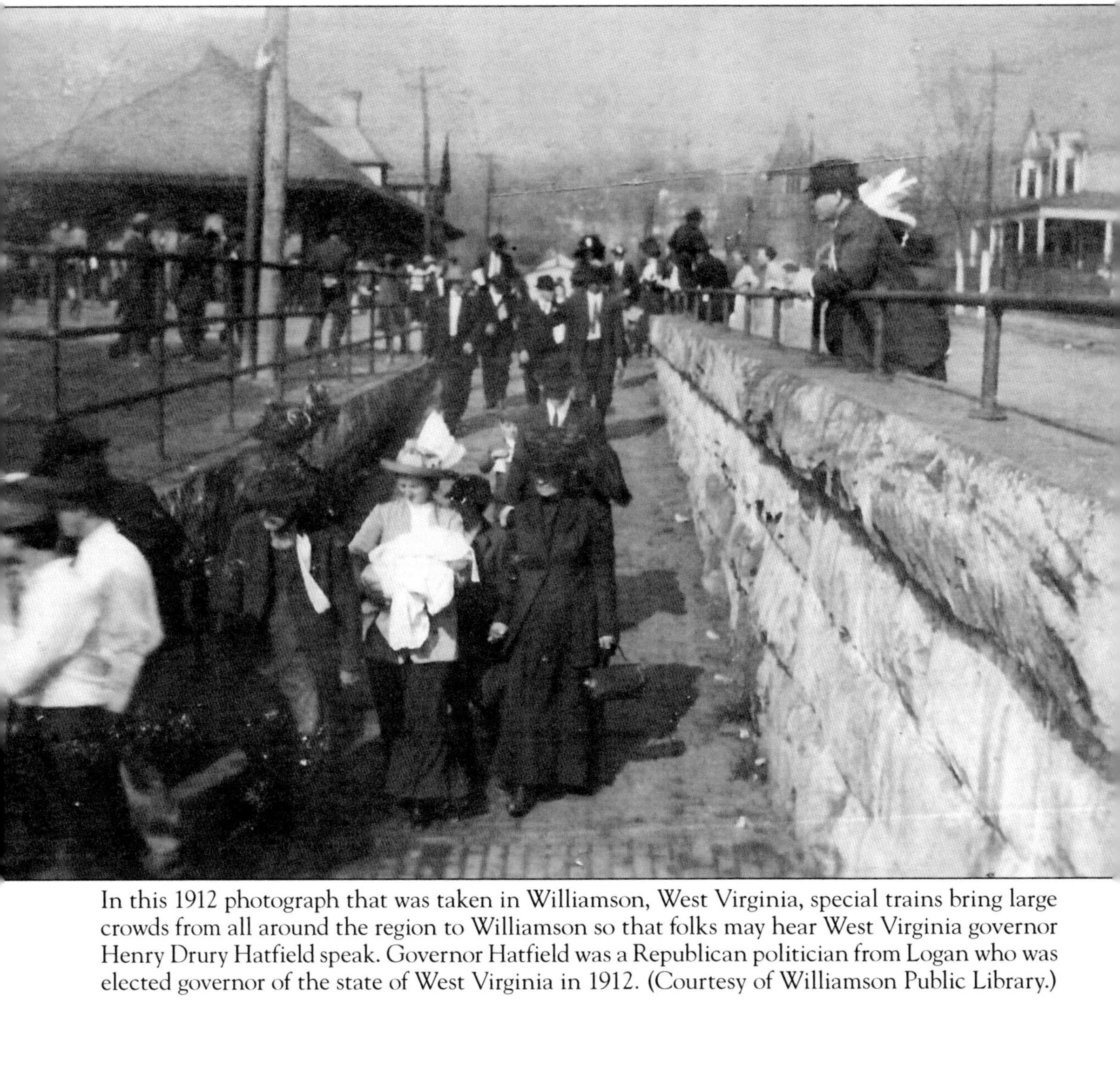

In this 1912 photograph that was taken in Williamson, West Virginia, special trains bring large crowds from all around the region to Williamson so that folks may hear West Virginia governor Henry Drury Hatfield speak. Governor Hatfield was a Republican politician from Logan who was elected governor of the state of West Virginia in 1912. (Courtesy of Williamson Public Library.)

Two

Business and Industry

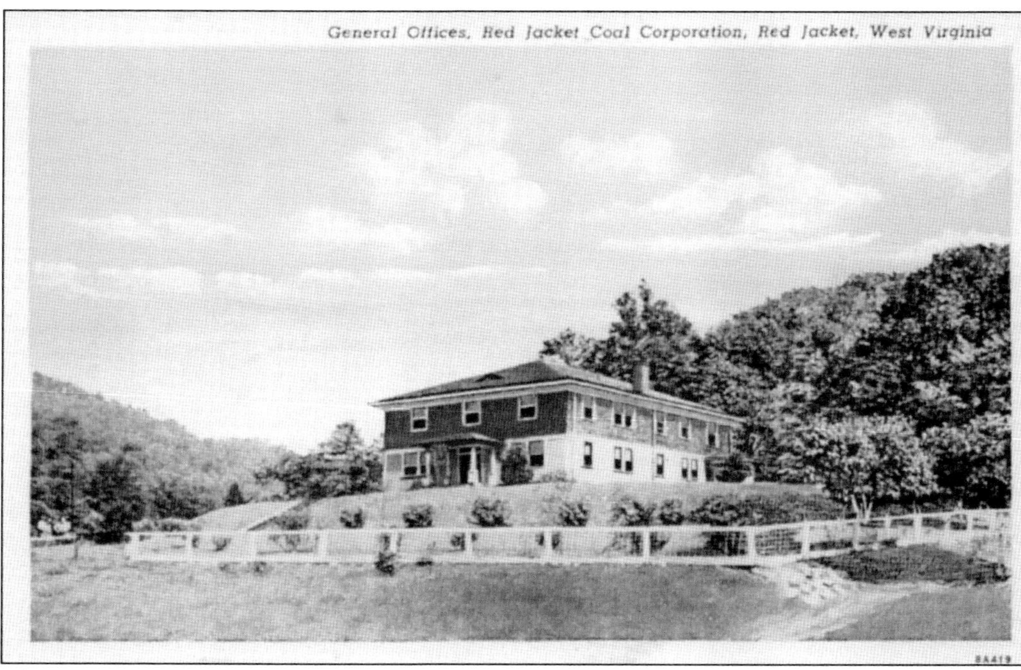

This postcard image shows the Red Jacket Coal Corporation General Offices, located in Red Jacket, West Virginia. In 1920, the operators of the Red Jacket Coal Company did not want to honor the demands for a union contract and tried to entice the laborers with increased wages for miners who did not join the union. Those who did join the union were blacklisted. This ultimately led to the involvement of the Baldwin-Felts detectives and the removal of miners from their company-owned homes. (Courtesy of William Woodward.)

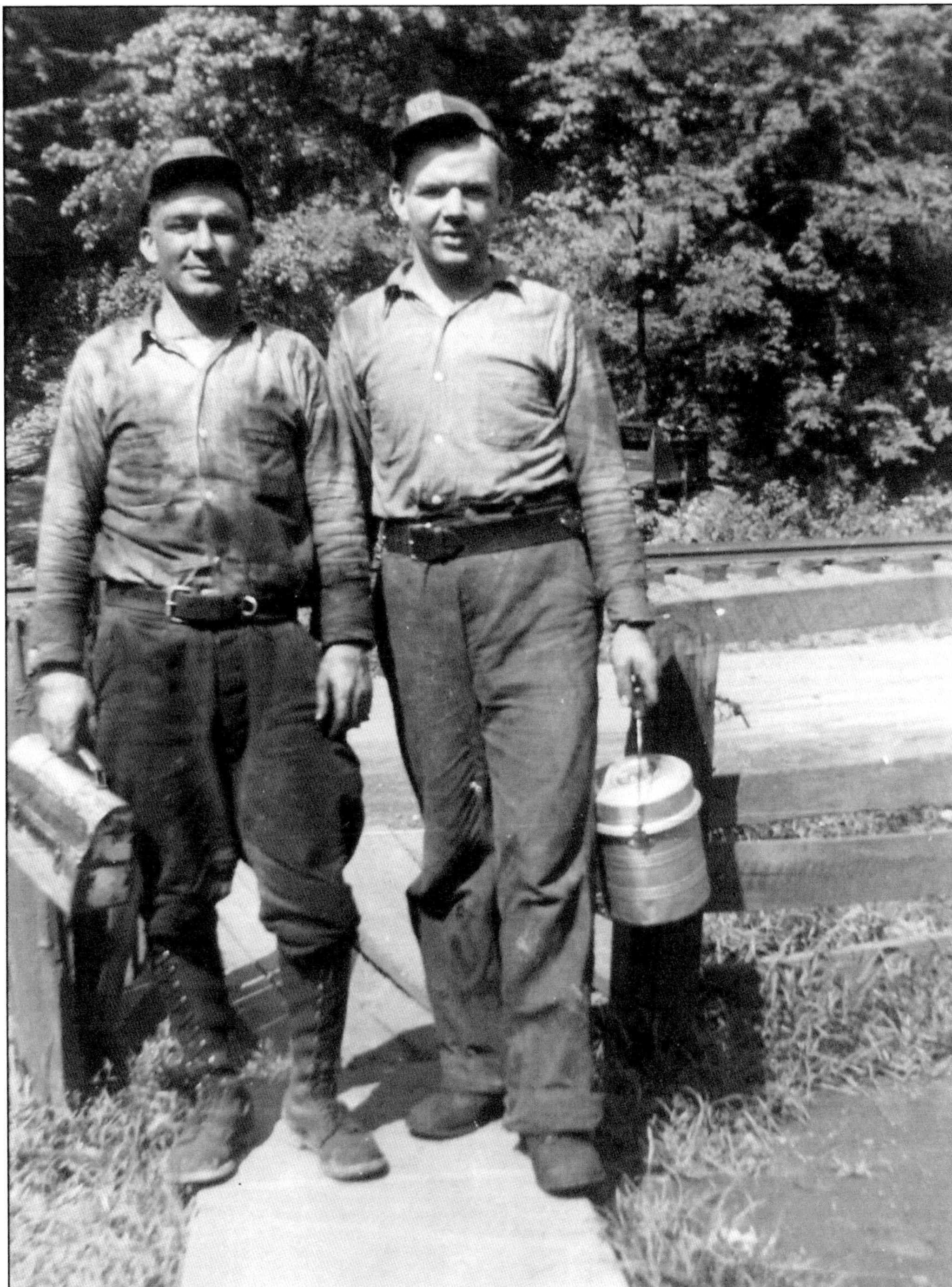

Pictured here are Raymond Newton Woodward, left, and his brother William Woodward. Both brothers worked for the Red Jacket Coal Company. The dinner bucket was an important part of any work shift in the mines. The dinner bucket held by William Woodward allowed for water to be carried in it. Often, an apple would be placed in the water to keep it cool while being transported. (Courtesy of William Woodward.)

This 1940s photograph shows Ella Chafin and Tommy Isaac in front of the New Town grocery store. Ella was the daughter of Allen and Lydia Chafin; Lydia was the daughter of Ellison Hatfield, who was killed by the McCoys on election day in 1882. The killing of Ellison blossomed into the Hatfield-McCoy Feud. Tommy was the son of Charles and Georgia Isaac. (Courtesy of Hazel M. Chafin.)

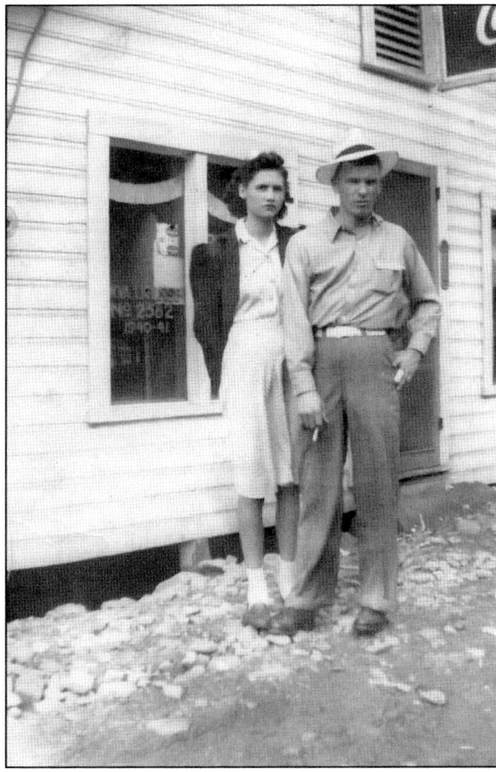

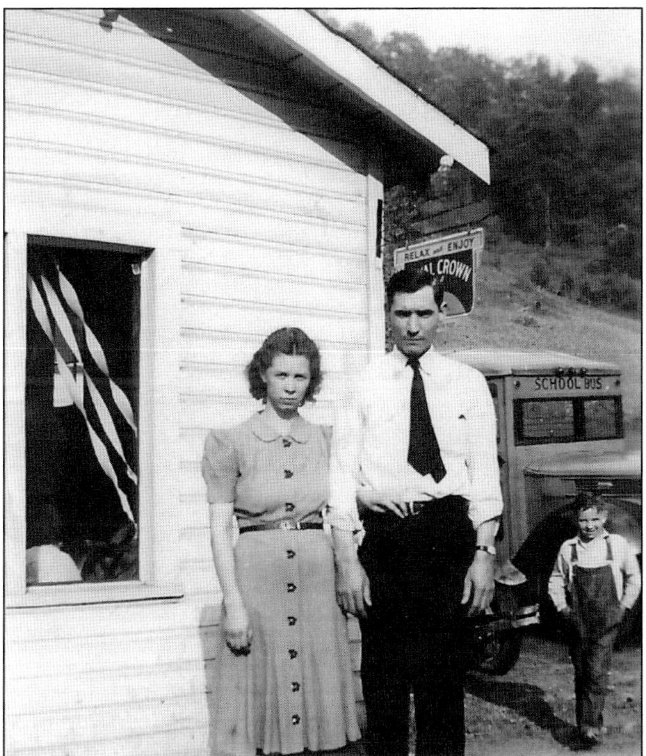

Pictured here are Hazel Isaac Chafin, left, and her husband Tom C. Chafin. The young man in the background is Alfred Steele. There is also a school bus in the background. In addition to operating the store, Tom also drove a bus. (Courtesy of Hazel M. Chafin.)

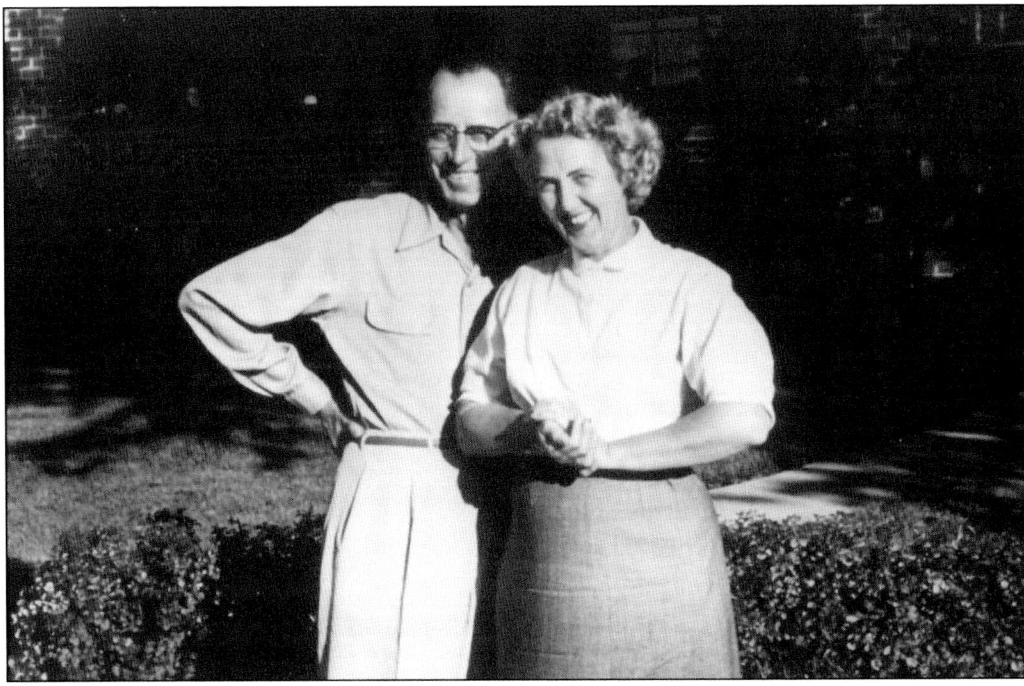

Emmitt E. Brown, left, and his wife, Marie Allara Brown, owned the B&C Oil Company in Matewan. The gas station was located near the downtown underpass. They are pictured here, happy to smile for the camera on a warm day in Matewan in the 1950s. (Courtesy of Dimple Tiller Allara.)

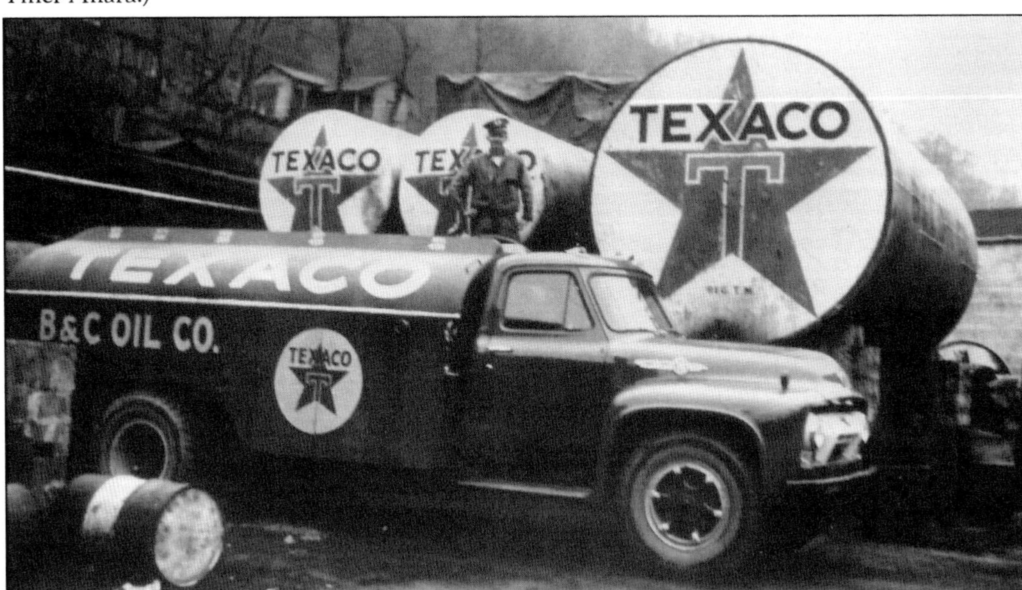

Ellis Brown, the twin brother of Emmitt Brown, was driving one of the family's B&C Oil Company fuel trucks down Mary Taylor Mountain when the brakes went out. Ellis stayed with the truck instead of jumping out of it. He ran it into Pigeon Creek and was killed. Most believe if he had jumped out he would have lived. He saved many lives with his courageous act. (Courtesy of Dimple Tiller Allara.)

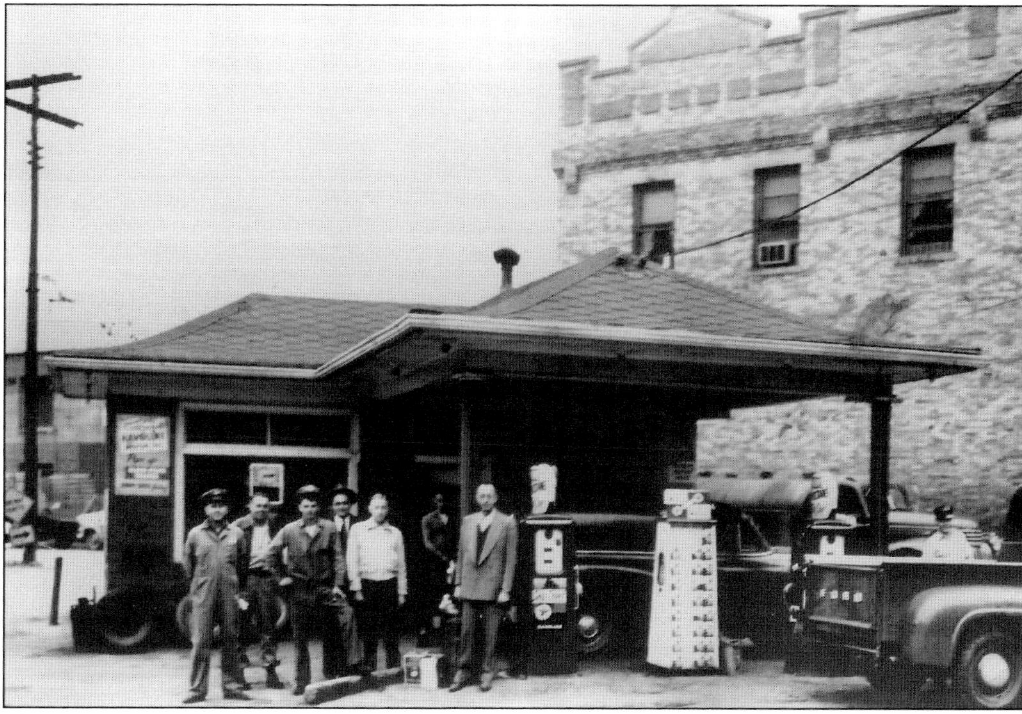

This picture of E.E. Brown's Texaco gas station was taken in the 1940s. Those pictured are, from left to right, E.E. Brown, Ellis Brown, Jack Stewart, Frank Morrell, and Vinchie Morrell. The 1977 flood in Matewan went all the way to the upstairs in the Buskirk Building, seen here in the background. (Courtesy of Dimple Tiller Allara.)

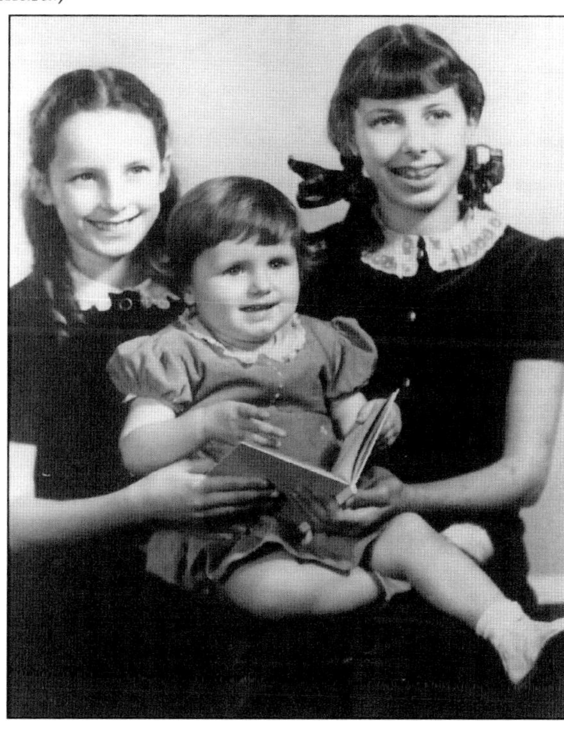

This sweet picture is of the three children of Emmitt and Marie Allara Brown. From left to right are Ernestine, Linda, and Betty Jo Brown. Their parents owned and operated B&C Oil Company in Matewan in the 1940s. (Courtesy of Dimple Tiller Allara.)

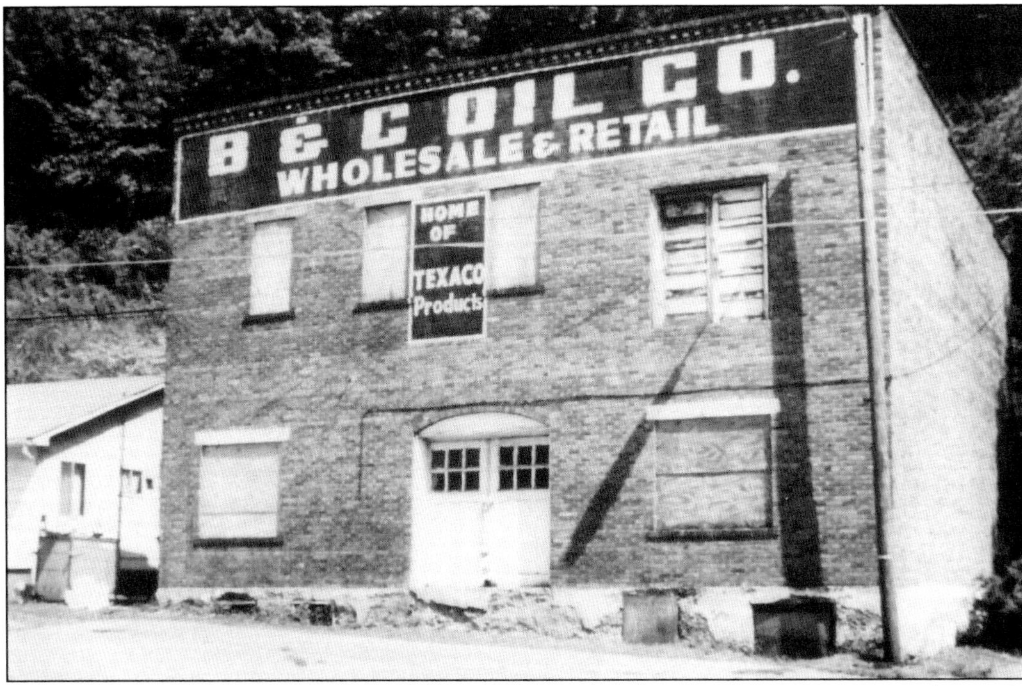

This is a picture of E.E. Brown's Texaco B&C Oil Company property in Matewan in the 1940s. This building has since been torn down; the Matewan United Methodist Church now sits on this site. (Courtesy of Dimple Tiller Allara.)

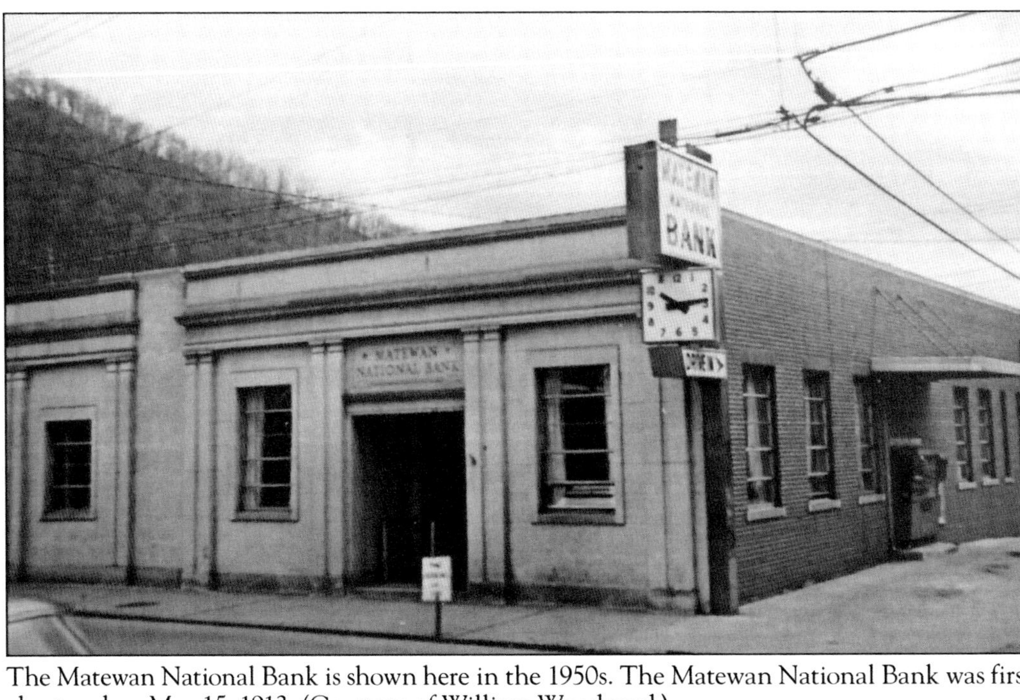

The Matewan National Bank is shown here in the 1950s. The Matewan National Bank was first chartered on May 15, 1913. (Courtesy of William Woodward.)

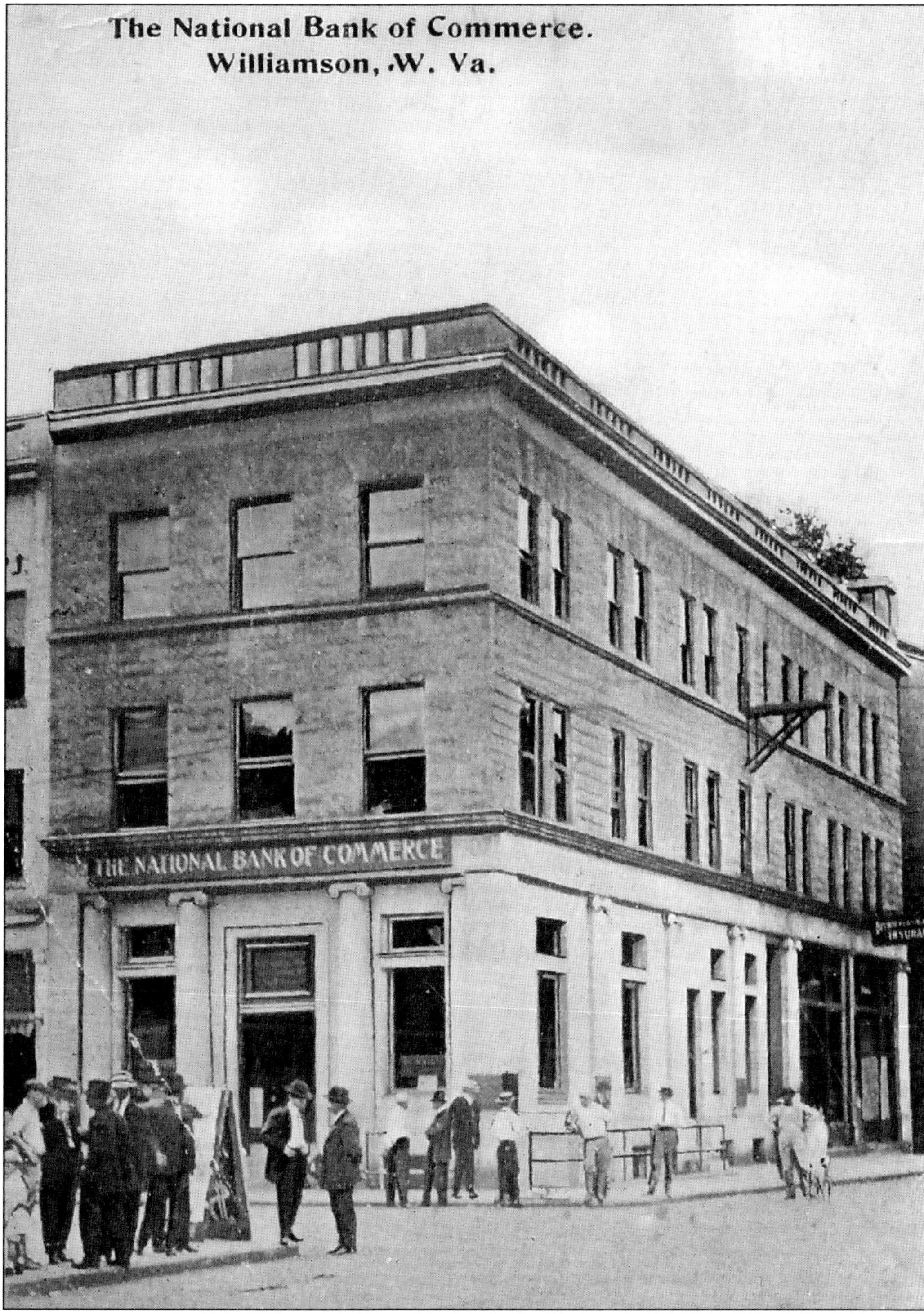

Pictured here is the National Bank of Commerce at its corner location in downtown Williamson. This picture is from the 1950s. The National Bank of Commerce in Williamson West Virginia was first opened on June 11, 1903. (Courtesy of Williamson Public Library.)

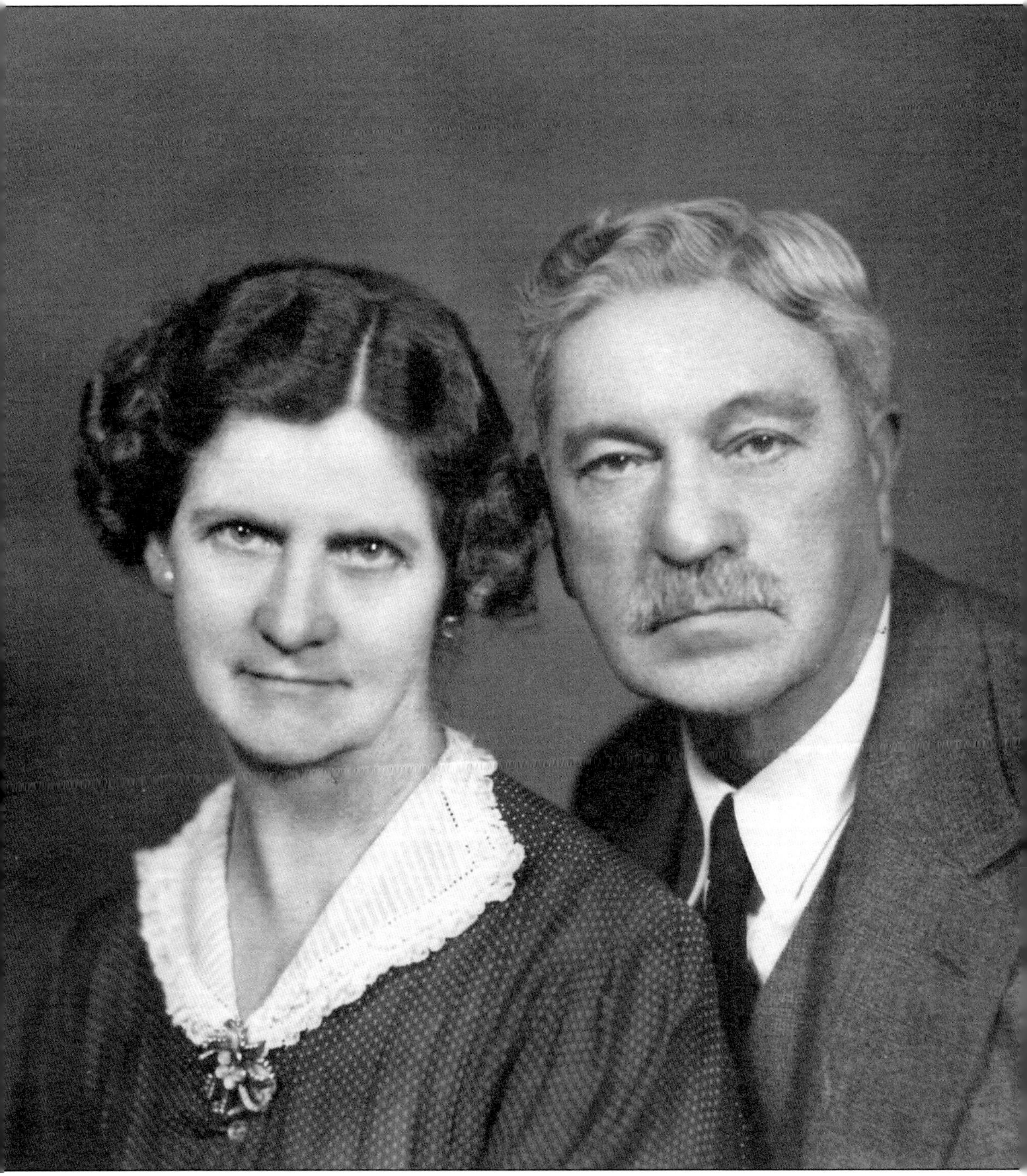

This photograph shows Parlee Justice Farley, left, and her husband, James A. "Jim" Farley. James Farley was born in 1873 in Chattaroy, West Virginia. He was first married to Mary Maynard; following her death, he married Parlee Justice. Farley, known as Daddy Jim to family, later lived on a large farm on Elk Creek near Delbarton, West Virginia. He was known as a son, husband, father, farmer, US marshal, mercantile operator, and a well-respected friend to all. (Courtesy of Lahoma Lee Farley Schuller.)

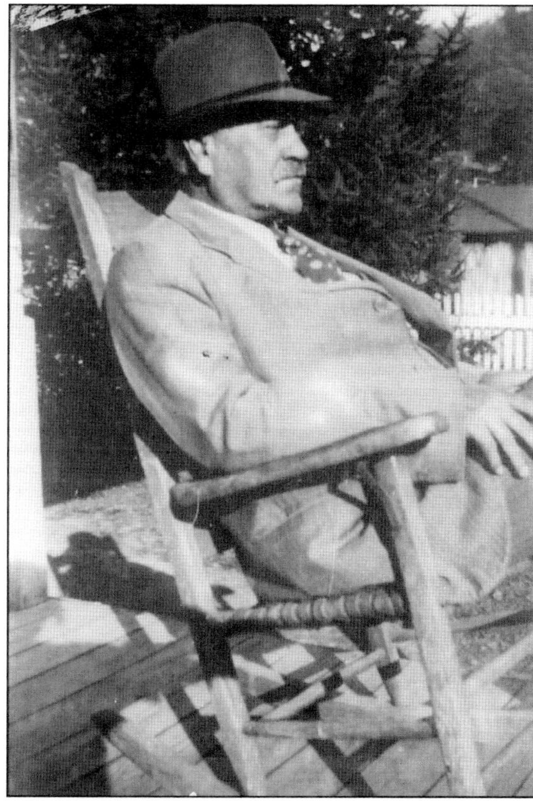

In this picture of James A. "Jim" Farley, he is sitting on the front porch of his large farm on Elk Creek near Delbarton. He loved life on his farm and took pleasure in the work of it. His grandchildren especially remember the cows and the pumpkins. Jim and his wife, Mary Maynard, had seven children. Five of their children became doctors. Jim Farley lived from 1873 to 1946. (Courtesy of Lahoma Lee Farley Schuller.)

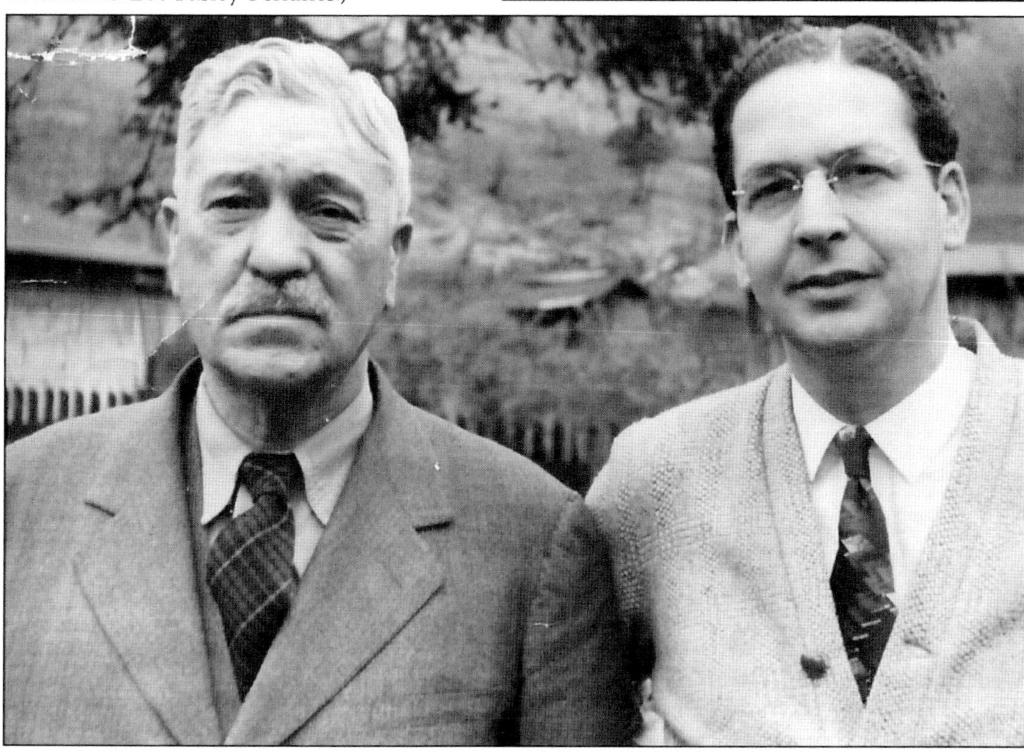

Shown here are James A. "Jim" Farley, left, and the Reverend Gibson. This picture was taken at Farley's farm on Elk Creek. Sunday dinners down at the farm after church were a regular occurrence. Family and friends would gather to eat and enjoy the fellowship. It is believed that this photograph was taken during one of those dinners. (Courtesy of Lahoma Lee Farley Schuller.)

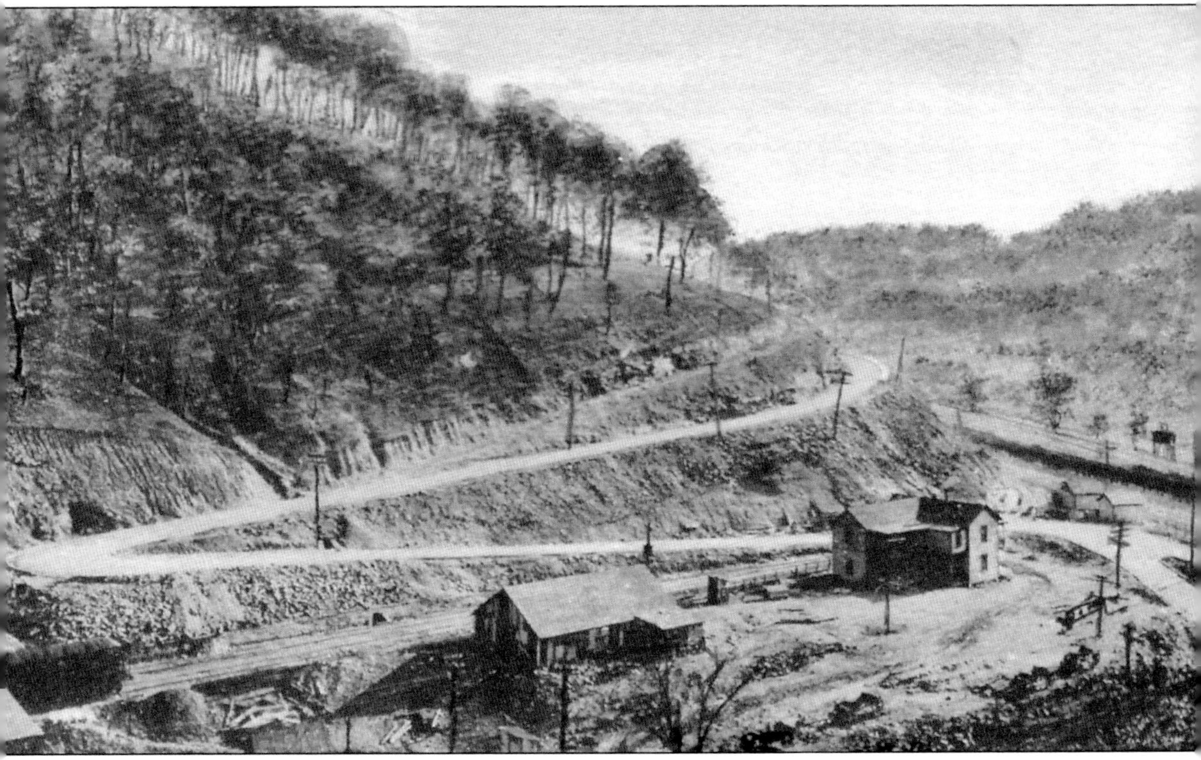

Pictured here is Hair Pin Turn in Williamson in the late 1800s. This site in Mingo County in the late 1800s would grow to become the city of Williamson and the county seat. In 1888, a company of railroad surveyors first broke a path along the Tug River while looking for a route for the railroads. Wallace Williamson had his farm laid out in lots and sold the lots at auction. The ones closest to the railroad sold for less but ultimately ended up being more valuable. The city would later become the heart of the billion-dollar coalfields. (Courtesy of Williamson Public Library.)

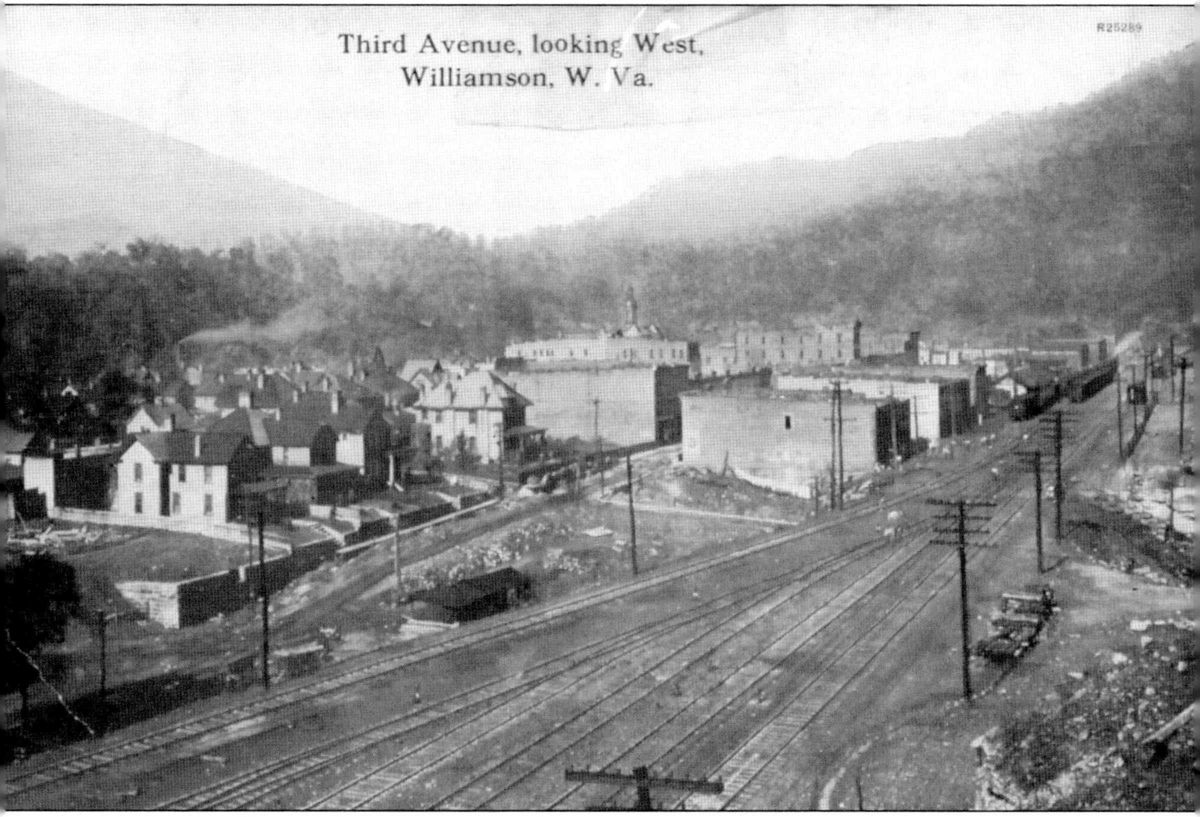

This is a 1910 photograph of Williamson that reflects a view of Third Avenue looking west. Williamson was incorporated in 1892 while Mingo County was still a part of Logan County. In 1895, Mingo County separated from Logan County and N.T. Keadle was elected the first sheriff of the county. Several of Keadle's descendants still reside in the county. (Courtesy of Williamson Public Library.)

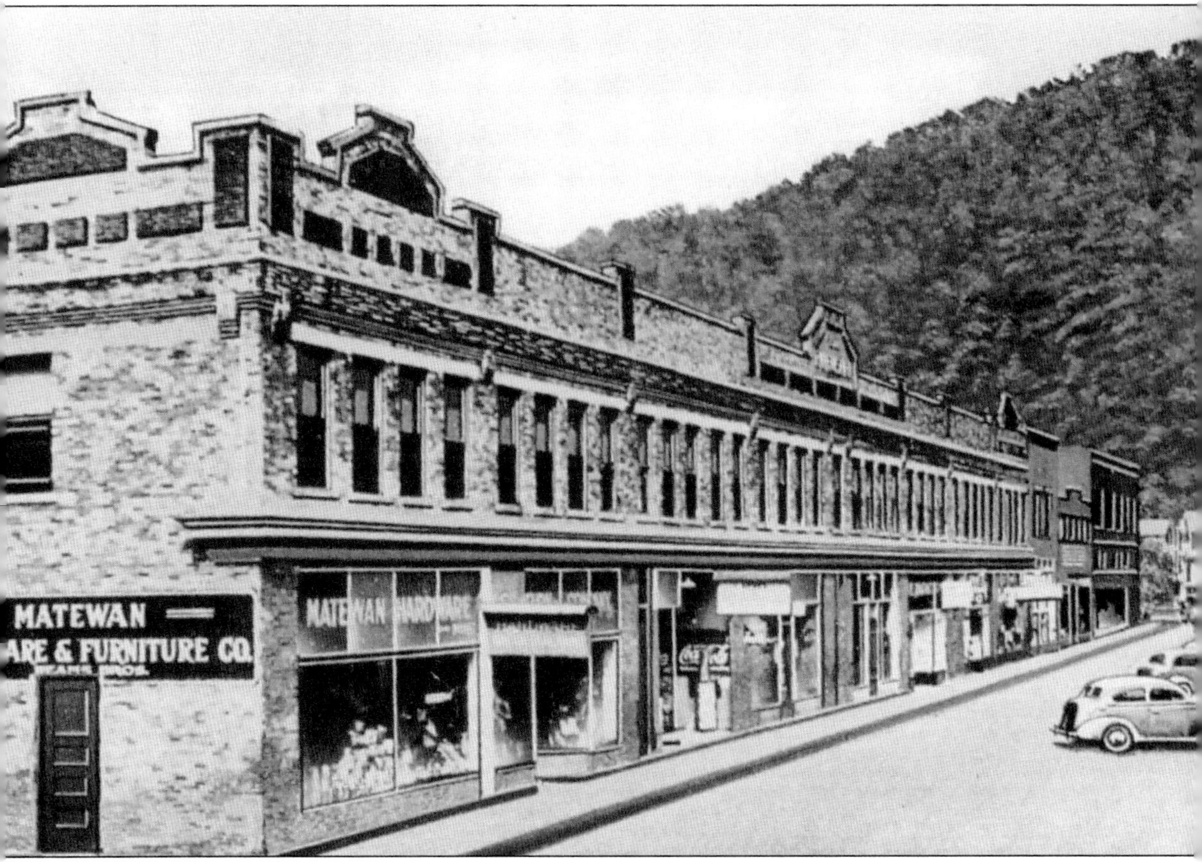

The Buskirk Building is pictured here at the time of the Matewan Massacre in 1921. This building housed the Urias Hotel and was the headquarters for the Baldwin-Felts detectives. Nearby buildings included the Chambers Hardware and the Hope Building. Matewan's commercial core has retained much of what existed at the time of the Matewan Massacre. Fire destroyed the Buskirk Building in 1992. (Courtesy of Eddie Nenni.)

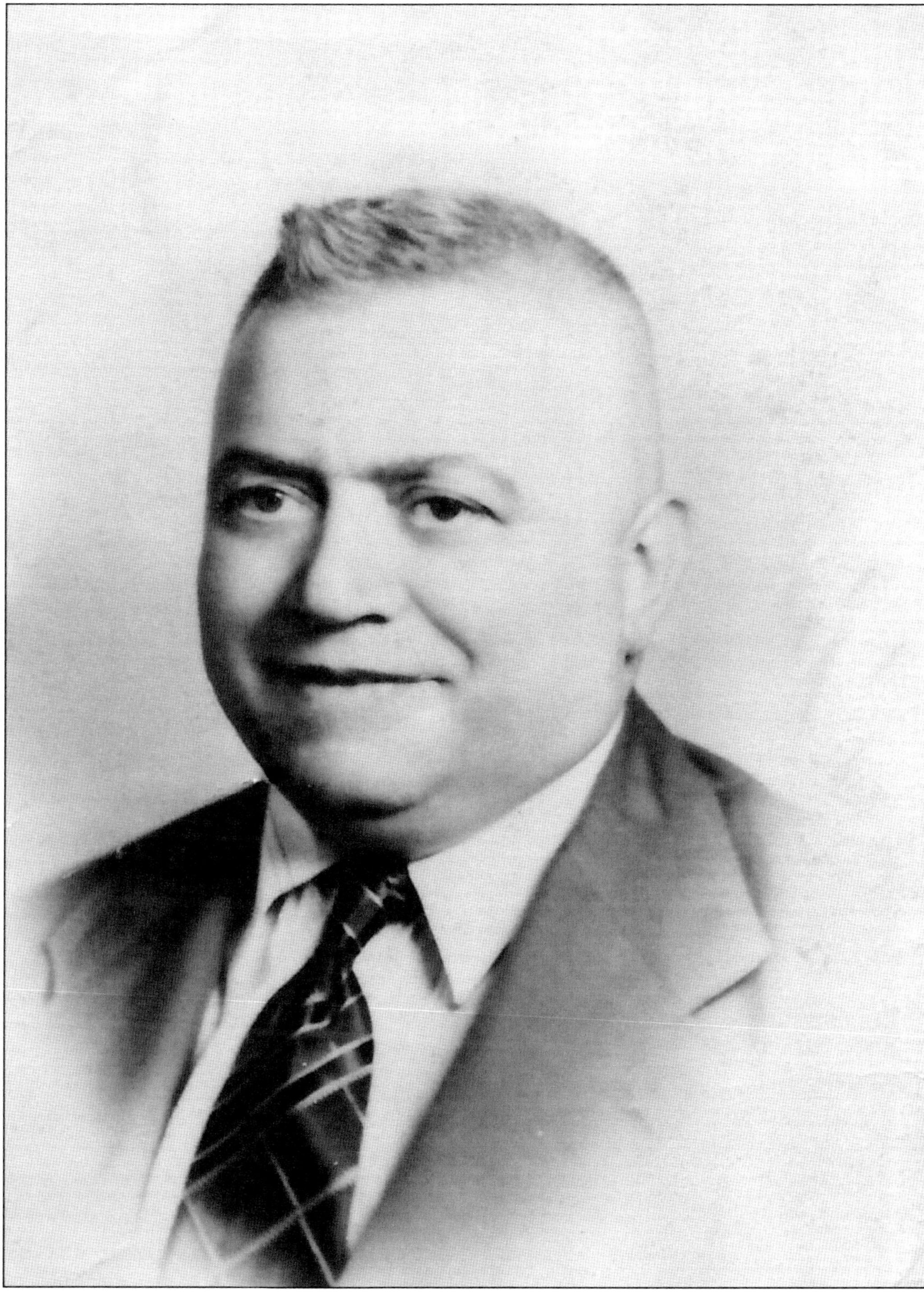

John Nenni, pictured here, emigrated from Rome, Italy, to America in 1909. Although he and Attitilo Nenni lived only 15 miles apart in Rome, they never knew each other until they met in Mingo County. Coincidentally, they lived also 15 miles apart in Mingo County before meeting each other in the early 1900s. (Courtesy of Eddie Nenni.)

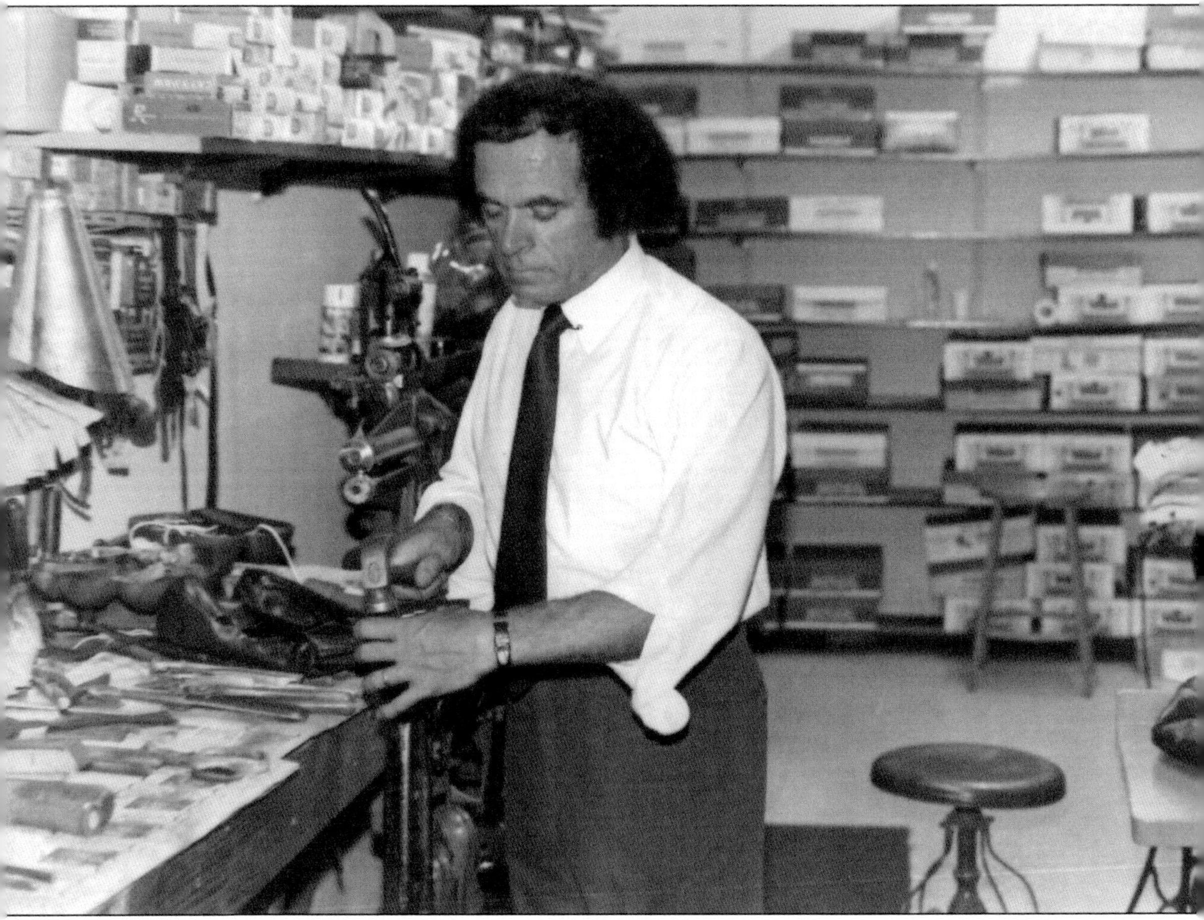

In this picture, Eddie Nenni plies his shoe repair at the Nenni Department Store in Matewan. Attitilo Nenni, Eddie's father, opened the shoe store in 1909, which was followed in 1919 with the opening of the department store. Nenni's is still open today. Eddie is the leader of a popular band, the Jaguars, which provides dance music. (Courtesy of Eddie Nenni.)

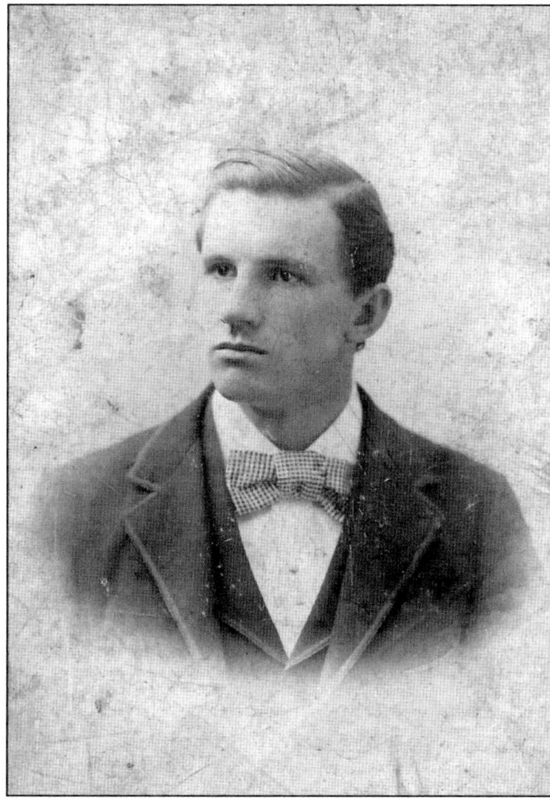

This picture is of Wells Goodykoontz, who came to Mingo County around 1894. Goodykoontz was a Republican leader while W.J. Williamson was a Democratic leader. Together, the two, along with others, worked hard to help insure that the land which was formerly part of Logan County would indeed be separated, leading to Mingo County being established in 1895. (Courtesy of Williamson Public Library.)

This photograph was taken at the "Rockefeller for Governor" campaign stop in Williamson in 1976. This event insured a strong turnout of loyal supporters. Seen here from left to right are Tom C. Chafin, Steve Adkins, Sen. Edward Kennedy, Sen. Jennings Randolph, and an unidentified man. Chief Field Deputy Sheriff Ernest Hatfield stands guard. Rockefeller served two terms as governor and later became West Virginia's US senator in 1984. (Courtesy of Hazel M. Chafin.)

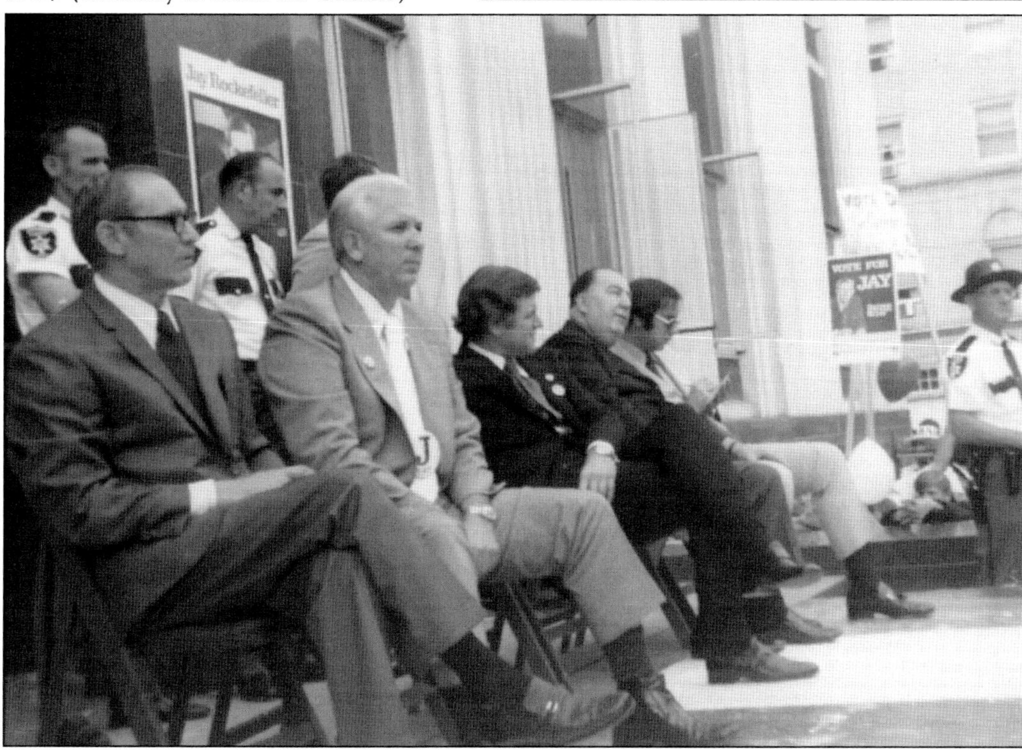

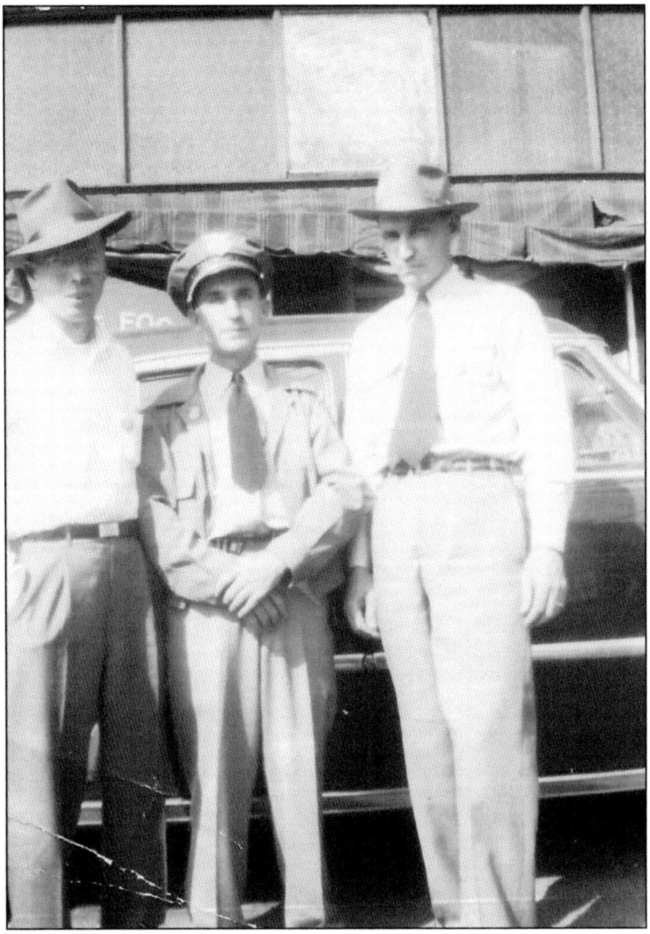

Pictured here from left to right are Joe Phillips, constable; Huff Ferrell, constable; and Tom C. Chafin, justice of the peace. This photograph was taken in the 1950s in Matewan. Tom C. Chafin was born on April 30, 1911. In 1928, at the age of 16, he went to work in the mines. He left the mines in 1941 and went into business for himself and drove a school bus until 1962. He was elected constable in November 1944. Tom was elected justice of the peace for four terms: 1948, 1952, 1956, and 1960. He served until he was elected county clerk in November 1962, serving out his term that lasted until 1968. He was elected to a second term as county clerk which was from November 1968 until 1972. He was elected sheriff in November of 1972 and again in 1976 and remained in that position until he retired on December 30, 1980. (Courtesy of Andrew Chafin.)

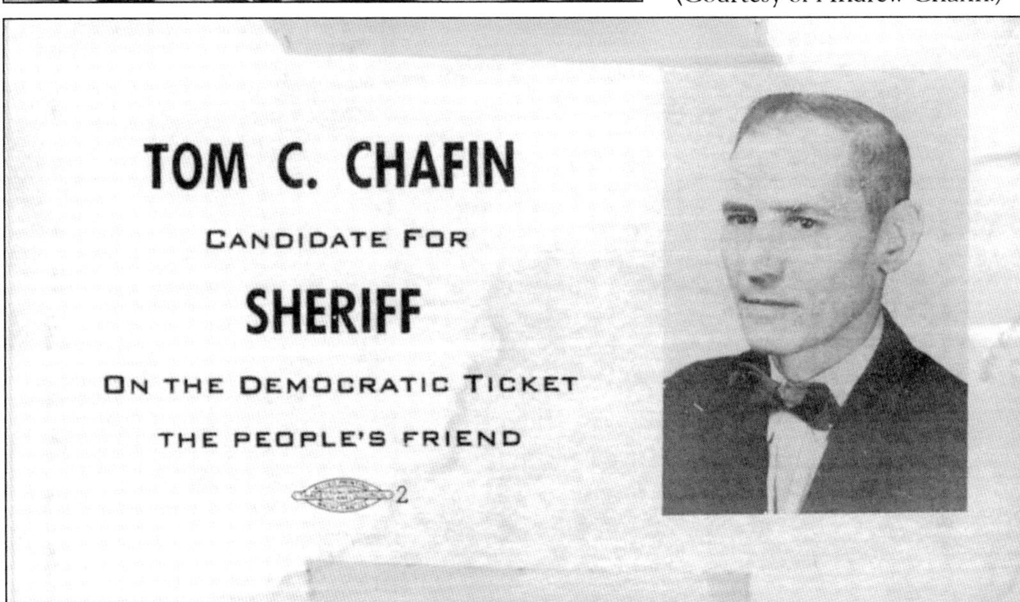

Three

Sports and Education

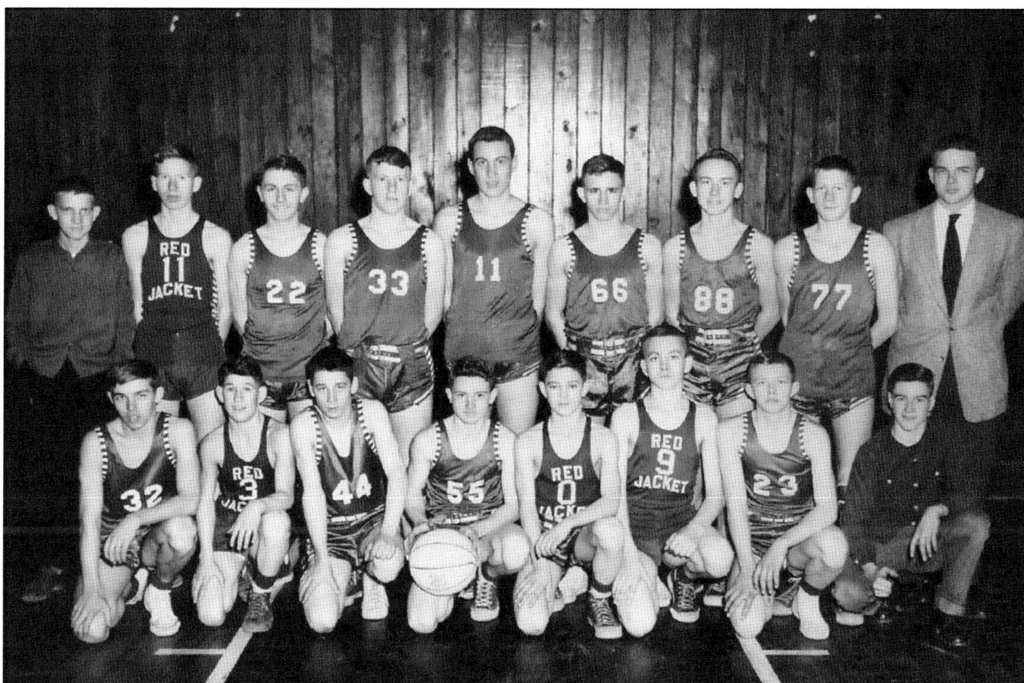

Pictured here is the Red Jacket Junior High School basketball team. The Red Jacket Junior High School consisted of grades 7–9. Graduates of Red Jacket went on to attend Matewan High School before the school was closed. A new consolidated high school was constructed and opened in August 2011. The new high school was named Matewan Central. Sports were always important to residents of Mingo County. Many young people were recognized for their athletic skills and abilities, and some later returned to coach at the facilities they had attended as students. (Courtesy of Andrew Chafin.)

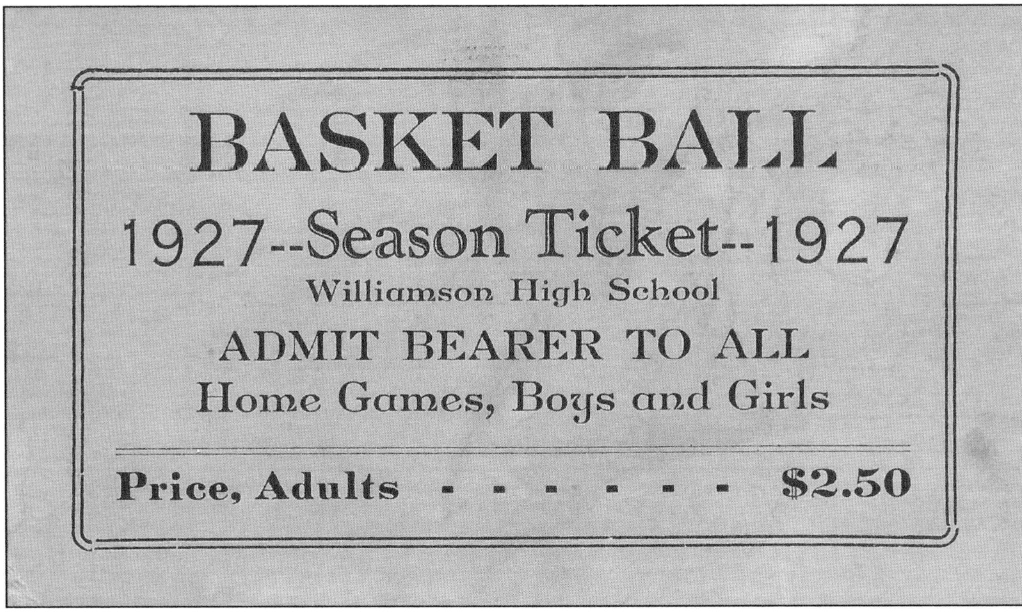
BASKET BALL

1927--Season Ticket--1927

Williamson High School

ADMIT BEARER TO ALL

Home Games, Boys and Girls

Price, Adults - - - - - - - $2.50

The season ticket for basketball at Williamson High School dated 1927 is an example of just how seriously the folks of Mingo County felt about their young people and the sports in which they participated. The price for adults was $2.50, and folks were proud to support their school sports and their young participants. (Courtesy of the Williamson Public Library.)

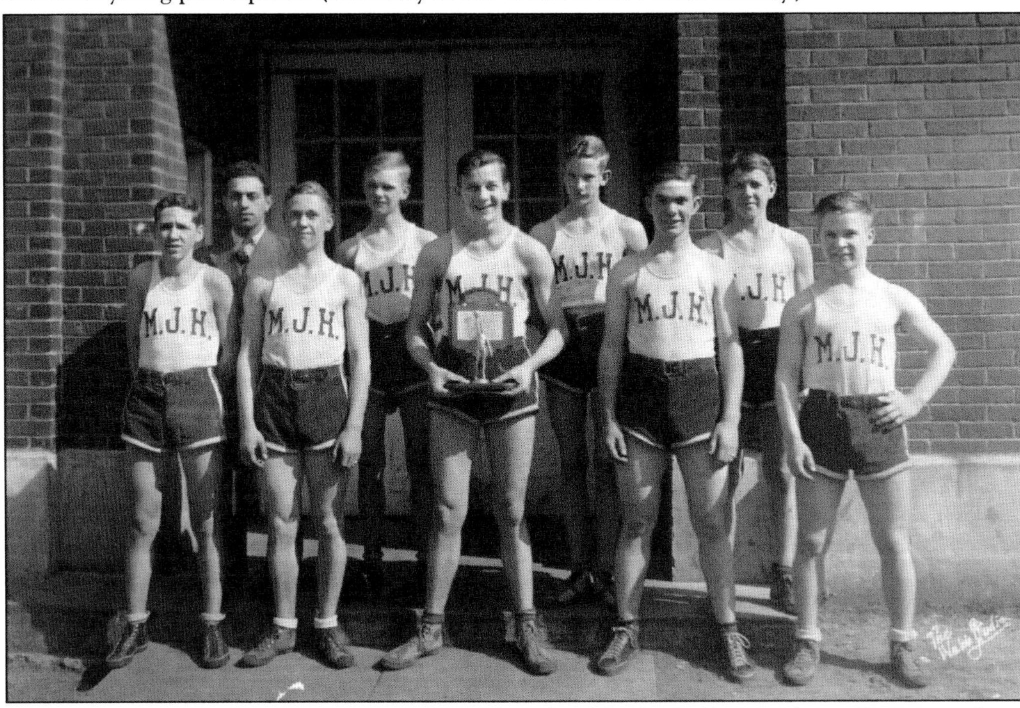

This is a picture of the Matewan Junior High School basketball team for 1937. Pictured and identified here are, from left to right, (first row) Frankie Morrell, unidentified, ? Ritter, Robert McCoy, and unidentified; (second row) coach Bill Nenni, James Gobble, Harry Roberson, and unidentified. (Courtesy of Hester Kinder Keatley.)

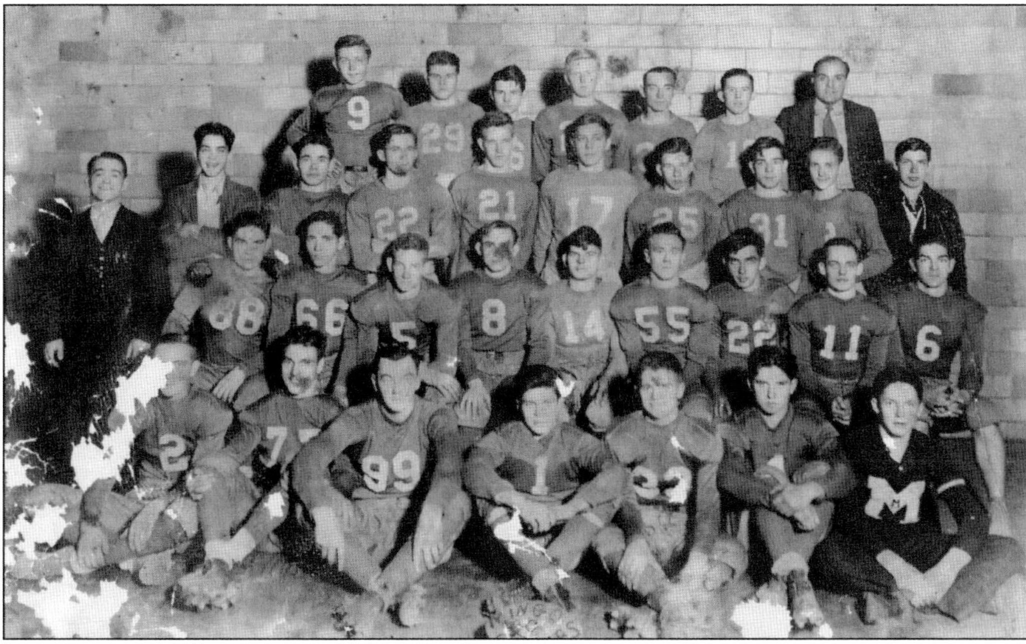

Matewan High School was also known as Magnolia High School of Matewan. Pictured here is the 1937 football team. Shown here are, from left to right, are (first row) (2) Rush Fields, Henry Schnell, (99) Tennis Mounts, (1) Winfield Cooper, (33) Ernest Renn, Millard Phillips, and M. Harod Dickens: (second row) Coach Oswald Rometo, (88) John Sipple, (66) Mackie Morrell, (5) Harry Roberson, (8) William Fedora, (14) Armal Howard, (55) Bob Ritter, (22) Russell Fields, (11) Ernest Smith, (6) David Daniels; (third row) Burnis Copley, Manuel Barrios, (22) Tom Weaver, (21) Sam McCoy, (17) Sam Kowallo, (25) Dorsel Steele, (31) Albert Vinciguerra, Steve Svetlick, and Mack Dotson; (fourth row) (9) Paul Hatfield, (29) Hubert Dishman, (26) Earl Bowes, Harry Chafin, Lawrence Smith, J.L. Williams, and Coach Hofstetter. (Courtesy of Hester Kinder Keatley.)

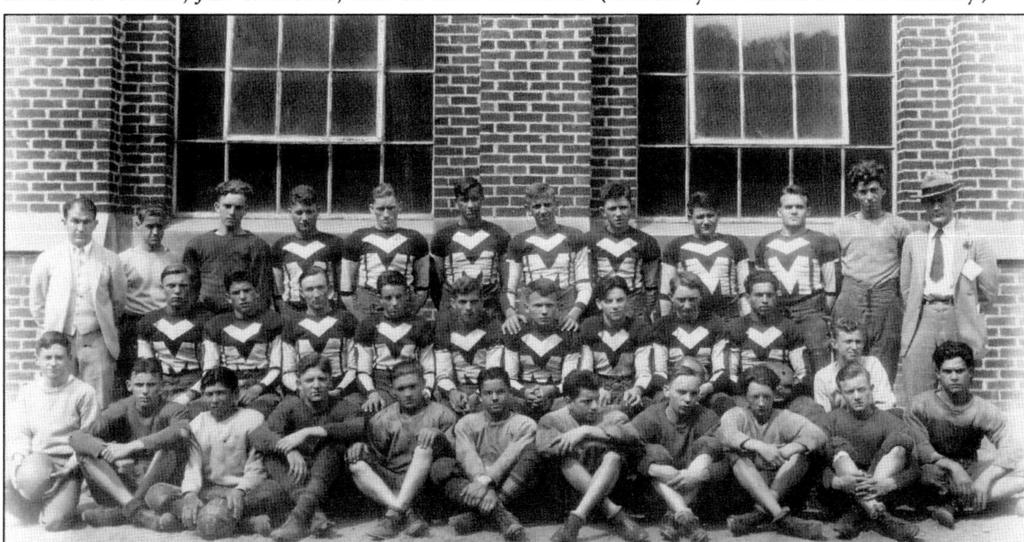

This picture of Matewan High School's football team was taken in the 1930s. The first person on the left is coach Glenn Taylor. The fifth person from the left is Hiram Keatley, father-in-law of Hester Kinder Keatley. (Courtesy of Hester Kinder Keatley).

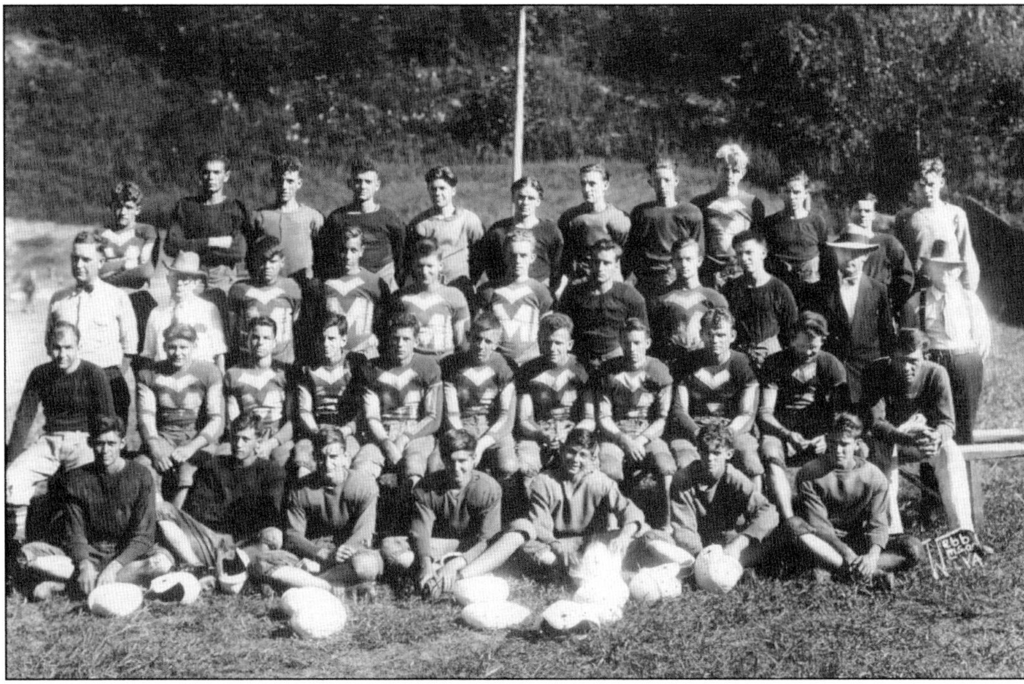

Pictured here is the 1932–1933 Matewan High School football team. Webb Studio was often the photographer for the school pictures. Stuart Gose is pictured here on the second row, the last one on the right. (Courtesy of Hester Kinder Keatley.)

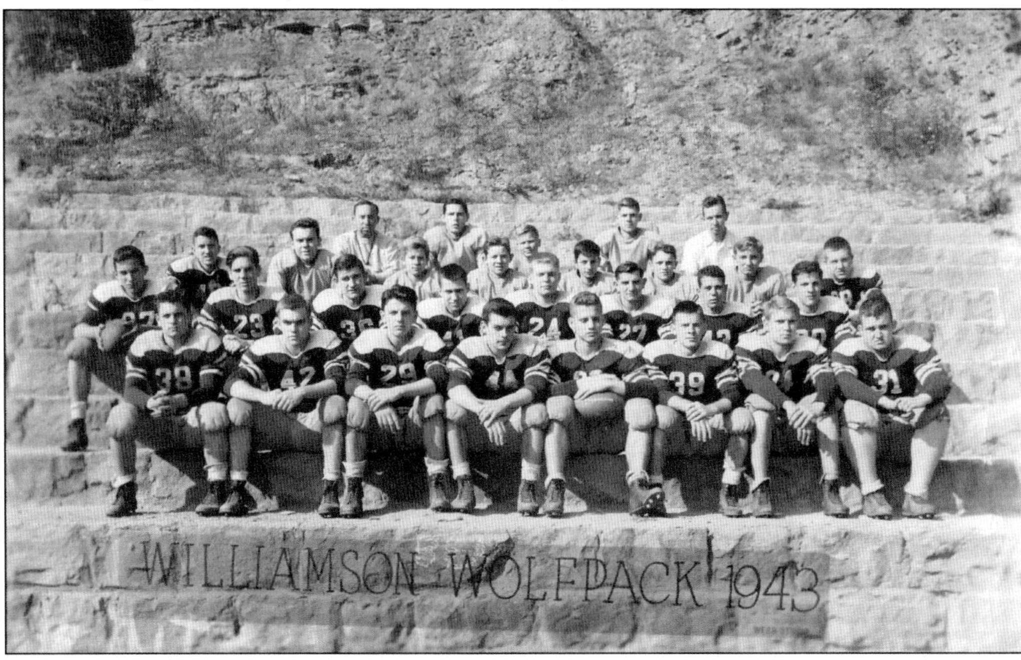

The Williamson Wolfpack High School football team poses here for a group portrait. The team has a long history of success, and this 1943 photograph includes many players who went on to win the West Virginia High School Championship in 1944. The West Virginia Sports Writers Association named state football champions from 1937 to 1946. (Courtesy of Williamson Public Library.)

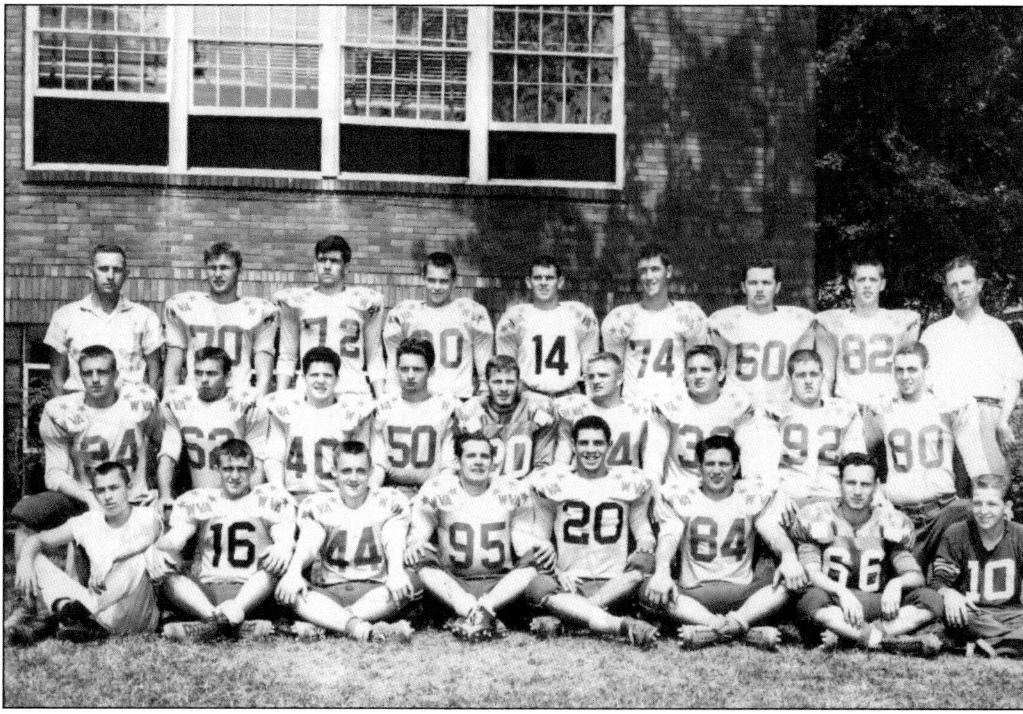

The first Kiwanis Senior Bowl was held in 1957. The game pitted the area's top senior football players against one another. The players identified here are number 14, Ronnie Whitt; number 80, Jim Keatley; number 20, Dick Barber; number 66, Al Warf; and number 80, Archie Bowen. (Courtesy of Hester Kinder Keatley.)

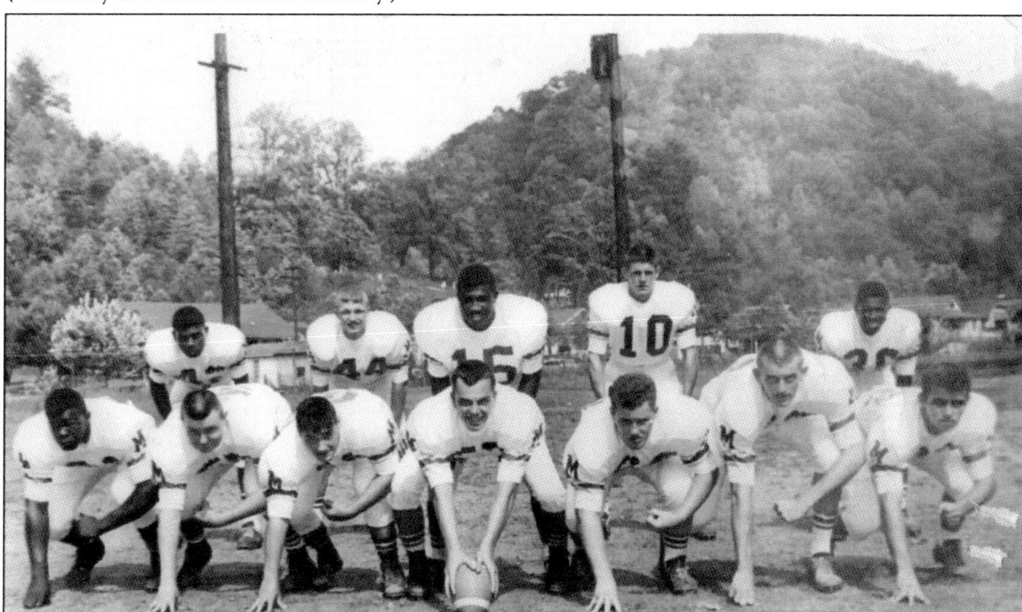

This Matewan football players' picture was taken in 1964. From left to right are (first row) ? Cook, Johnny Collins, Larry Smith, unidentified, David Kirk, Mose Tiller, David Cook; (second row) unidentified, Rod Cline, unidentified, and Eddie Queen. (Courtesy of Hester Kinder Keatley.)

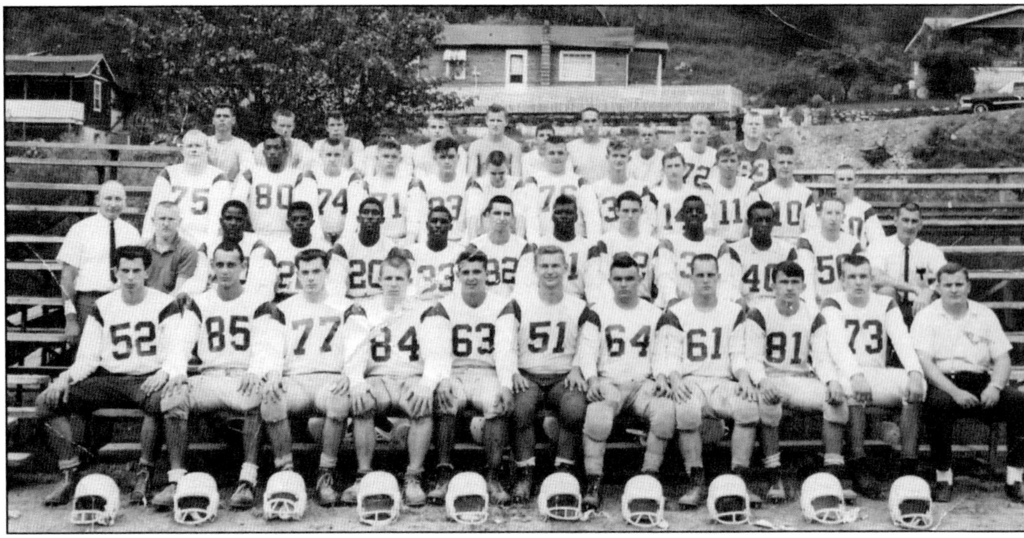

This photograph shows the entire 1964 Matewan football team. Those identified, from left to right, are (first row) L.R. Bruce Kinder (brother of Hester Kinder Keatley), David Kirk, Teddy Cisco, two unidentified, David Kiser, three unidentified, Danny Lemaster, and coach Jim Keatley (spouse of Hester Kinder Keatley); (second row) assistant coach Jack Elkins, manager Joe Bosen, four unidentified, Ronnie Williams, five unidentified, and assistant coach Jim Melmige. (Courtesy of Hester Kinder Keatley).

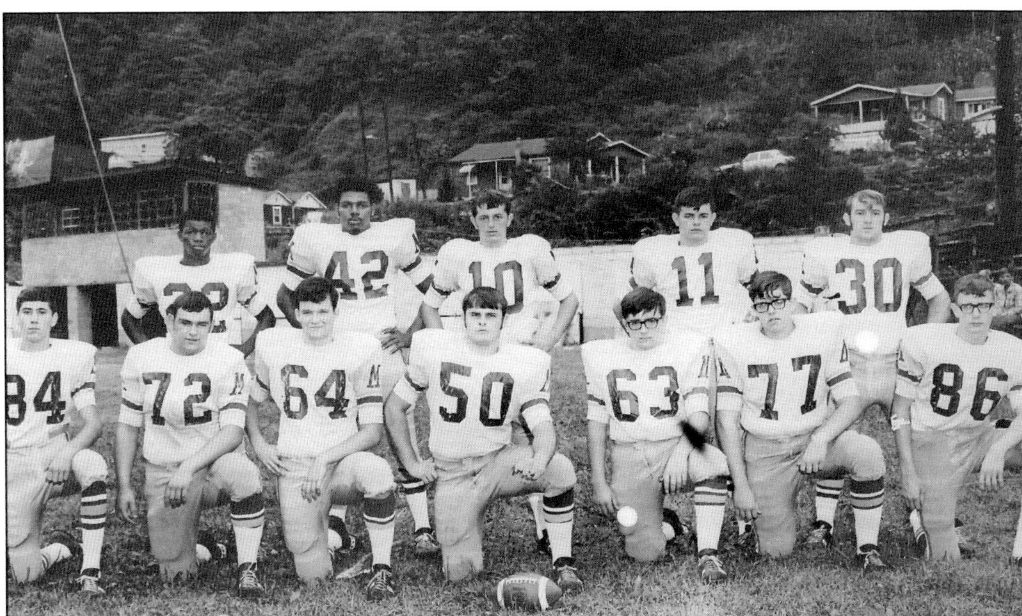

Members of the 1968 Matewan High School football team pictured here include, from left to right, (first row) unidentified, David Dudley, Sid Young, ? Hatfield, Eugene Kitts, and two unidentified; (second row) three unidentified, Mike Whitt, and Russell Hardesty. (Courtesy of Hester Kinder Keatley.)

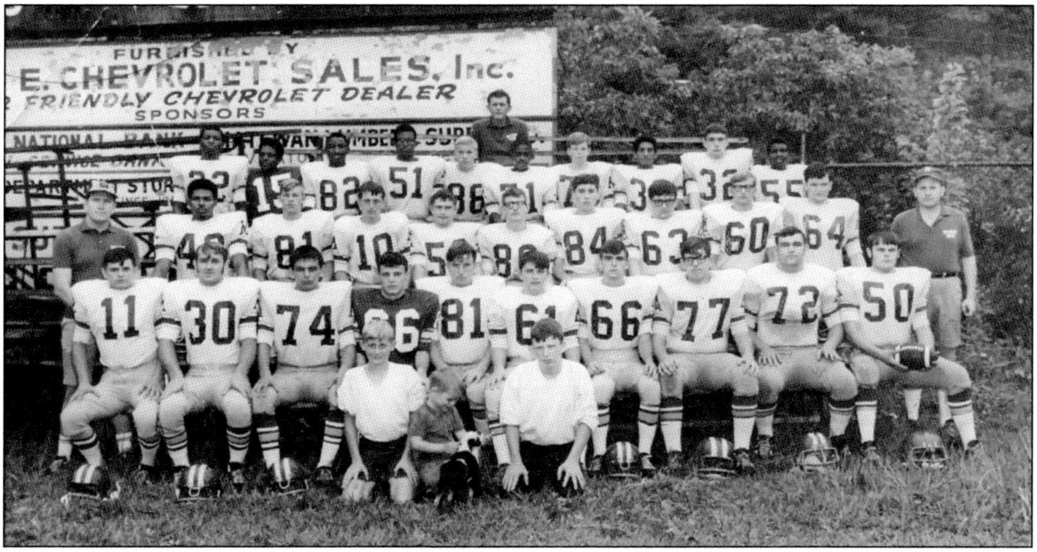

In this 1969 image of the Matewan High School football team are, from left to right, (first row) Princess Meade, Jimmy Keatley II (playing with the little dog), and Ricky Meade. Coach Jim Keatley is seen standing to the far right, and standing in the back in front of the sponsorship sign is assistant coach Joe Clusky. (Courtesy of Hester Kinder Keatley.)

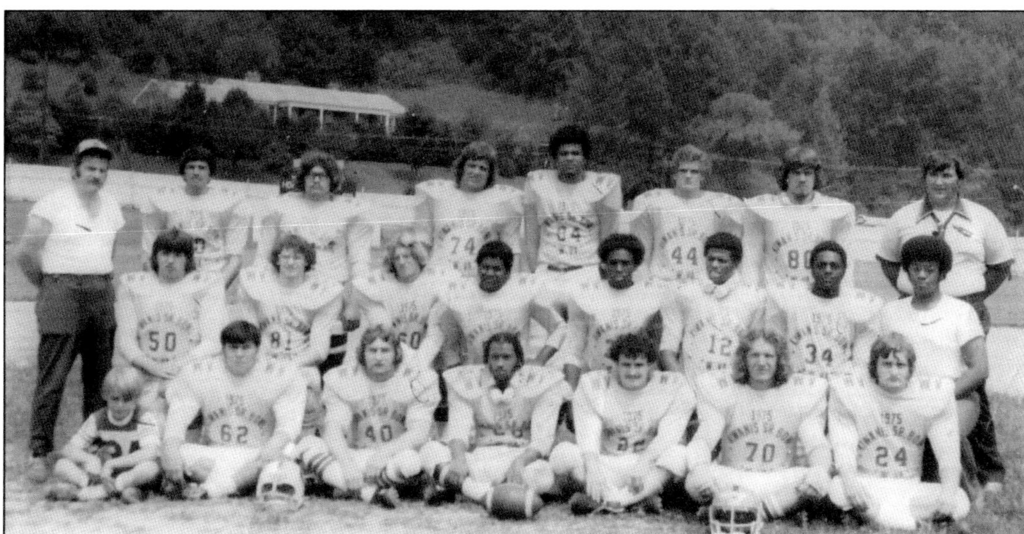

This photograph features participants in the 1975 Kiwanis Senior Bowl. Coach Jim Keatley is standing to the far left. (Courtesy of Hester Kinder Keatley.)

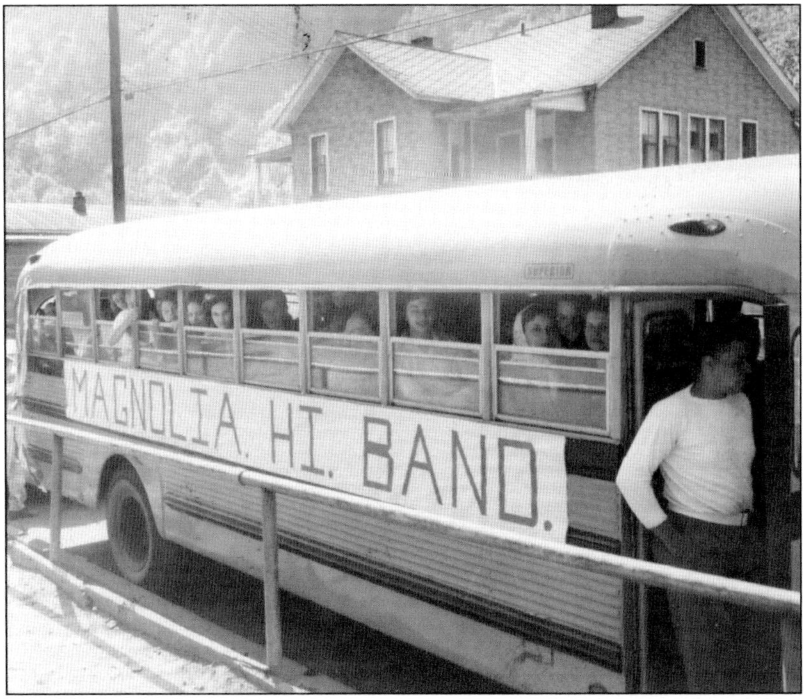

This photograph of the bus carrying the Matewan High School Band was taken in the 1950s. The county high school bands entertained at football and basketball games and were an integral part of the education and sports programs at the schools. (Courtesy of Hazel M. Chafin.)

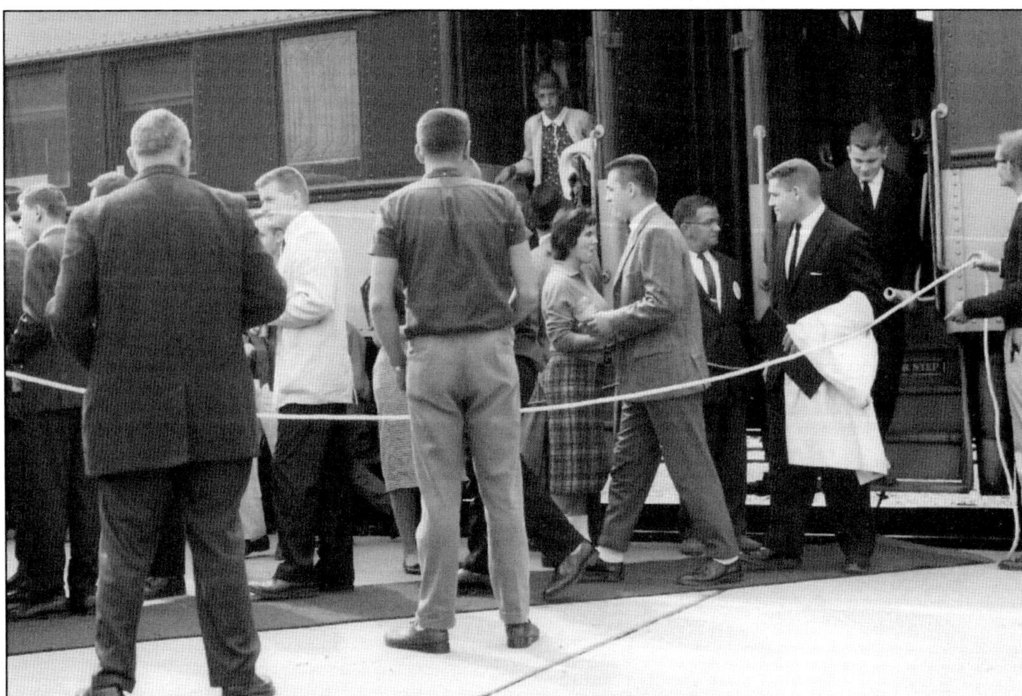

Jim Keatley, son of Hiram Keatley, is pictured here. He is the young man to the far right who is stepping down from the arriving train. This is Jim during his sophomore year at Marshall University. Here, the players are arriving to play football against the University of Kentucky in Lexington, Kentucky. (Courtesy of Hester Kinder Keatley.)

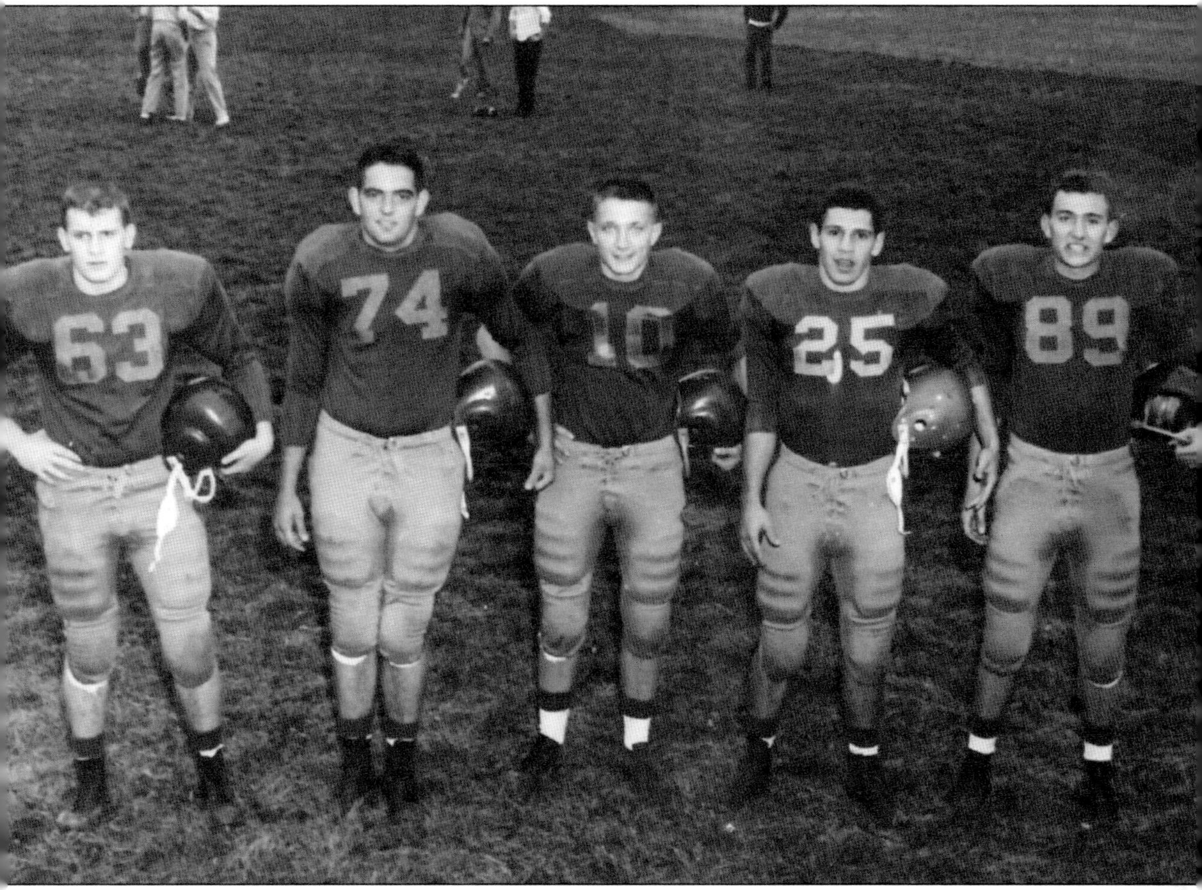

Members of the 1957–1958 Greenbrier Military School football team are pictured here. Jim Keatley was a student there at the time and a member of the team. From left to right are Jim Keatley, Bob Pennu, Tom ?, Dick Barber, and Jay Rutherford. (Courtesy of Hester Kinder Keatley.)

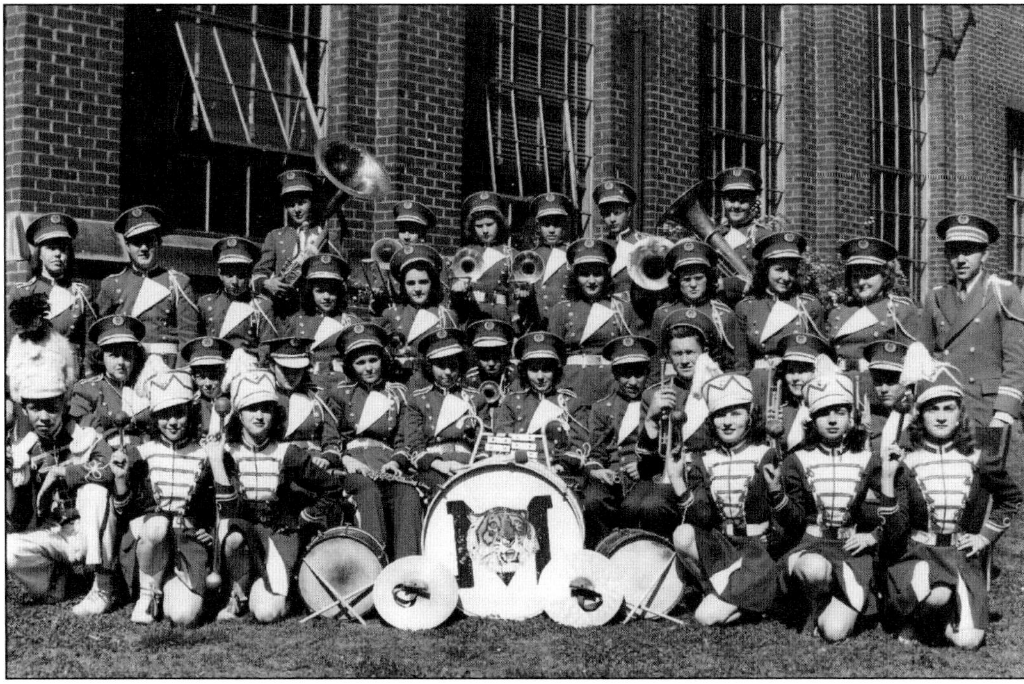

In this 1950s image, the proud Matewan Tigers marching band and its majorettes have their picture taken outside the Matewan High School. Music and team spirit ran high with the Matewan Tigers. Victor G. Allara played the trumpet in the band. (Courtesy of Dimple Tiller Allara.)

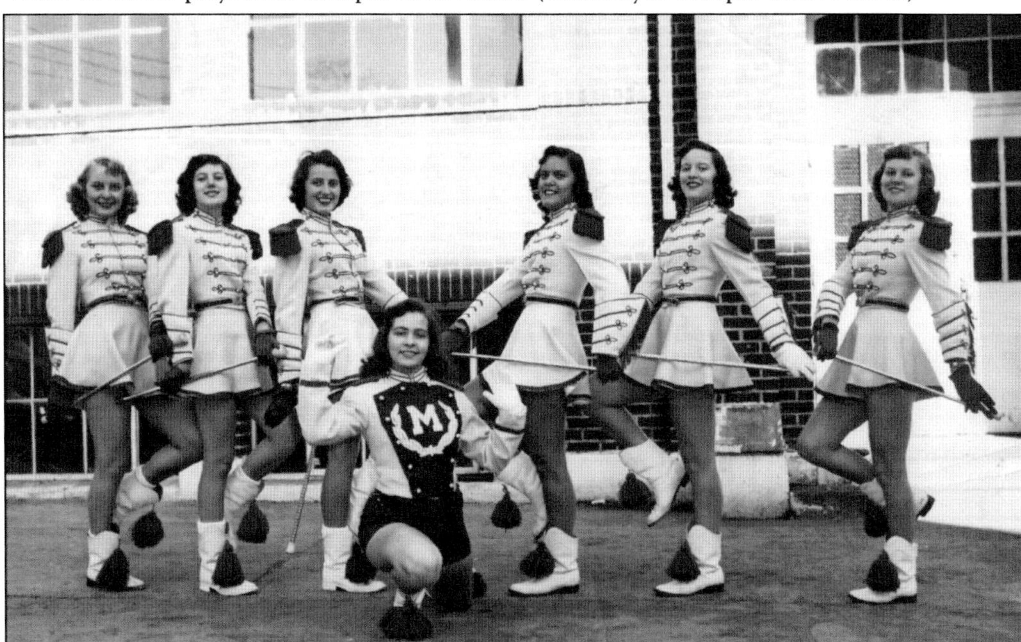

Pictured here are the Matewan majorettes in the mid-1950s. From left to right are Loretta Pinson, the director; Elaine Starr; Linda Brown (Stevenson); Toby Varney (Chafin); Doris Starr (Hatfield); Shirley DeHart (Blackburn); and head majorette Susan (O'Brien) Mankin. (Courtesy of Dimple Tiller Allara.)

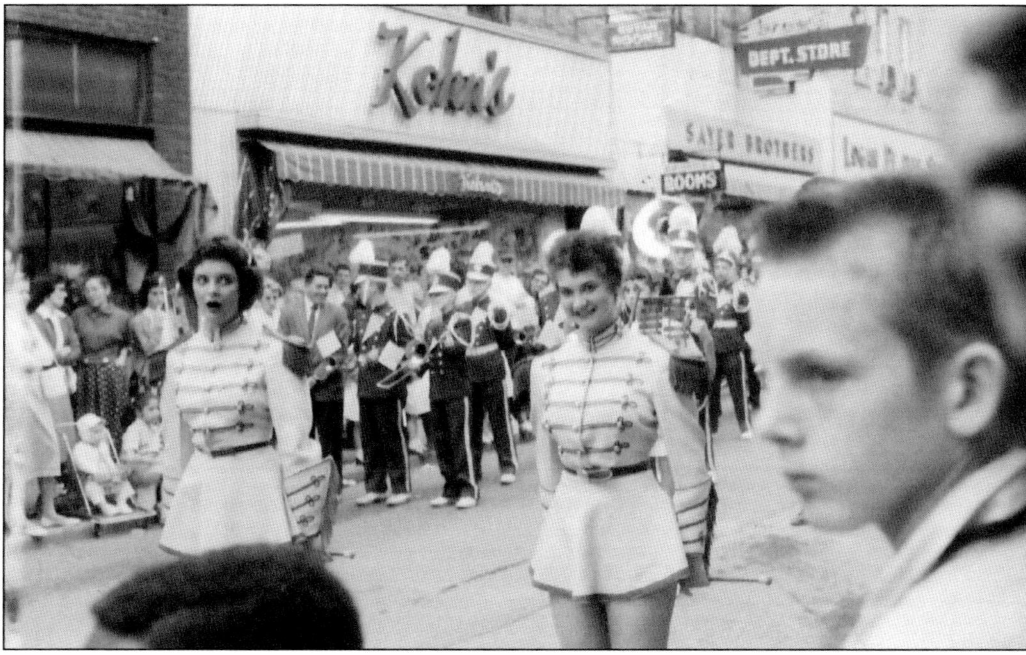

As the Matewan Tigers Band and majorettes made their way down the street, this picture was snapped in May 1958. It would be hard to say just what prompted these lovely young ladies to have such interesting expressions. The young lady to the right is Georgia Ann (Chafin) Griffith; the lady to the left is not identified. (Courtesy of Hazel M. Chafin.)

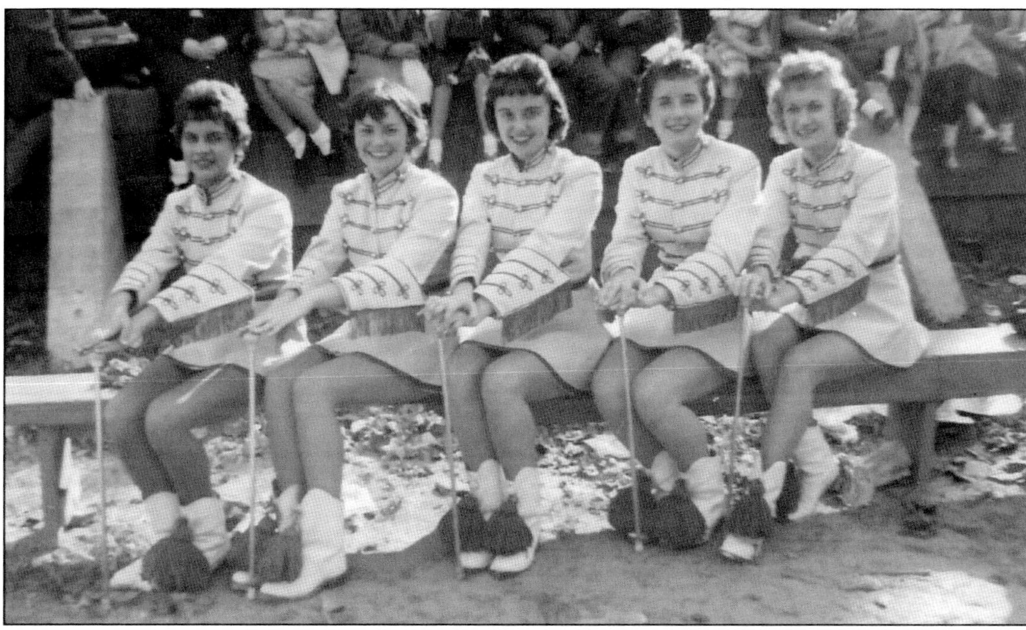

Pictured here are the lovely Matewan Tigers majorettes for the 1959–1960 school year. This photograph was taken at the homecoming game, which saw the Matewan Tigers play against the team from Birch. Matewan won with a final score of 32-6. Pictured here from left to right are Brenda Copley, Jeanne Chafin, Peggy ?, Fay Layne, and Judy Hatfield. (Courtesy of Hazel M. Chafin.)

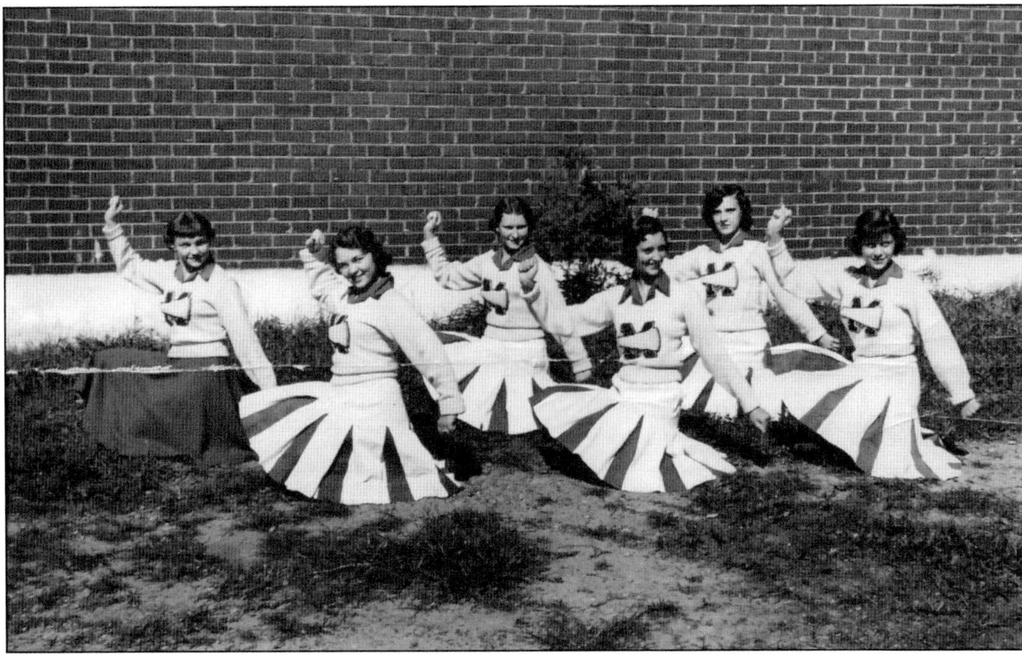

The Matewan High School (also known as Magnolia High School) cheerleaders are pictured here in October of the 1955–1956 school year. From left to right are Carol Edwards, Nina Steele, Christa Shields, Shirley Ferrell, Barbara Vagost, and Hester Kinder Keatley. (Courtesy of Hester Kinder Keatley.)

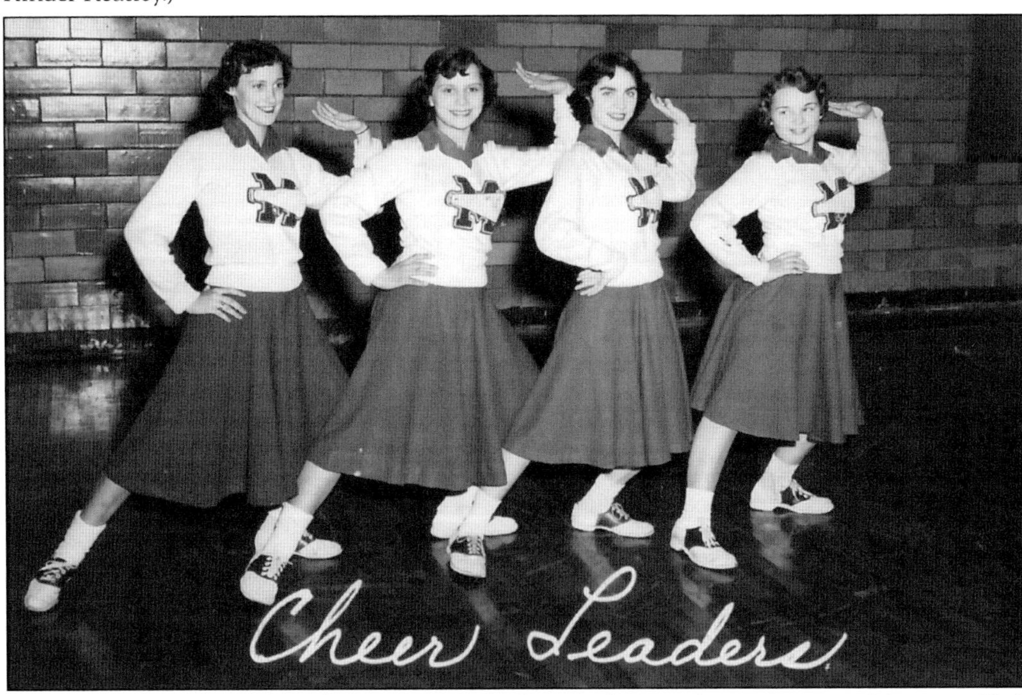

This photograph was taken during Hester Kinder Keatley's sophomore year at Matewan High School. From left to right are cheerleaders "Tinkey" Barrett, Hester Kinder, Shirley Curry, and Nina Steele. (Courtesy of Hester Kinder Keatley.)

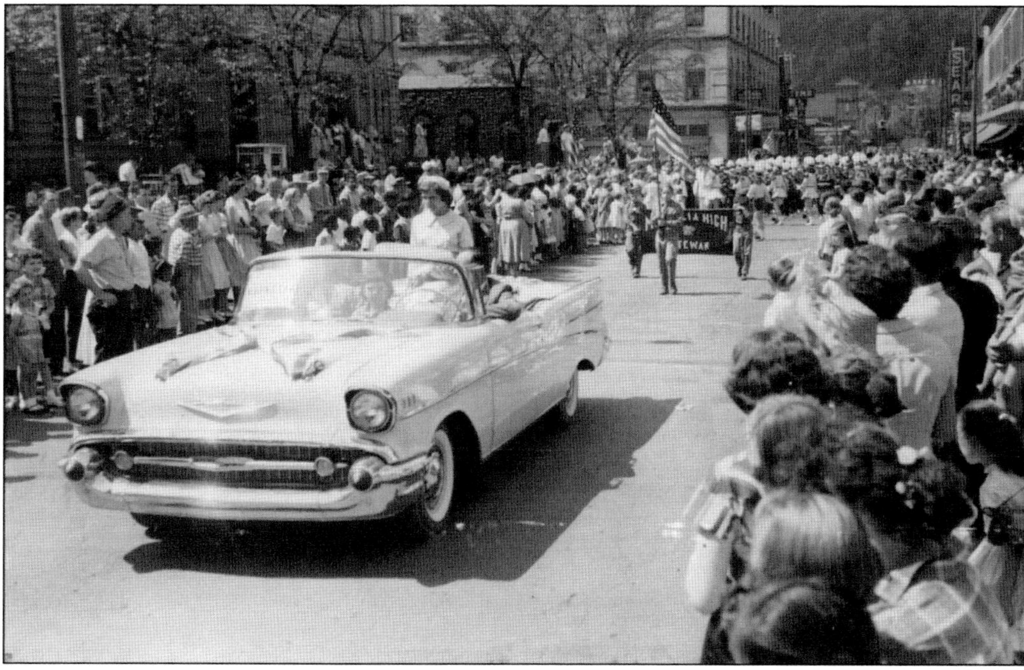

This 1957 photograph, taken in Williamson, shows the Kiwanis Senior Bowl Parade. The homecoming queen was Hester Kinder. The homecoming queen's car was followed by the marching bands of local high schools. Directly behind the car is the Magnolia High School of Matewan's marching band. Many referred to Magnolia High School as Matewan High School. The Kiwanis Senior Bowl was an annual event that gave senior football players the opportunity to show their skills to visiting college scouts. (Courtesy of Hester Kinder Keatley.)

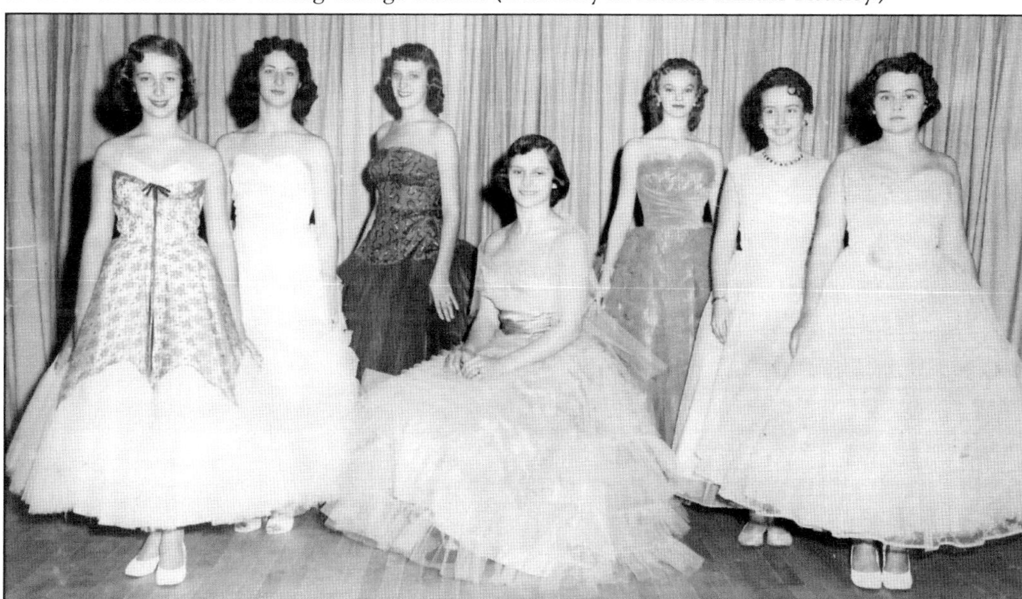

The 1957 homecoming court for the Kiwanis Senior Bowl football game is shown here. From left to right are Patricia Harris, Peggy Justice, Gladys Sue Hatfield, Homecoming queen Hester Kinder, Wyonna Chafin, Margaret Tinsley, and Nina Steele. (Courtesy of Hester Kinder Keatley.)

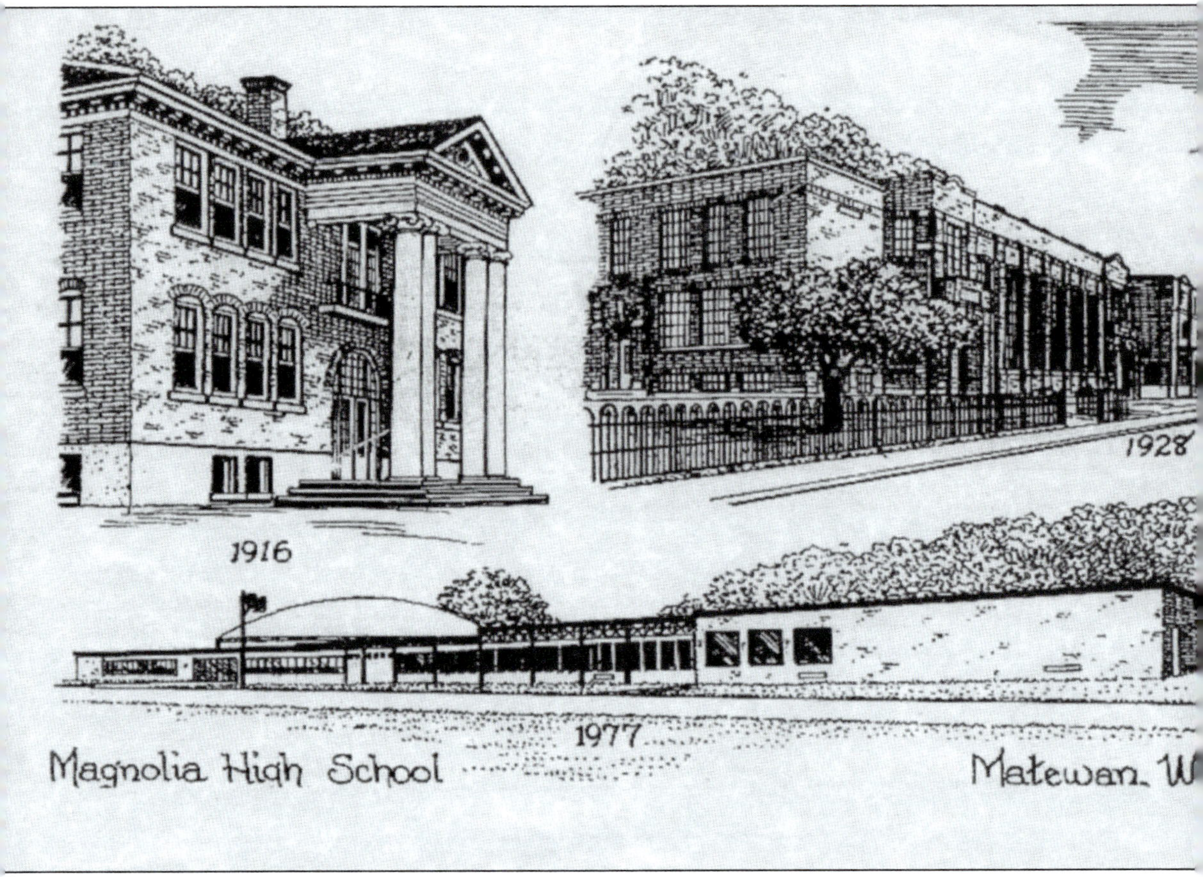

These etchings are of the old Magnolia Schools of Matewan as they existed and held the memories of the many young Mingo County families who received their education there. Now they have been replaced with consolidated schools that are state-of-the-art and bring new but different advantages to the young people who attend them. Many former classmates of the old schools have stayed in the area and made it the work of their lives to continue to educate the young Mingo County children as they prepare to find their place in the world. (Courtesy of Dimple Tiller Allara.)

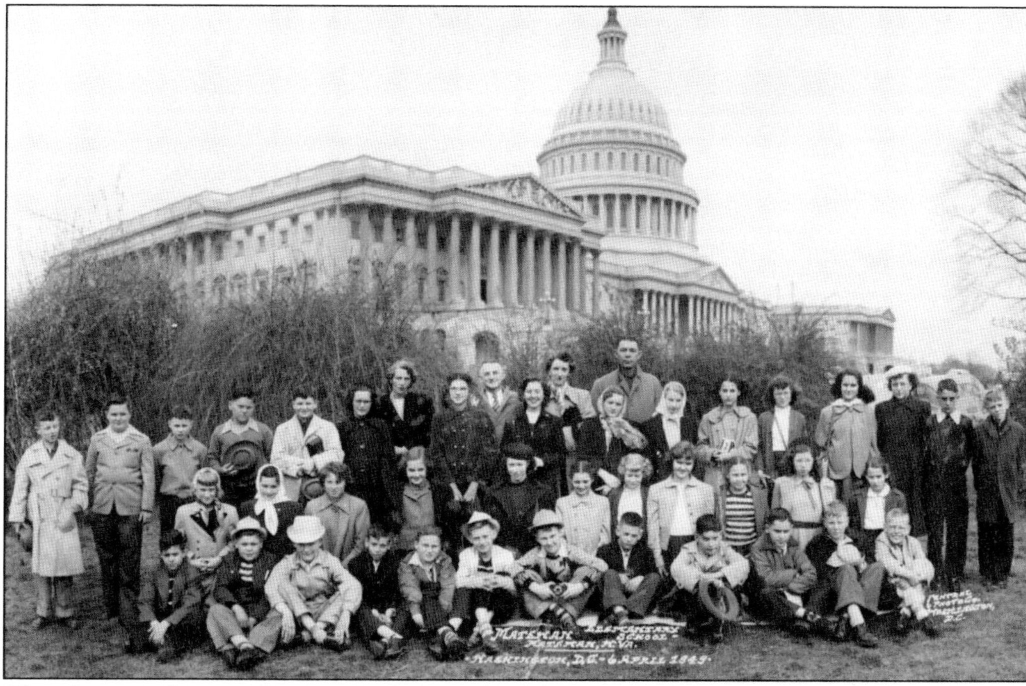

This photograph was taken in April 1949 when the Matewan Elementary School students and students from other Mingo County schools enjoyed a trip to the nation's capital. For many of the students, it was their first train ride and their first stay in a hotel. Five teachers accompanied the group on the three-day trip. This photograph was taken by the Central Photograph Company of Washington, DC. (Courtesy of Andrew Chafin.)

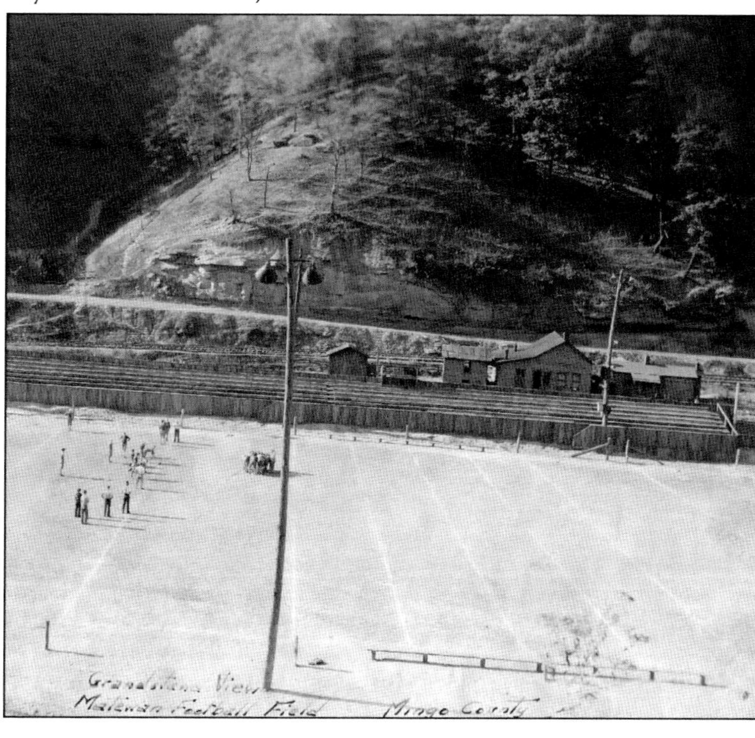

This grandstand view features the Matewan football field. This was the second football field built for Matewan High School. The first football field was located in North Matewan near where the Montgomery's Super Market was located. (Courtesy of Hester Kinder Keatley.)

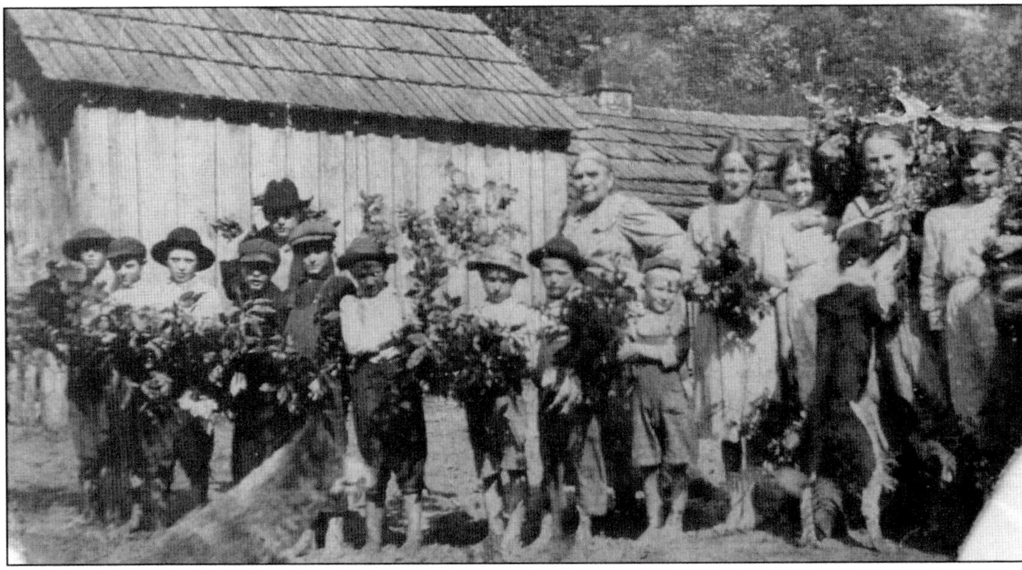

This photograph shows schoolchildren from Elk Creek literally on a field trip. Their teacher, Aunt Lou (as known by her niece and the provider of this picture) Farley, decided that a great lesson in biology and botany was just outside the classroom, where many plants and flowers grew. This great experience was then captured on film. The older lady in the center of the photograph is Grandmother Pinson, who was able to enjoy and assist with the learning adventure. (Courtesy of Lahoma Lee Farley Schuller.)

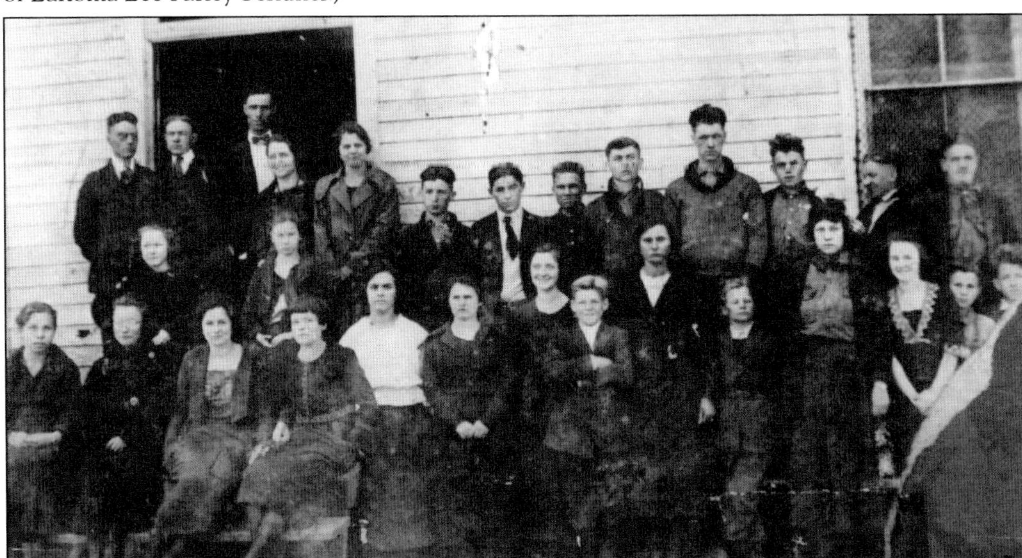

Pictured here is Burch High School in the 1918–1919 school year. This was the last year in the old school located on Elk Creek near Delbarton. Pictured from left to right are (first row) Elizabeth Row, Effie Conley, Lula Farley, Ethel Hatfield, Belle Varney, May White, Tilda Chafin Curry, Joe Hanners, Vicie Justice, Wayne B. Curry, May Floyd, Tina Duty, Stuart White, Forest Evans, Chloe Conley, Florence Hensley; (second row) Clarence Dove, Dr. Roy Curry, Claude C. Dove, Lulia Curry Toppings, Sally Farley Gates, Rush Curry, J.R. "Bob" Farley, Raymond Walker, Wallace Varney, Burt Curry, John Justice, Wirt Curry (Dr. W.W.), and Lace Curry. (Courtesy of Lahoma Lee Farley Schuller.)

Shown here are school days' pictures of New Town, grades one and two, taken for the 1947–1948 school year. No preschool was available at this time, so this was the first time these students experienced structured education. (Courtesy of Clarence and Sue Hatfield.)

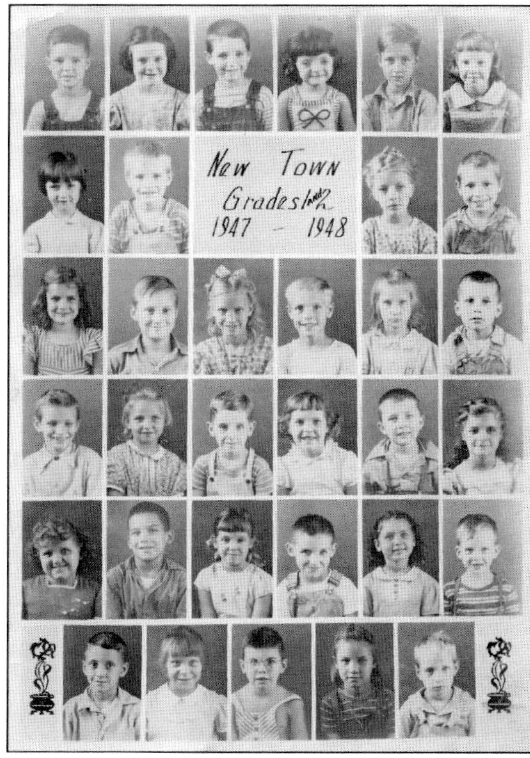

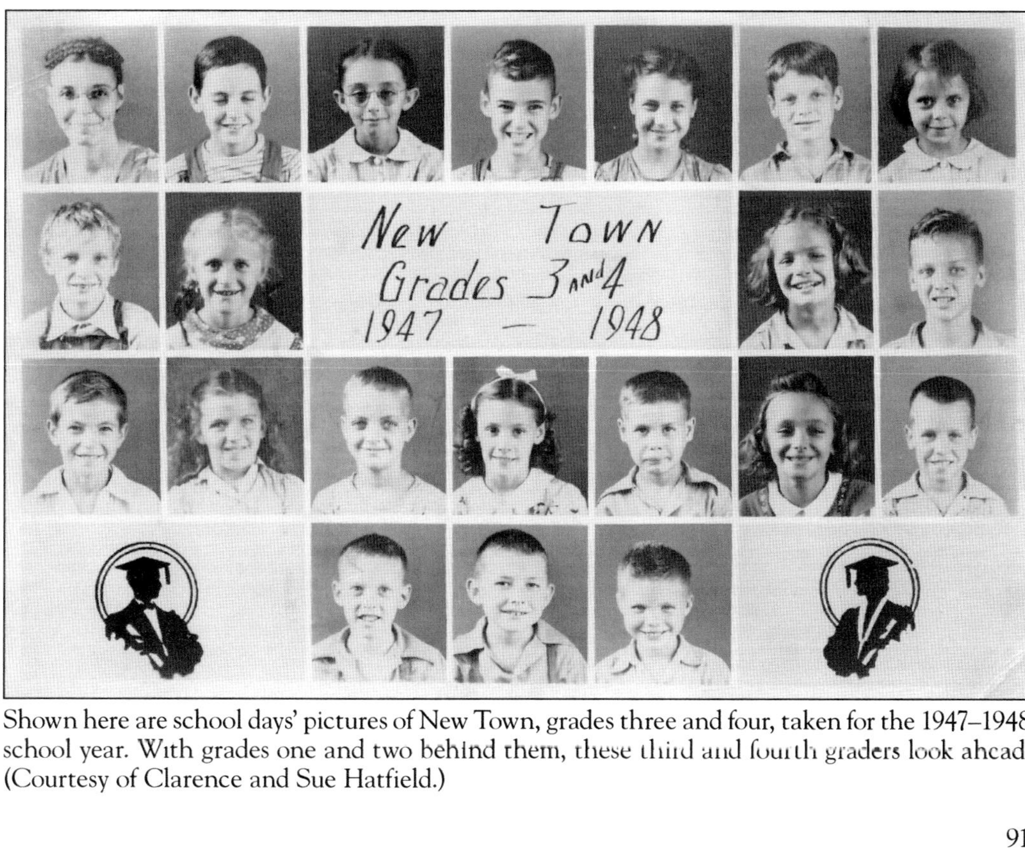

Shown here are school days' pictures of New Town, grades three and four, taken for the 1947–1948 school year. With grades one and two behind them, these third and fourth graders look ahead. (Courtesy of Clarence and Sue Hatfield.)

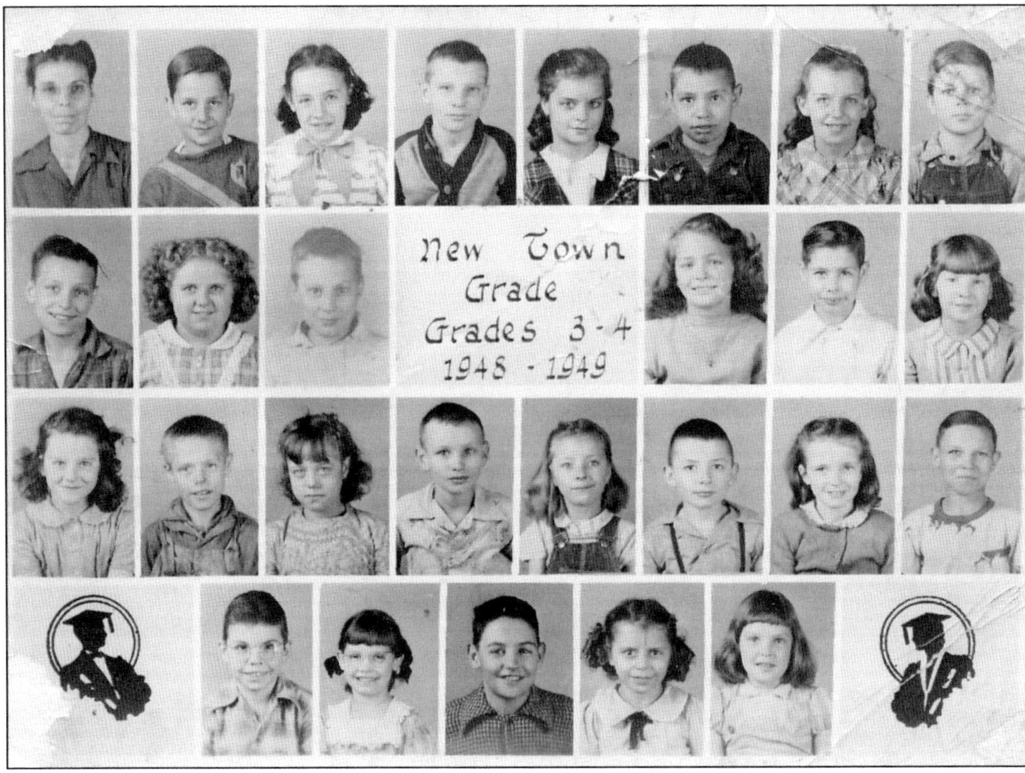

Shown here are school days' pictures of New Town, grades three and four, taken for the 1947–1948 school year. The New Town Elementary School taught first through sixth grade. (Courtesy of Clarence and Sue Hatfield.)

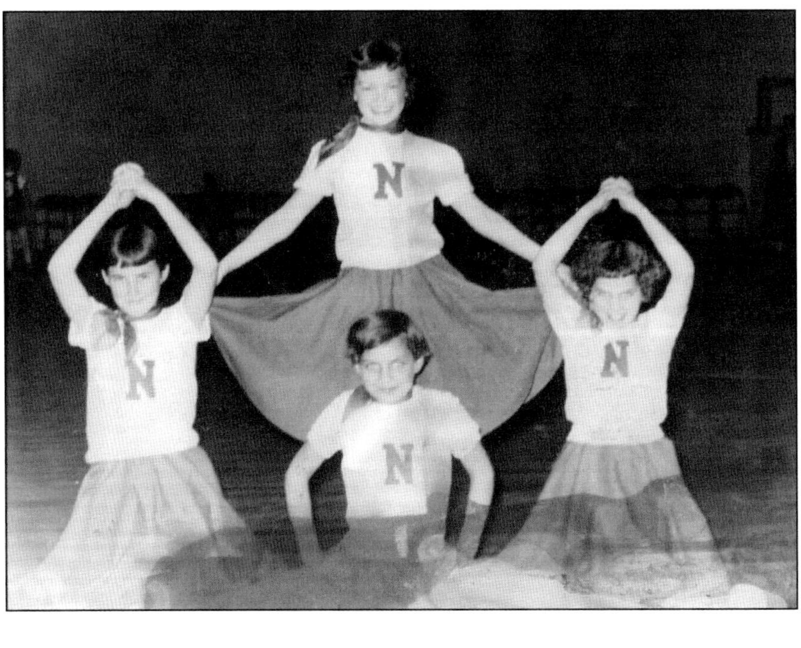

School days' pictures of New Town cheerleaders at the Burch Gym are seen here. From left to right are Lou Chafin, fifth grade; Jeanne Chafin (standing), sixth grade; Pat Mitchell, fourth grade; and Brenda Copley, sixth grade. (Courtesy of Hazel M. Chafin.)

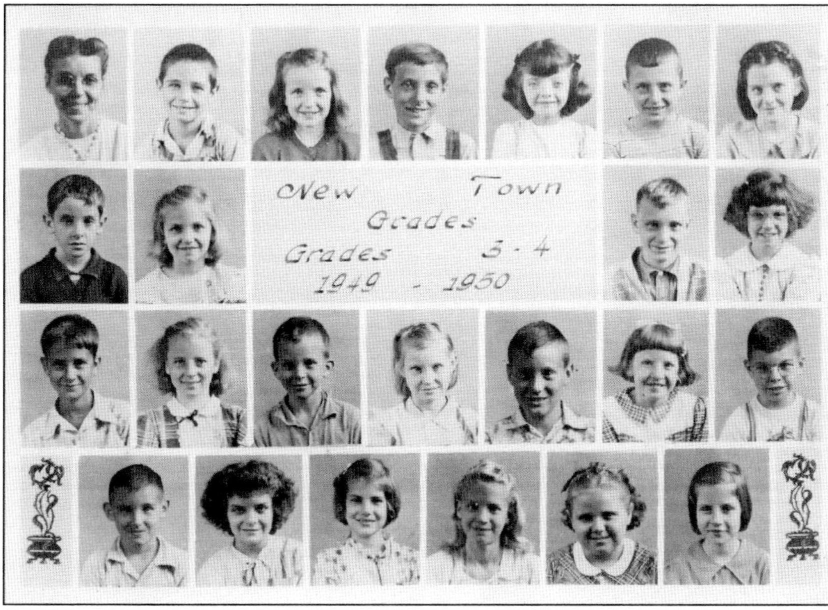

Shown here are school days' pictures of New Town, grades three and four, taken for the 1949–1950 school year. This class moved on to the fifth and sixth grades prior to junior high school at Red Jacket. (Courtesy of Clarence and Sue Hatfield.)

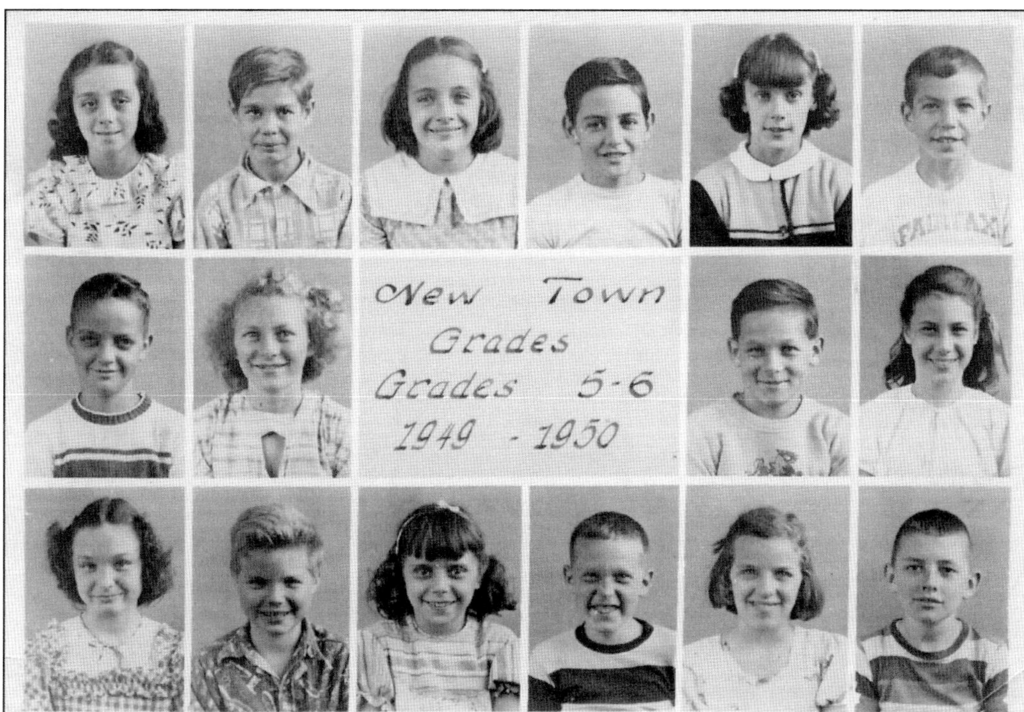

Shown here are school days' pictures of New Town, grades five and six, taken for the 1949–1950 school year. Grade six would move on to Red Jacket Junior High school for the seventh grade. (Courtesy of Clarence and Sue Hatfield.)

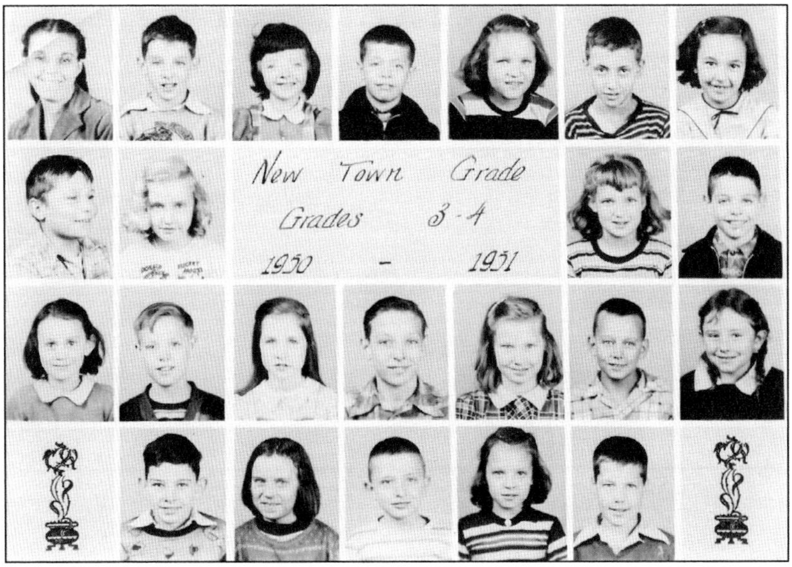

Shown here are school days' pictures of New Town, grades three and four, taken for the 1950–1951 school year. Fourth grade was considered one of the harder grades. Math and English were the focus, as it was felt the students were ready for more intense learning. (Courtesy of Clarence and Sue Hatfield.)

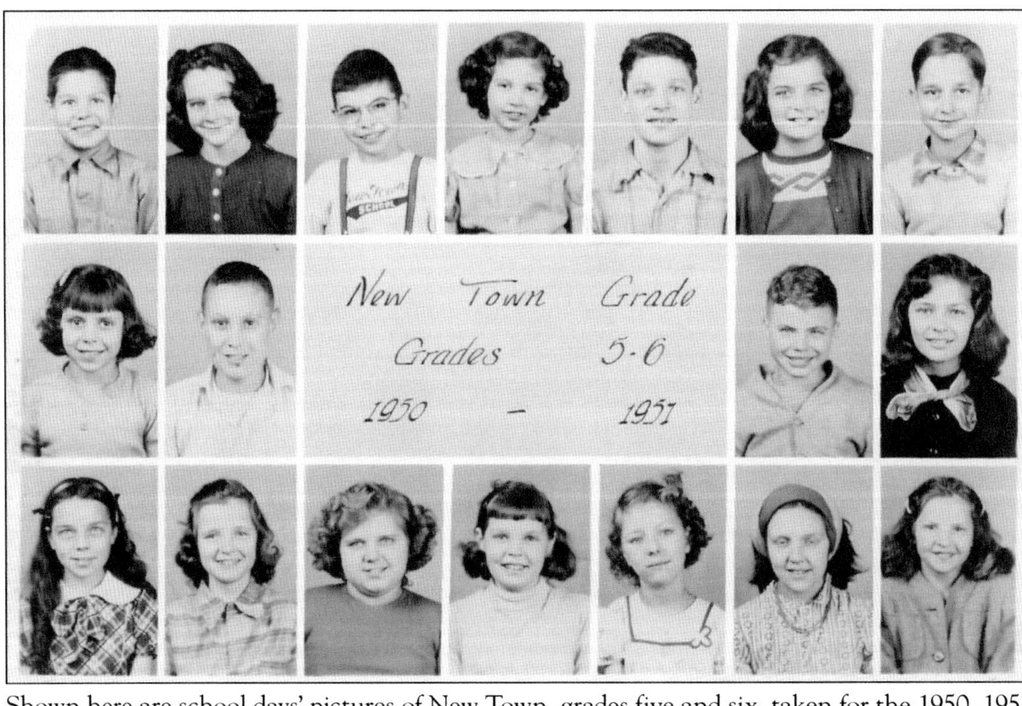

Shown here are school days' pictures of New Town, grades five and six, taken for the 1950–1951 school year. Red Jacket Junior High School taught grades seven through nine. Students then moved on to Matewan High School. (Courtesy of Clarence and Sue Hatfield.)

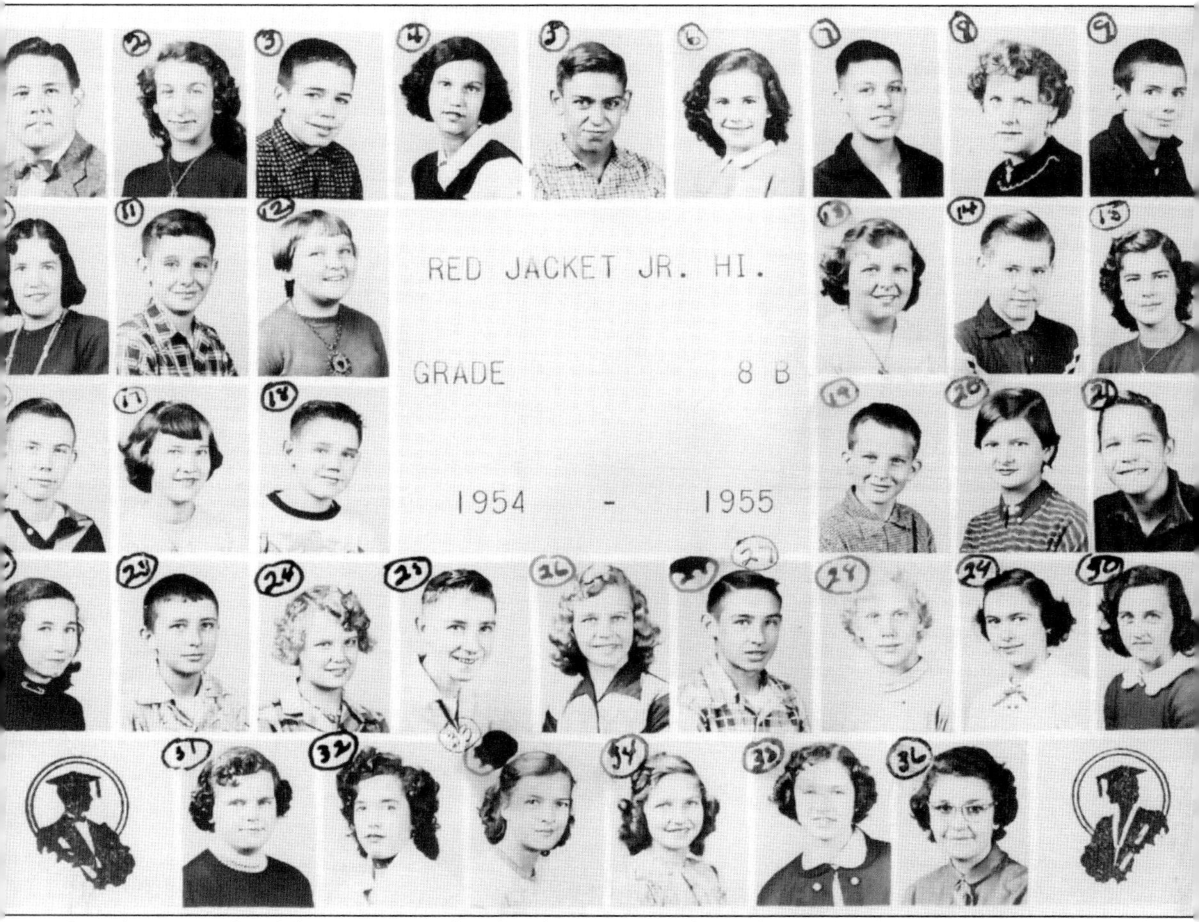

Seen here are school days' pictures of Red Jacket Junior High, grade 8-B, for the 1954–1955 school year. Corresponding names are listed numerically: (1) Robert Simpkins (principal), (2) Alice Staten, (3) Anthony Barrios, (4) Anna Varney, (5) Alvin Dudley, (6) Louise Cooke, (7) Larry Adkins, (8) Phyllis Browning, (9) Ted Cooke, (10) Rena Chumley, (11) Joe Hatfield, (12) Maysha Blankenship, (13) Mary Osborne, (14) Eugene Mills, (15) Alene McCoy, (16) Charles Kennedy, (17) Carol Staten, (18) Raymond Hale, (19) Joe Chafin, (20) Geneva Clusky, (21) Jimmy Fitch, (22) Doris Wallace, (23) Clarence Hatfield, (24) Phyllis Rice, (25) Ronald Kirk, (26) Callie Mitchell, (27) Roger Steele, (28) Mary Sykes, (29) Glenna Maynard, (30) Margie Vaggot, (31) Linda Musick, (32) Barbara Kennedy, (33) Doris Simpkins, (34) Linda Kinder, (35) Maggie Fields, and (36) Mary Jo Wessel. (Courtesy of Clarence and Sue Hatfield.)

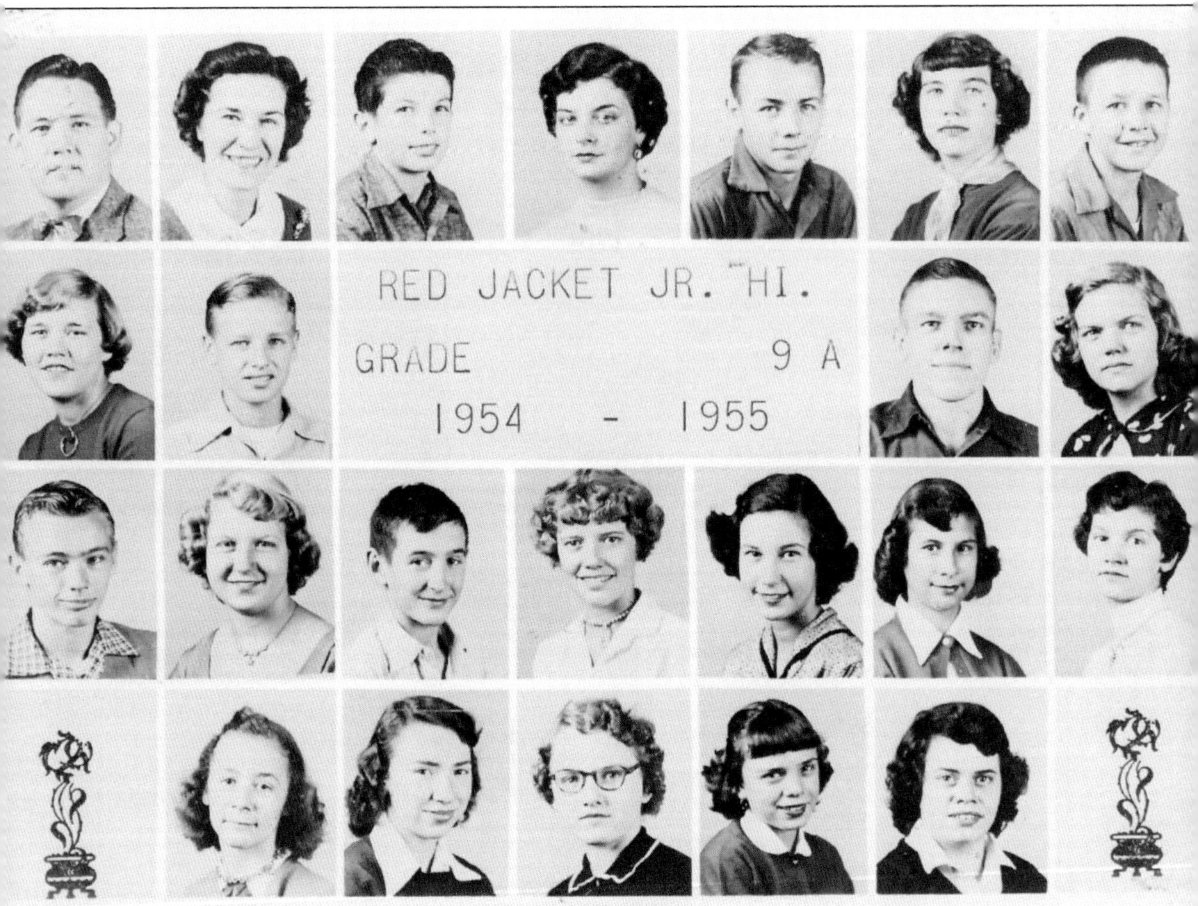

Seen here are school days' pictures of Red Jacket Junior High, grade 9-A, for the 1954–1955 school year. (Courtesy of Clarence and Sue Hatfield.)

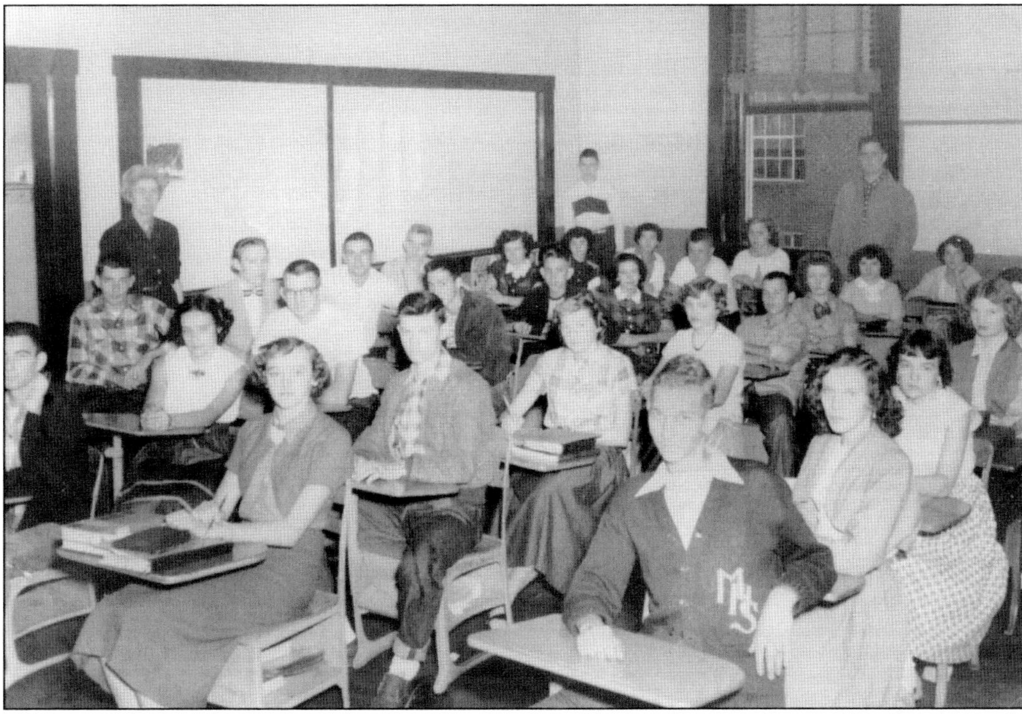

The 1954 English class at Matewan High School was taught by Marion Montgomery. She had a reputation as a stern but well-loved taskmaster. Her students graduated with a strong background in English. The gentlemen identified to the far left are Jack McGuire, left, and Eugene Hatfield. The girls to the far left are Brenda Mitchell, left, and Shirley Harth. Andrew Chafin is seated directly behind Shirley Harth. To the far right, the first person in the row is Howard Shields; directly behind him is Toni Kinder. Montgomery is standing to the left side of the room. (Courtesy of Andrew Chafin.)

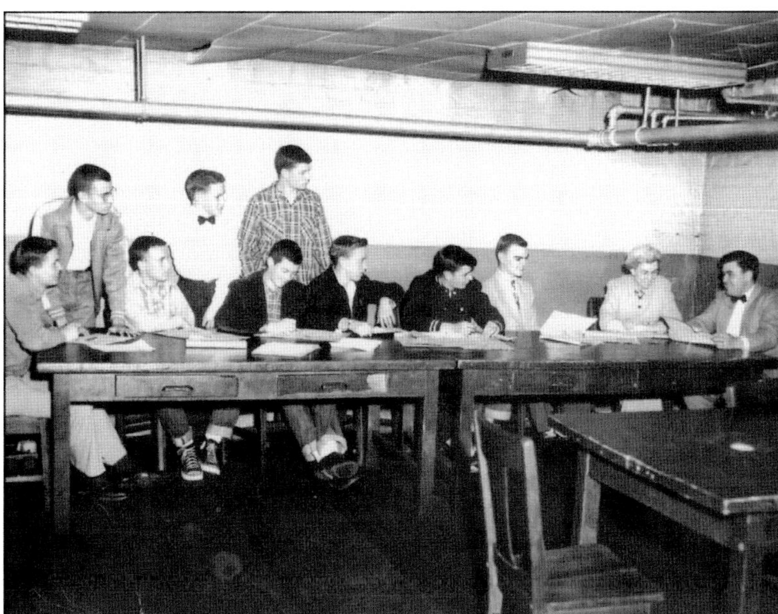

The 1954 journalism class of Marion Montgomery at Matewan High School is pictured holding a work session with a guest speaker. The class was charged with producing the school newspaper, the *Green and White Echo*. Due to a lack of space, the class met in the basement of the high school. (Courtesy of Andrew Chafin.)

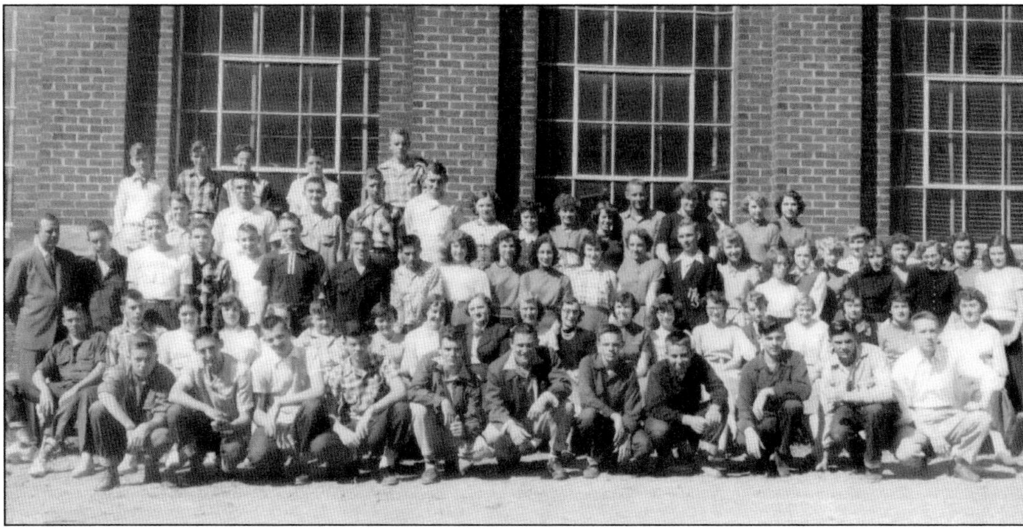

This photograph is of the 1954 graduating class of Matewan High School. Eleanor Thompson was class president, Alfred Steel was vice president, and Frances Henson was the secretary-treasurer. James Loudermilk was the class valedictorian. The class motto was, "He who fails to plan, plans to fail." Pictured here on the far left is the principal, John D. Anderson. (Courtesy of Andrew Chafin.)

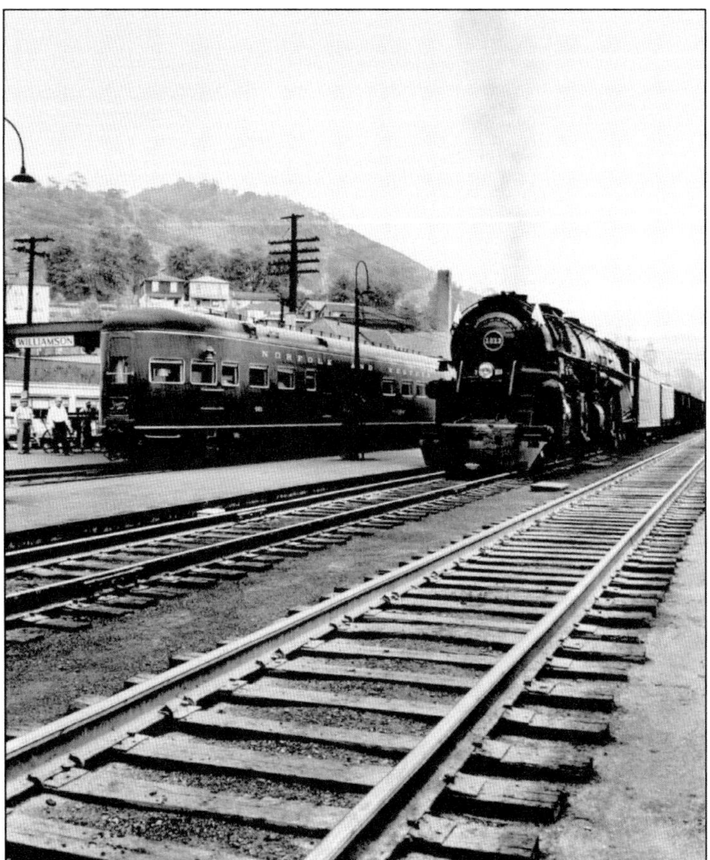

This photograph was taken at the railroad station in Williamson. Since the 1930s, this area has been considered the heart of the billion-dollar coal industry. Large-scale mining began before World War I and continues today. At one time, Mingo County was one of the top five coal-producing counties in the eastern United States. In addition to the movement of coal, passenger-train travel was a popular method for getting from town to town. During World War II, due to rationing of gas and tires, railroad travel reached an all-time high in 1944. After that time, the use of automobile and air travel slowly began to lessen the need for train travel. (Courtesy of West Virginia State Archives Collection.)

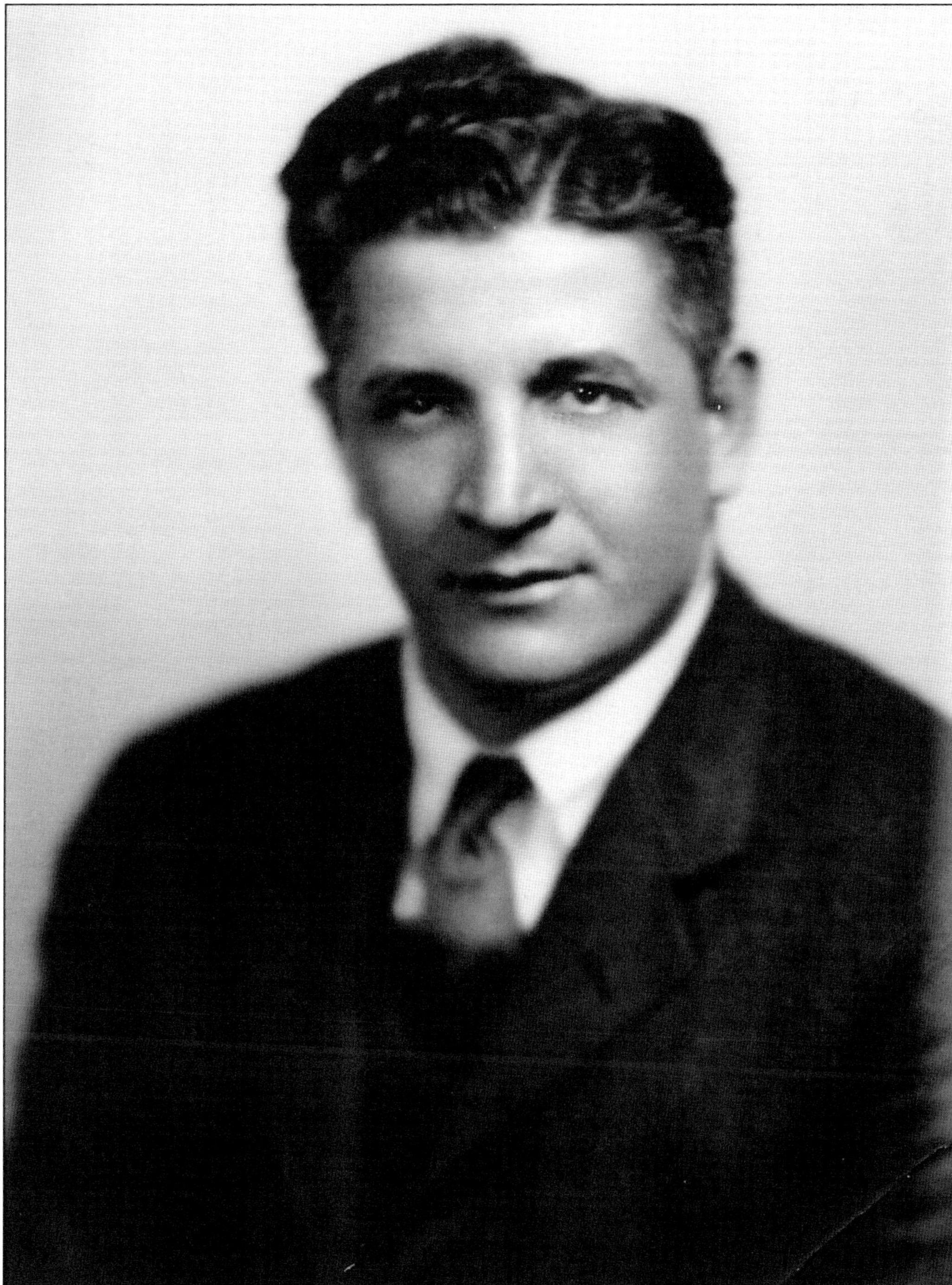

A.R. Tony Gentile, pictured here, was a well-respected and longtime coach for Williamson High School. As a coach for Williamson High School, Coach Gentile won the baseball state championship in 1948 and the state basketball tournament in 1950. He was named area coach of the year in basketball and served as president of the West Virginia Coaches Association. (Courtesy of Eddie Nenni.)

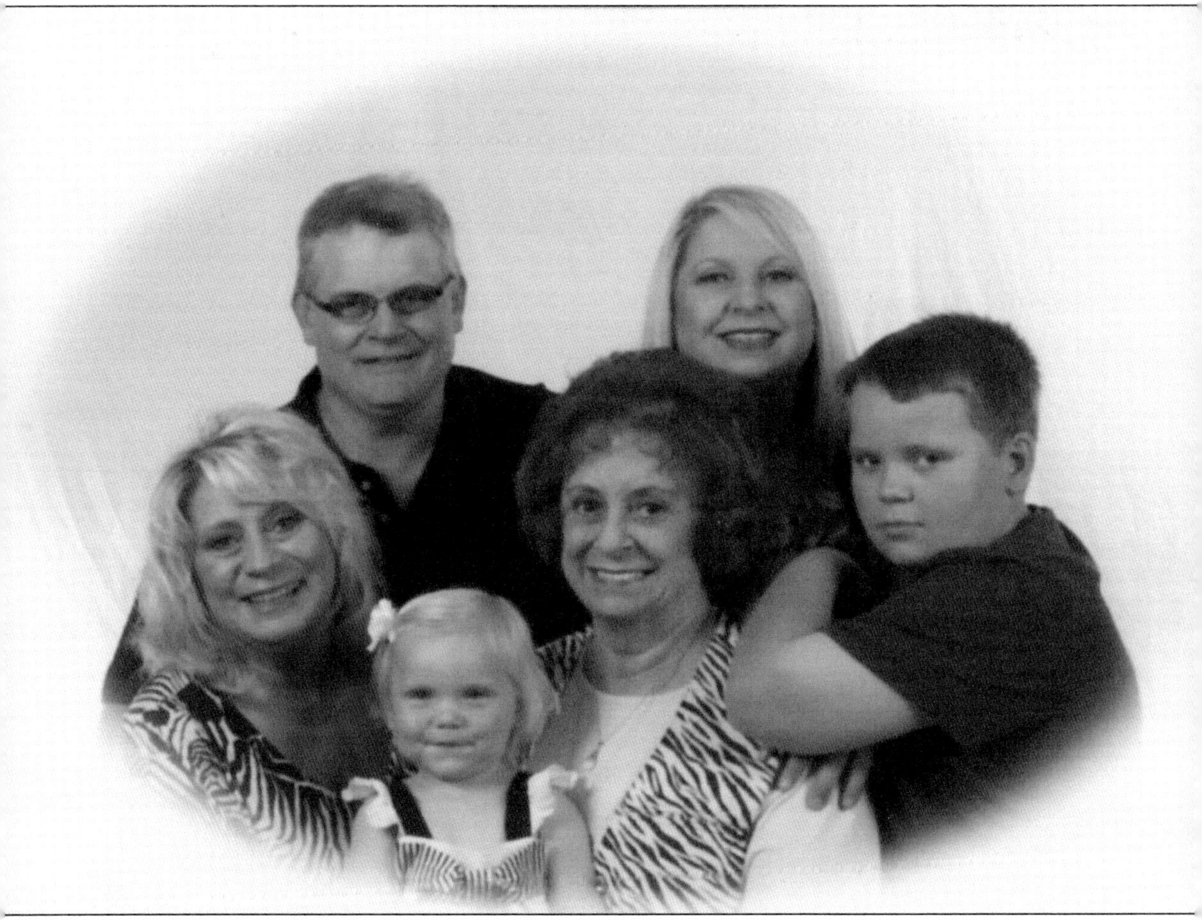

This photograph shows Hester Kinder Keatley and her family. Hester is very active in her community and is as much a part of the education system as she was when she was a student. She and a band of others hold together the memories and treasures of this area so that others can have them to enjoy. Pictured here from left to right are Rebecca Keatley, James Hiram Keatley II, MaKenley Keatley (the baby), Hester Kinder Keatley, Elizabeth Dawn Keatley, and James Hiram Keatley III, representing four generations of the Keatleys in Mingo County. (Courtesy of Hester Kinder Keatley upon request of Andrew Chafin.)

Four

Essence of Mingo County

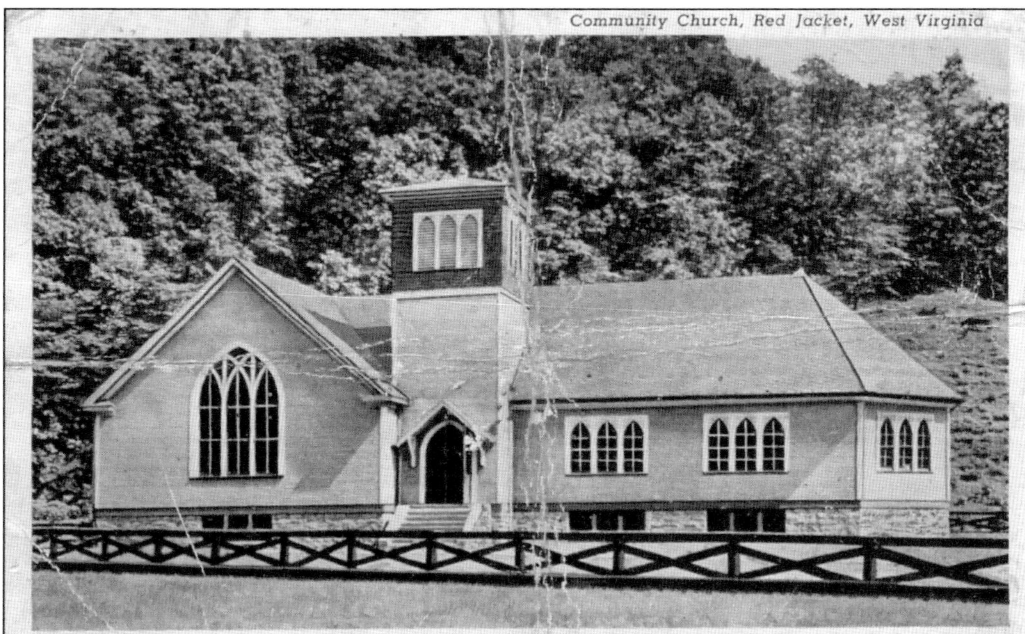

This photograph is of the community church in Red Jacket. Churches, to the folks of Mingo County, represent their love of God and country. The churches of Mingo County have long supported their members during the best and the worst of times. (Courtesy of William Woodward.)

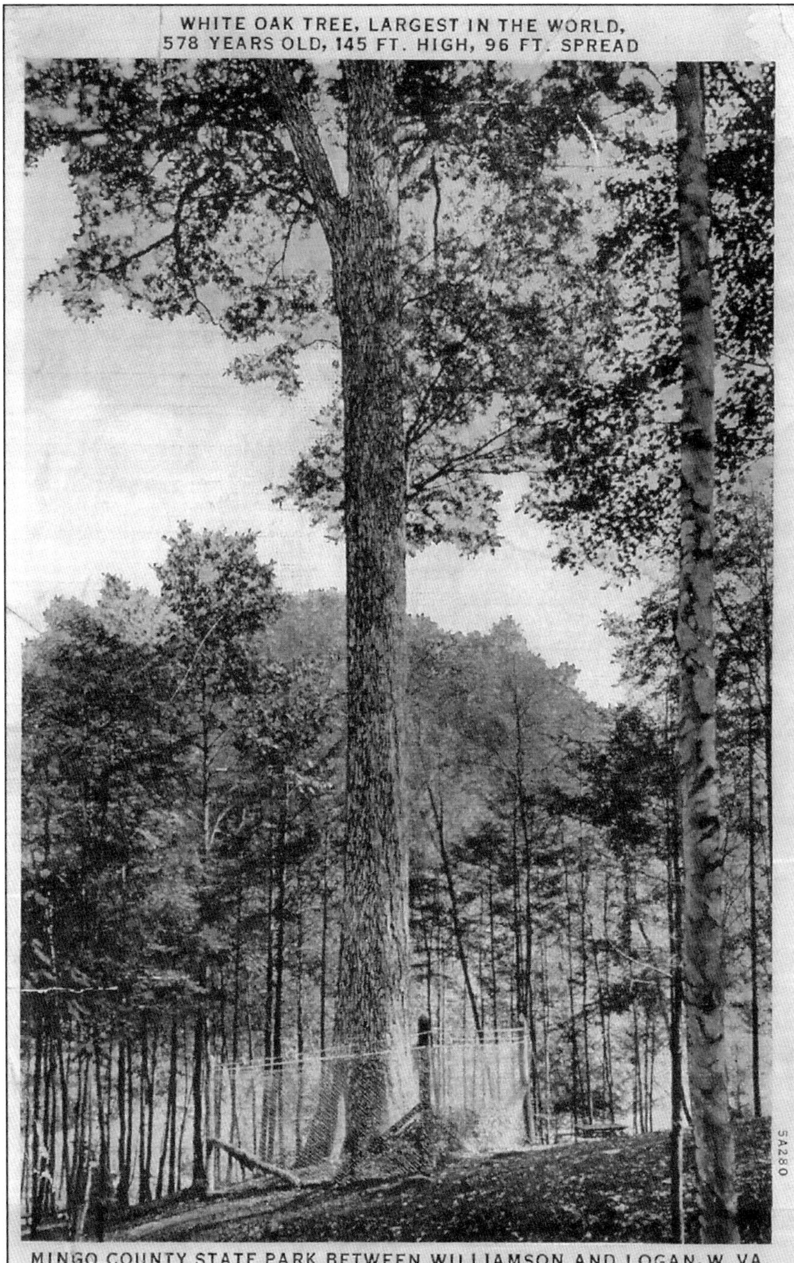

This white oak tree in the photograph is reported to have been the largest of its species in the world at the time. It was believed to be between 576 and 578 years old, stood 145-feet high, and had a 96-foot spread. It was located in the Mingo County State Park. This tree attracted national attention in the 1930s when it was pronounced dead after failing for the first time to put forth leaves in the spring and thus required removal. On September 23, 1938, with a crowd of 2,500 observers, the great tree was felled. It was intended to be taken down at 10:30 a.m., but the great giant fought back, finally falling to the ground around 11:00 a.m. Portions of the mighty oak tree were sent to the Smithsonian Institute in Washington, DC, for preservation. (Courtesy of Williamson Public Library.)

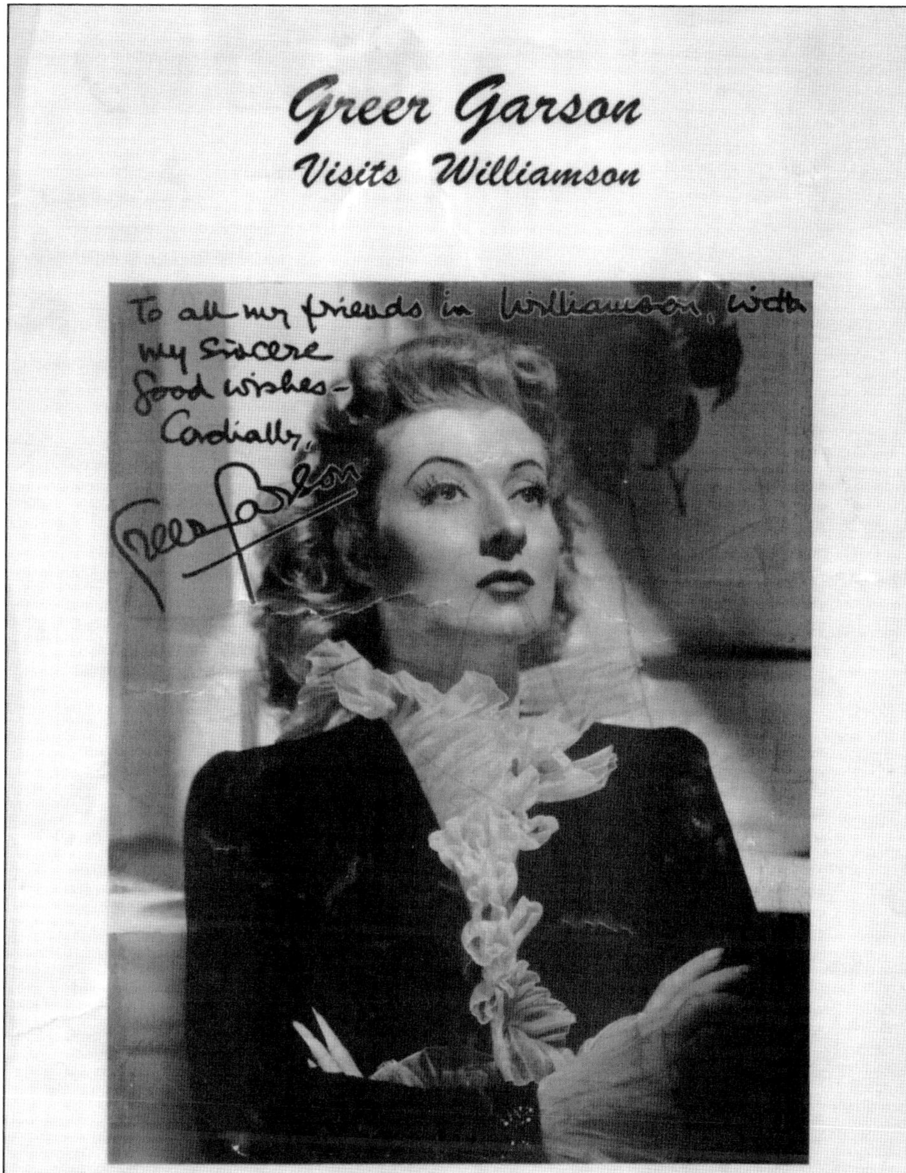

One of the most memorable visitors to Williamson was Greer Garson in 1943 during World War II on a savings bond drive. She stated in an article in *This Week* in November 1943, that the visit "was one of the most illuminating experiences of my life." She stated that she was concerned as to how to convince folks to buy war bonds, when war seemed so far away from the simple, peaceful life of the people and the beauty of the mountains. She later said that she need not have worried, as she was greeted with a grand parade down Main Street that included Boy and Girl Scouts, the Red Cross, the USO, civilian volunteers, miners, workers of the town, farmers, and lastly, the almost 600 mothers of men in service to their country, proudly wearing badges of honor, earned by their sons and pinned on their cotton dresses. She then knew the war was already very personal to these folks. It was their war, too. (Courtesy of Williamson Public Library.)

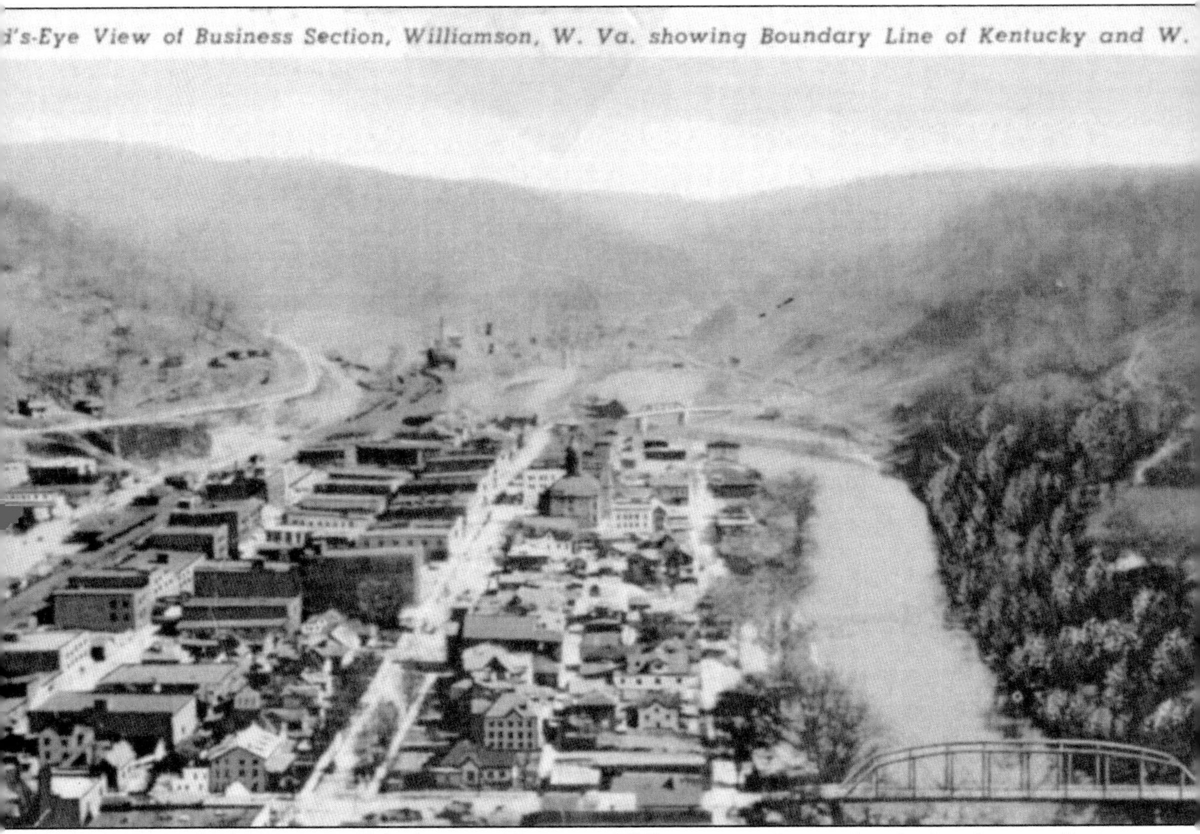

This is a bird's-eye view of the business district in Williamson and was taken before the installation of the floodwall. The Tug River is the boundary between West Virginia and Kentucky and is shown here. The Tug River often flooded, causing widespread damage and destruction. The flood in 1977 reached a record 52.56 feet, more than 25 feet above flood stage. (Courtesy of Williamson Public Library.)

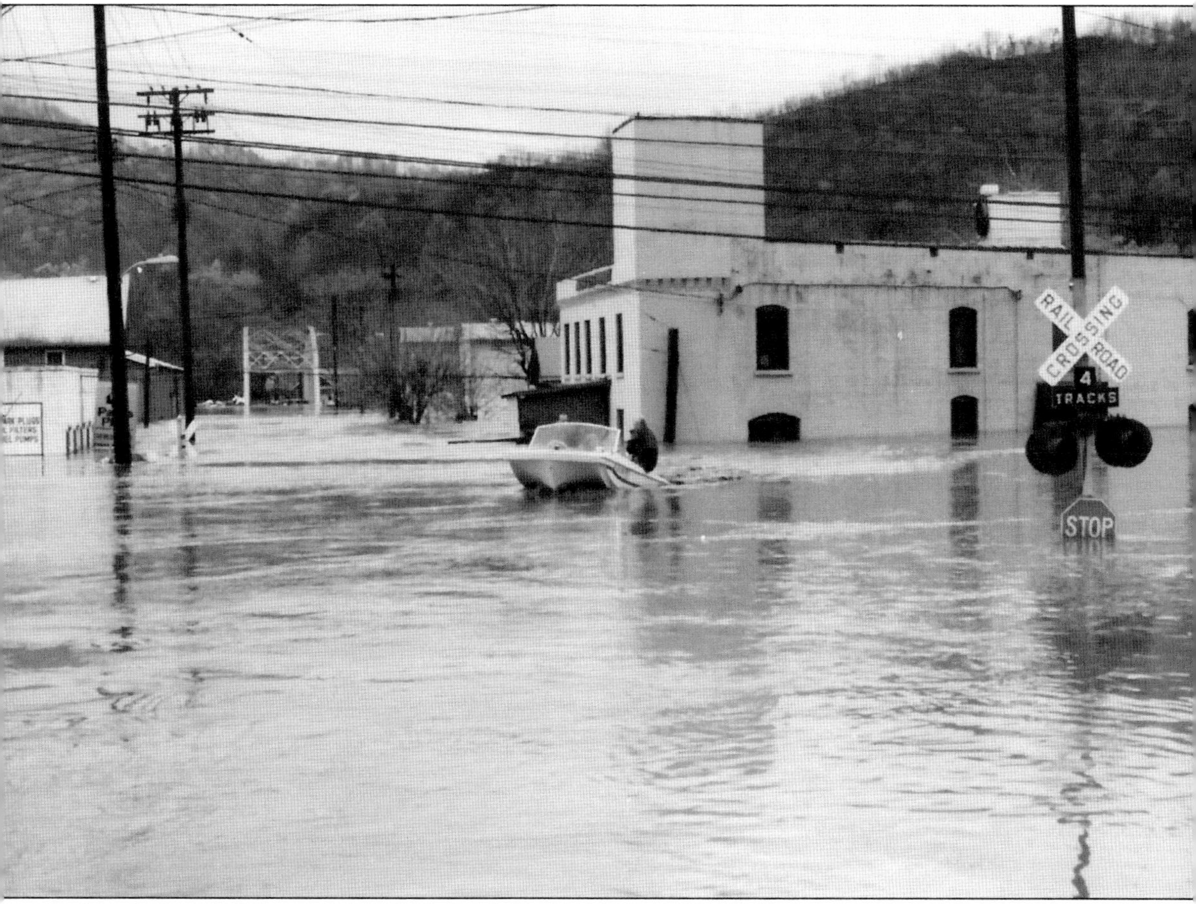

This close-up of the 1977 flood shows the water level above the stop sign at the railroad tracks in downtown Williamson. As pictured, the only means of transportation possible was by boat. (Courtesy of Williamson Public Library.)

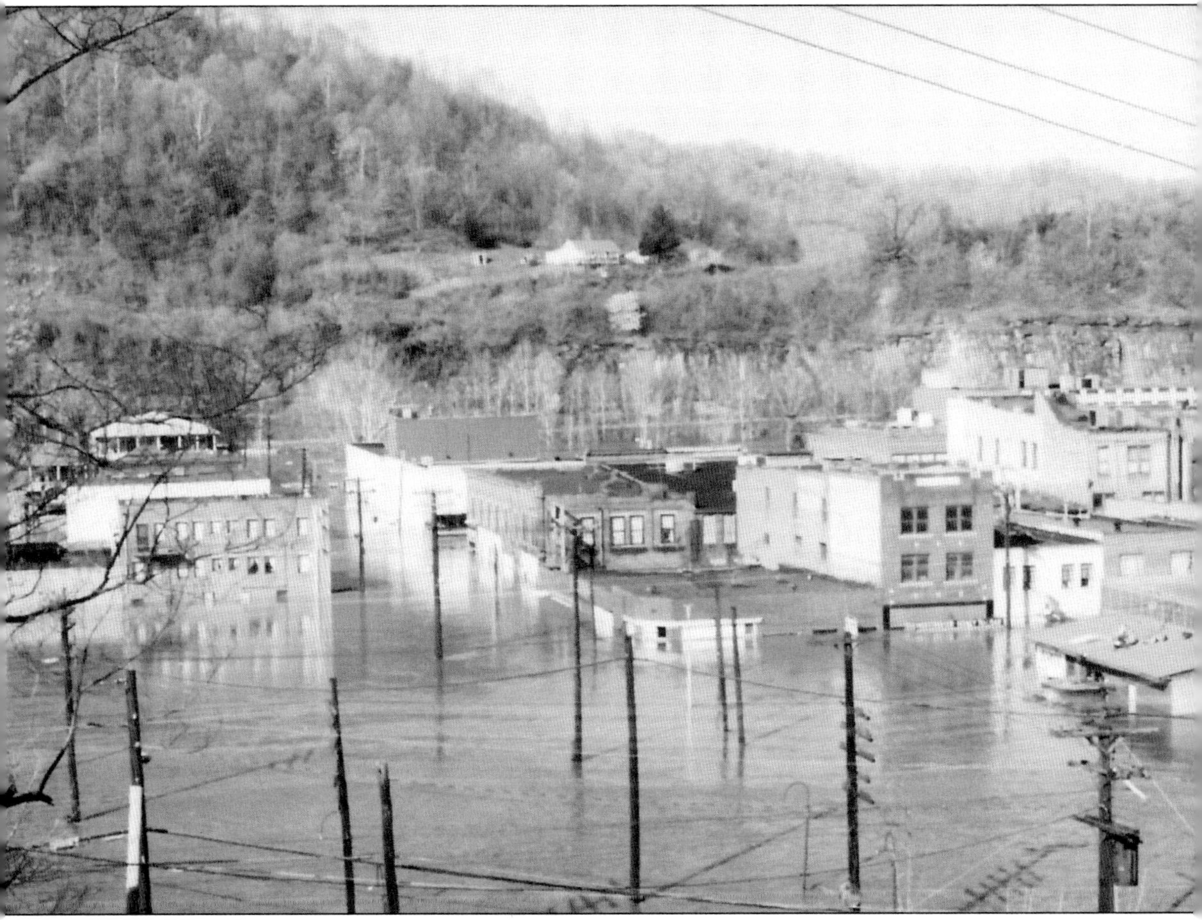

This image shows downtown Williamson during the flood of 1977. Drastic measures would be required to be prevent these conditions in the future. (Courtesy of Williamson Public Library.)

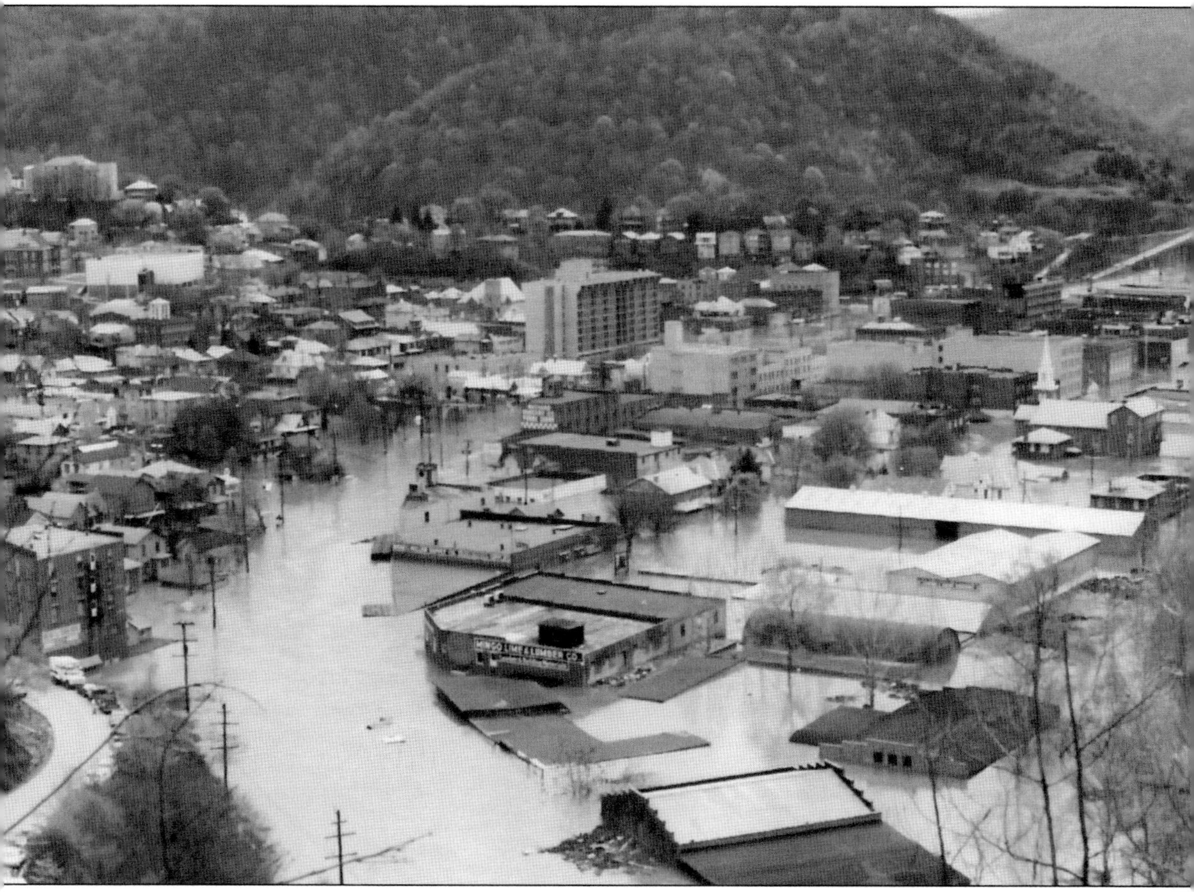

As pictured here, the flooding of the Tug River in 1977 involved the displacement of such vast amounts of water that there was no holding it back. (Courtesy of Williamson Public Library.)

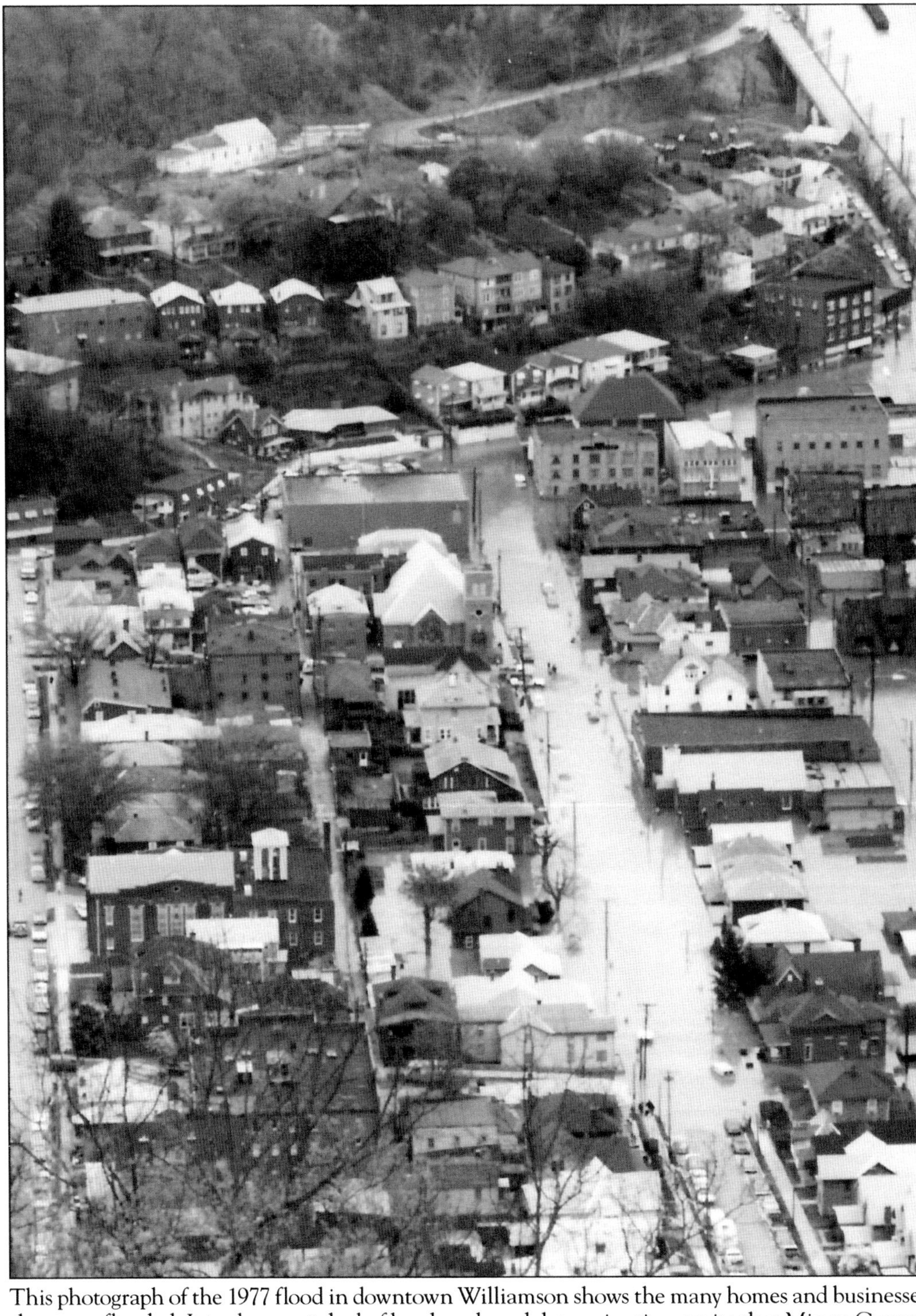

This photograph of the 1977 flood in downtown Williamson shows the many homes and businesses that were flooded. It took a great deal of hard work and determination, traits that Mingo County folks are known for, to bring life back to normal after so much destruction. (Courtesy of Williamson Public Library.)

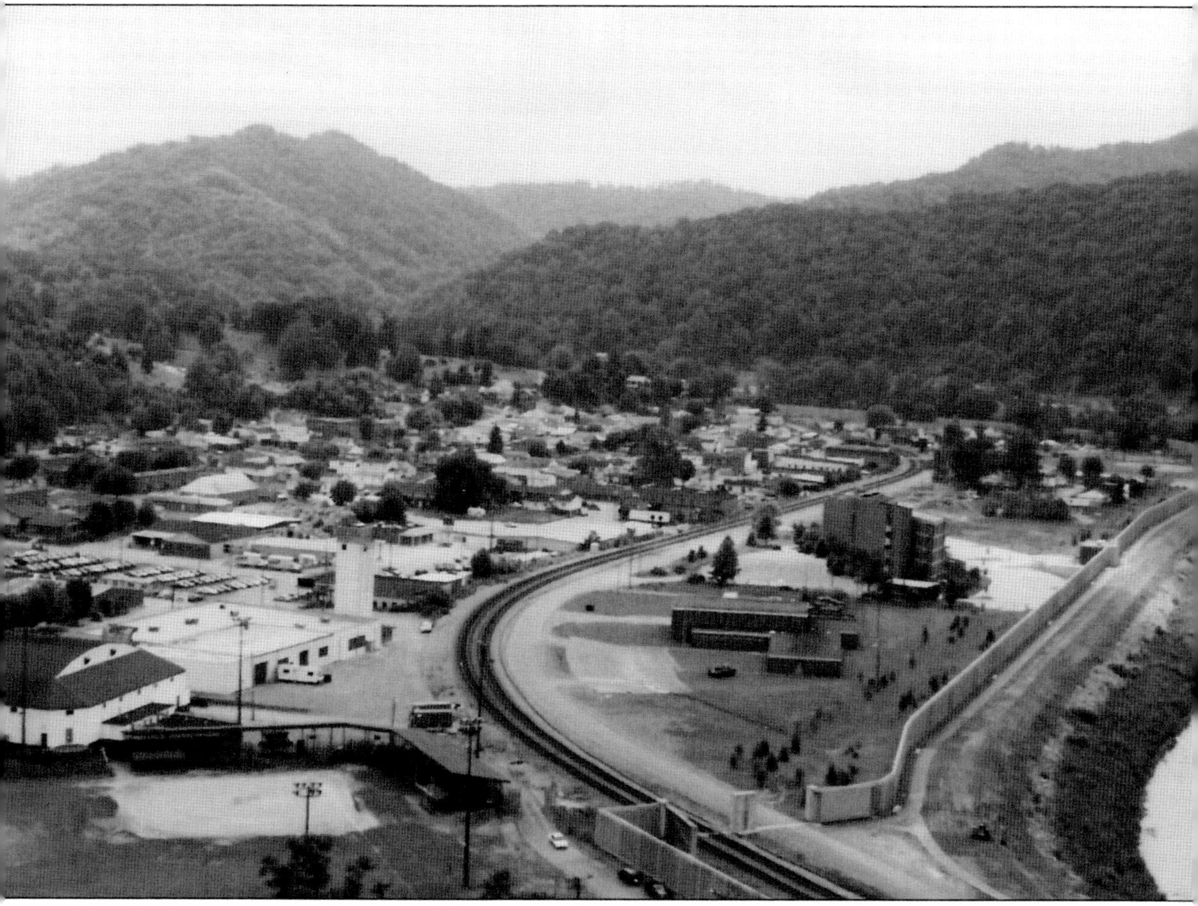

After the devastation and continual flooding of the Tug River, it was necessary to build a floodwall to prevent such future catastrophic flooding. Pictured here to the right is the floodwall, which now contains the Tug River. The Williamson Floodwall was built at a cost of more than $105 million. In 1980, Congress passed a law that specifically exempted several Appalachian waterways from the "cost benefit" equation that normally determined who received flood protection. Matewan also received a floodwall at a cost of $51.7 million. These 20-foot-high walls have gates that close when they are needed to protect the residents from the mighty Tug River. (Courtesy of Williamson Public Library.)

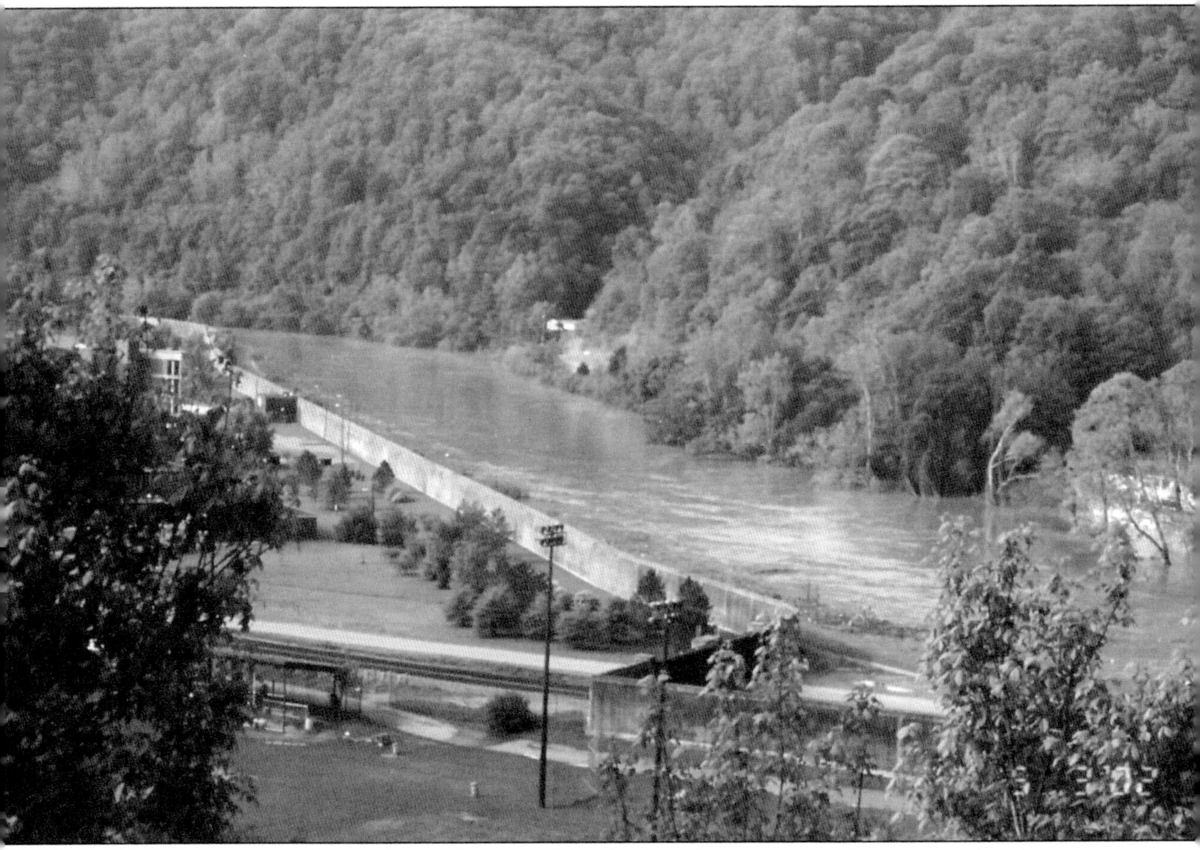

This close-up view shows the Williamson Floodwall. (Courtesy of Williamson Public Library.)

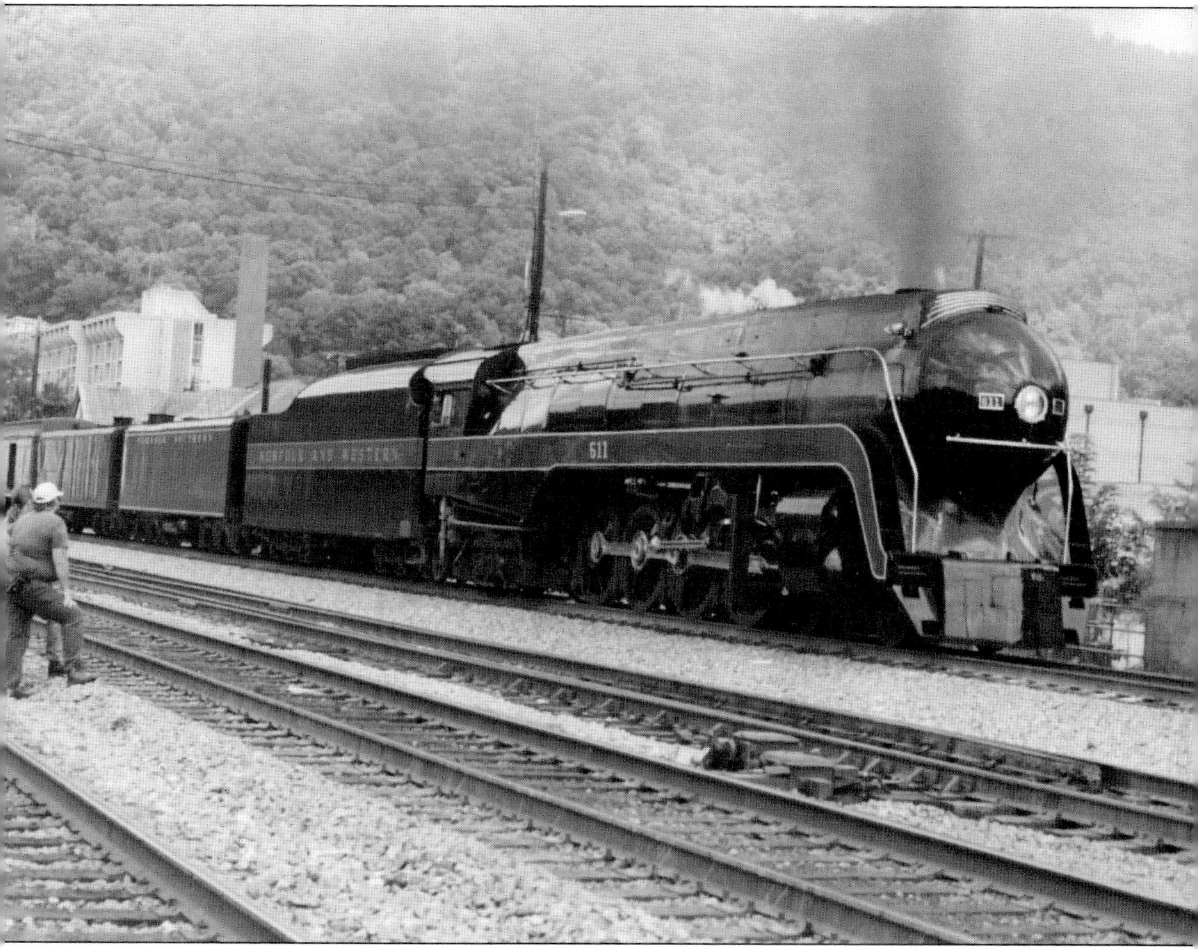

Pictured here is the Williamson Rail Yard with a Norfolk & Western train sitting on the tracks. The Williamson Rail Yard was built in 1902. At one time, it was the second largest train yard in the world. To this day, the coalfields of southern West Virginia have one of the highest concentrations of railroad tracks in America. These tracks, built to transport vast coal riches and timber resources, still see some of the highest train traffic in the United States. (Courtesy of Williamson Public Library.)

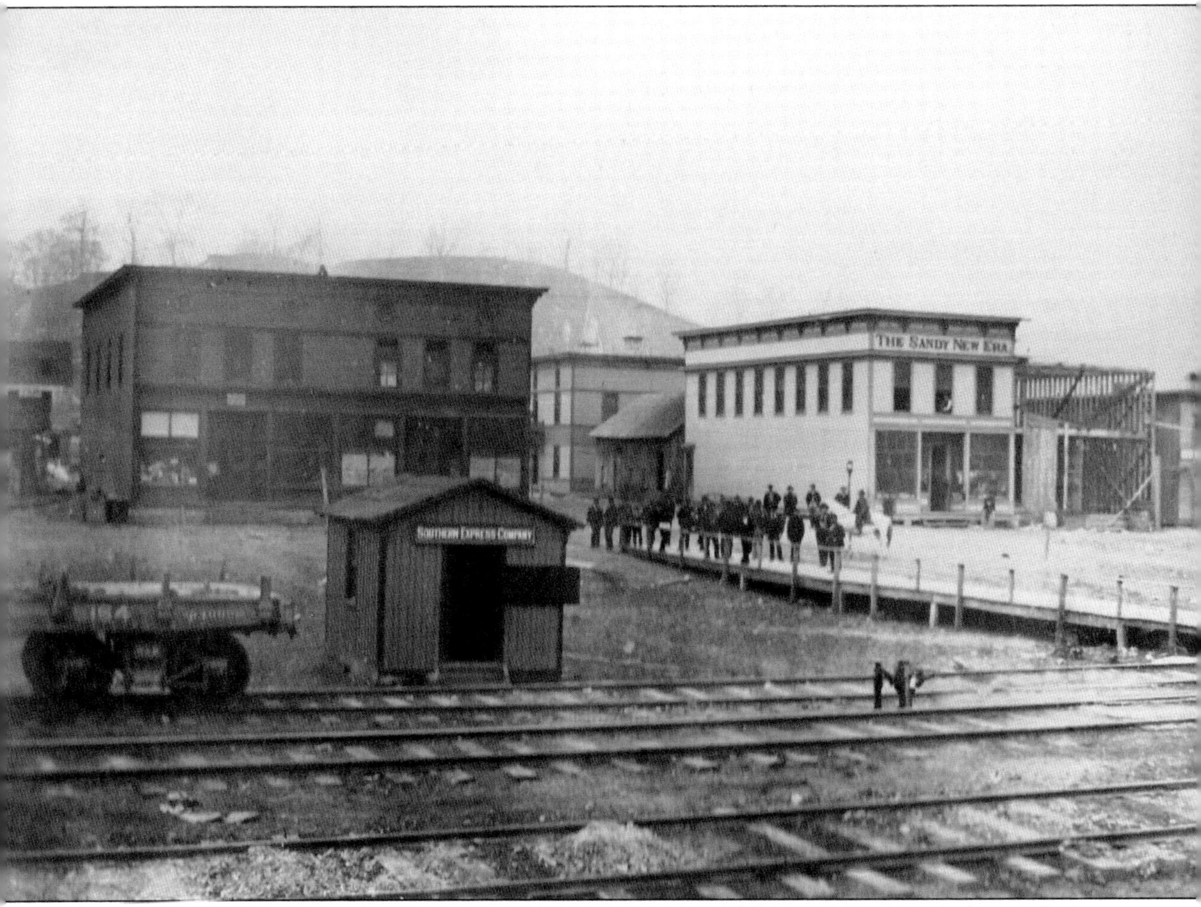

The Williamson railroad tracks in the early 1920s, pictured here, often attracted crowds. It was at the train stops that folks began and ended journeys, since most of the long-distance travel of the day took place by train. It was a place for socializing and catching up on the news of the day in addition to being an important part of the business of the people of Mingo County. With the increasing use of trains, items were brought for sale and folks had increased opportunities to purchase goods from across the country. (Courtesy of Williamson Public Library.)

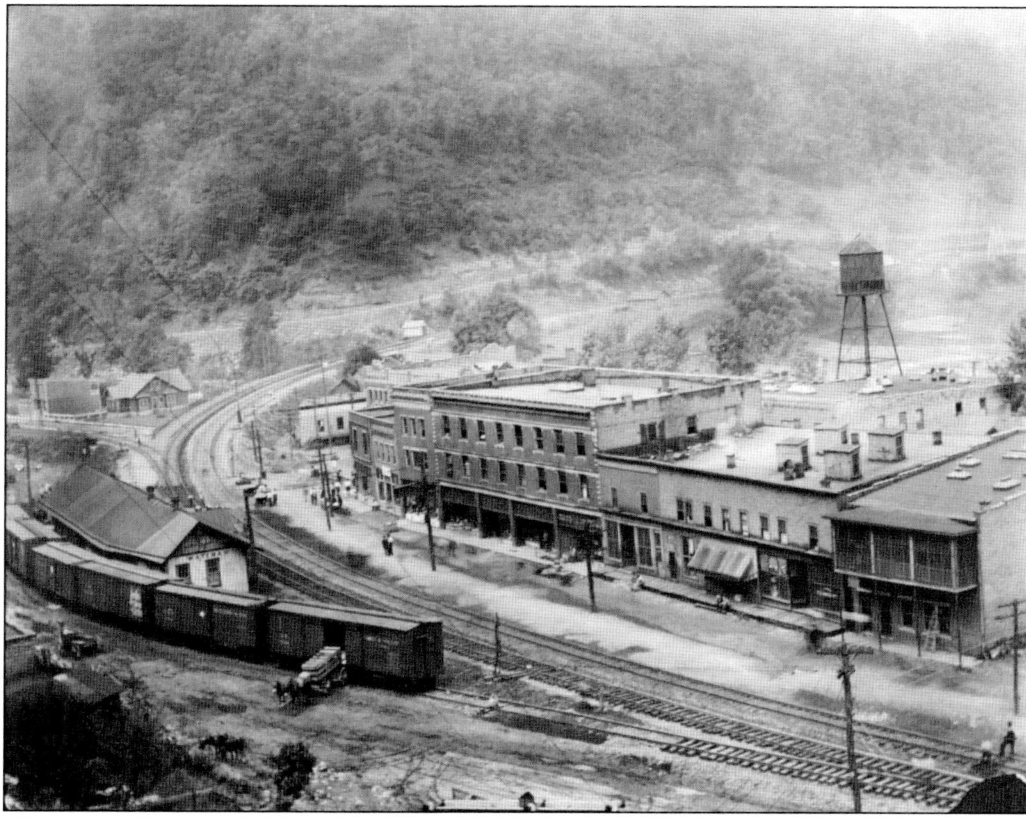

This 1920s photograph shows the scene of the Matewan Massacre. Coal miners intent on joining the union met a group of Baldwin-Felts detectives in the famous shootout. The detectives had evicted families from company-owned homes before they were confronted by police chief Sid Hatfield and the coal miners. Seven detectives and three townspeople were killed, including Matewan mayor Cabell Testerman. (Courtesy of West Virginia State Archives, Edward Hale Collection.)

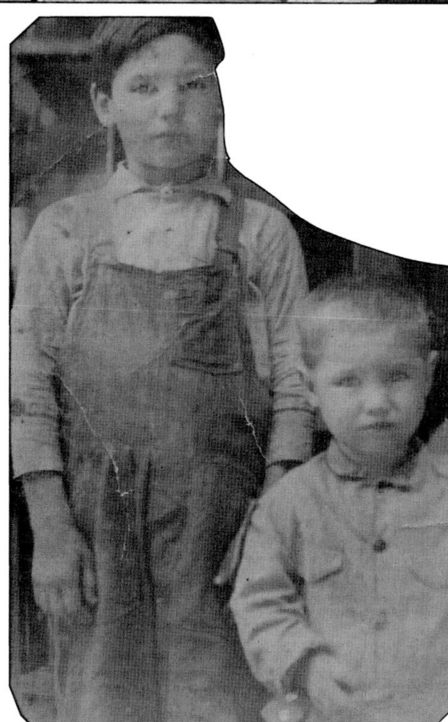

This rare photograph was taken in the 1920s and shows Tom Chafin, left, and his younger brother, Pete Chafin. These were the children of Allen and Lydia Chafin. Lydia Chafin was the daughter of Ellison Hatfield. Tom Chafin would grow up to have a family of five children and would serve the citizens of Mingo County in a number of different elected offices.

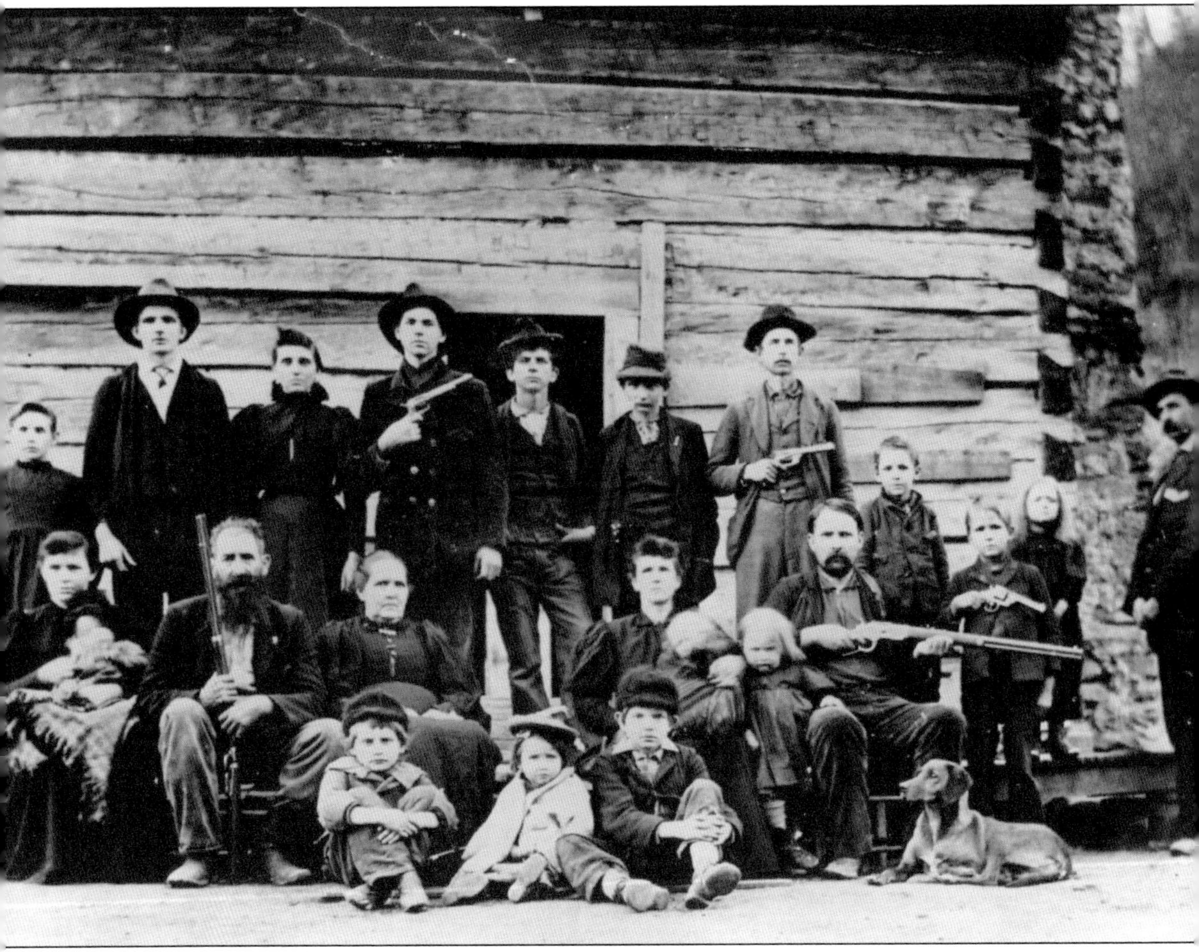

This photograph of the Hatfield family was taken around 1897 at the family home on Beech Creek in Mingo County, West Virginia. Seen here from left to right are (first row) Tennyson Hatfield, Louvisa Hatfield, Willis Hatfield, and "Devil Anse's" bear and coon dog; (second row) Mary Hensley-Simpkins-Howes, Vici Simpkins, William Anderson "Devil Anse" Hatfield, Levicy Chafin Hatfield, Nancy Elizabeth Hatfield, Robert Elliott Hatfield, Louise Hatfield, Cap Hatfield, and Coleman Hatfield; (third row) Rosa Lee Hatfield Browning, Detroit Hatfield, Betty Lee Hatfield Caldwell, Elias Hatfield, Tom Chafin, Joe D. Hatfield, hired hand "Ock" Damron, Shephard Hatfield, Levicy Emma Hatfield, and store manager William Borden. (Courtesy of Lahoma Lee Farley Schuller.)

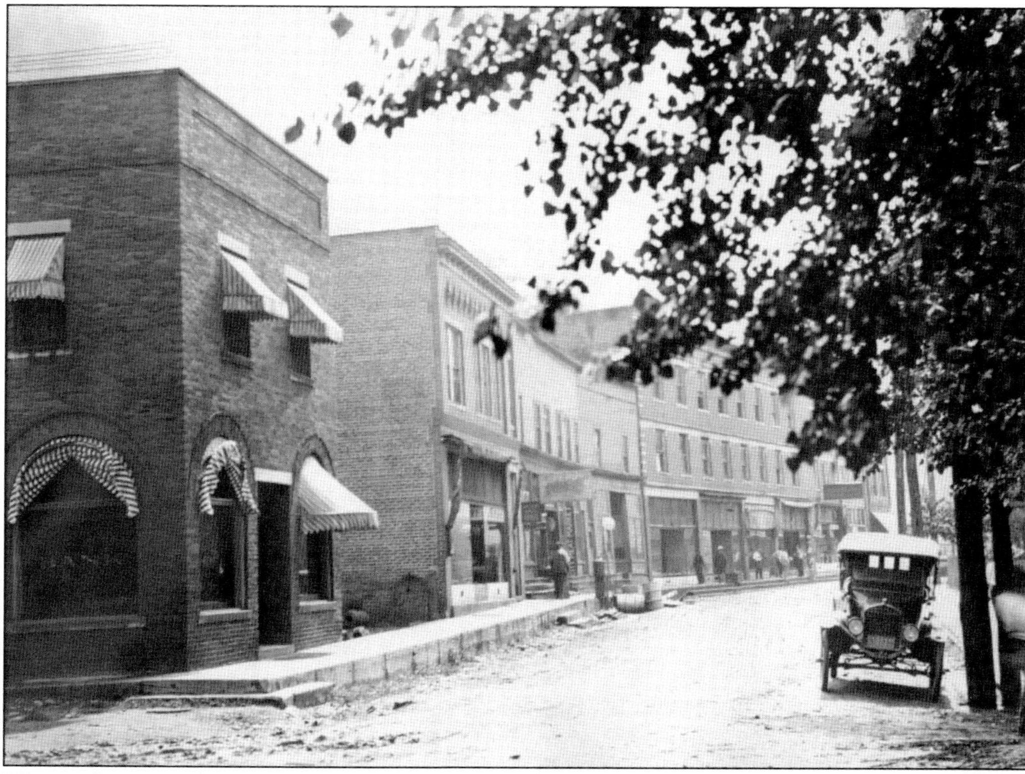

This early-1930s photograph shows Matewan's Main Street. Most of the buildings still stand, despite major flooding of the Tug River. Matewan is known for the Matewan Massacre in 1920 and the Hatfield and McCoy Feud, which erupted in the late 1800s. The town is now protected by a multimillion-dollar floodwall. (Courtesy of West Virginia State Archives, Edward Hale Collection.)

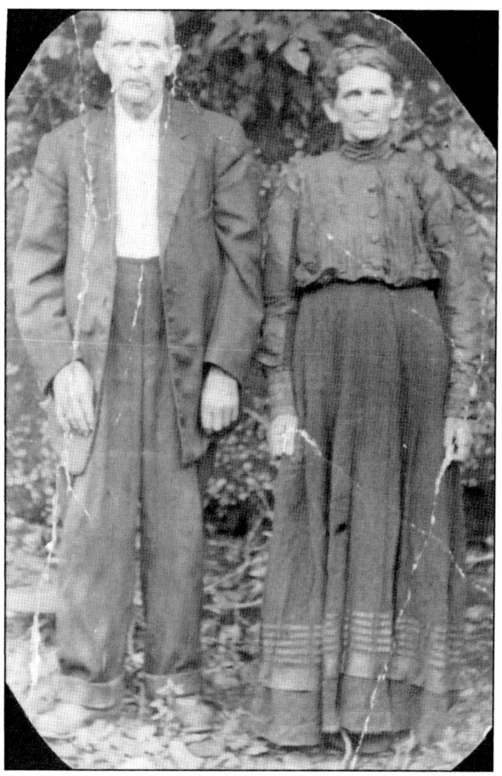

Shown here are Andrew Chafin, left, and Vicey Mounts Chafin, who pose here for this 1920s photograph. Vicey was the wife of Anderson "Devil Anse" Hatfield, the leader of the Hatfield clan during the Hatfield-McCoy Feud. It is said that Vicey gave the nickname Devil to Anderson after declaring he was mean as the devil. (Courtesy of Hazel M. Chafin.)

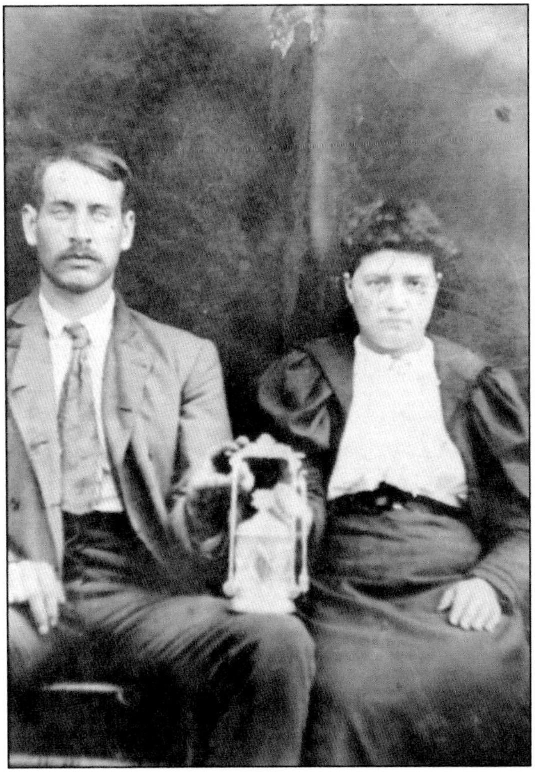

On the left in this image is William Johnson McCoy, and to the right is Sarah Sally Chafin. Johnson McCoy, as he was known, was born in 1836 and was the son of Hiram and Chloe Samson McCoy. Sally Chafin, as she was called, was born in the 1830s and was the daughter of Nathan and Matilda Varney Chafin. This photograph was taken on their wedding day. Sally was the sister of Devil Anse Hatfield's wife, Levicy Chafin Hatfield. (Courtesy of Lahoma Lee Farley Schuller.)

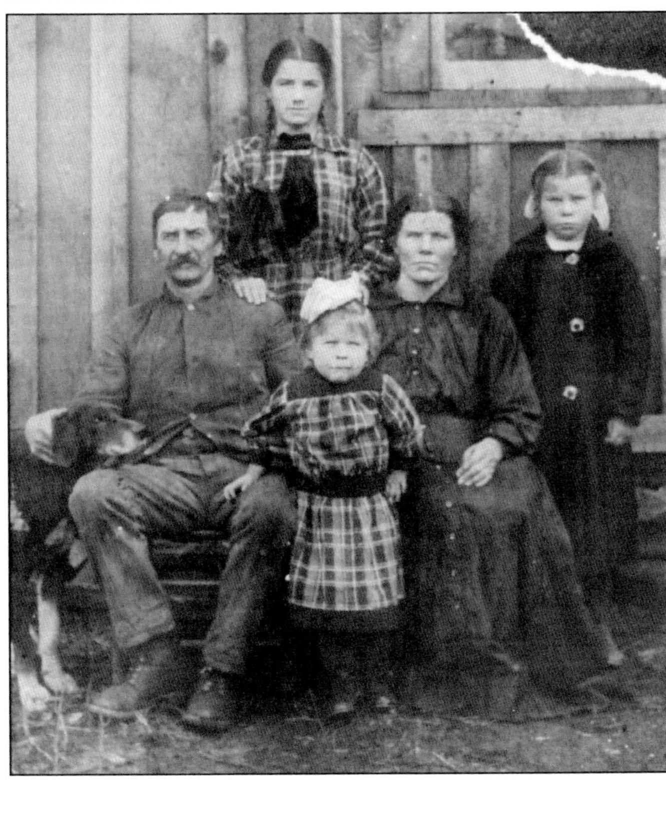

This early-1930s photograph is of Smith Hatfield and his family. Smith was the youngest brother one of the of Devil Anse Hatfield. Smith's twin brother was named Patterson Hatfield. This image shows Smith and his wife, Louise Hubbard Hatfield. Their oldest daughter, standing in the back, is Willie. On the right is Emma, and in front is Biddie. Both Emma and Biddie were named after Smith's sisters. (Courtesy of Hester Kinder Keatley.)

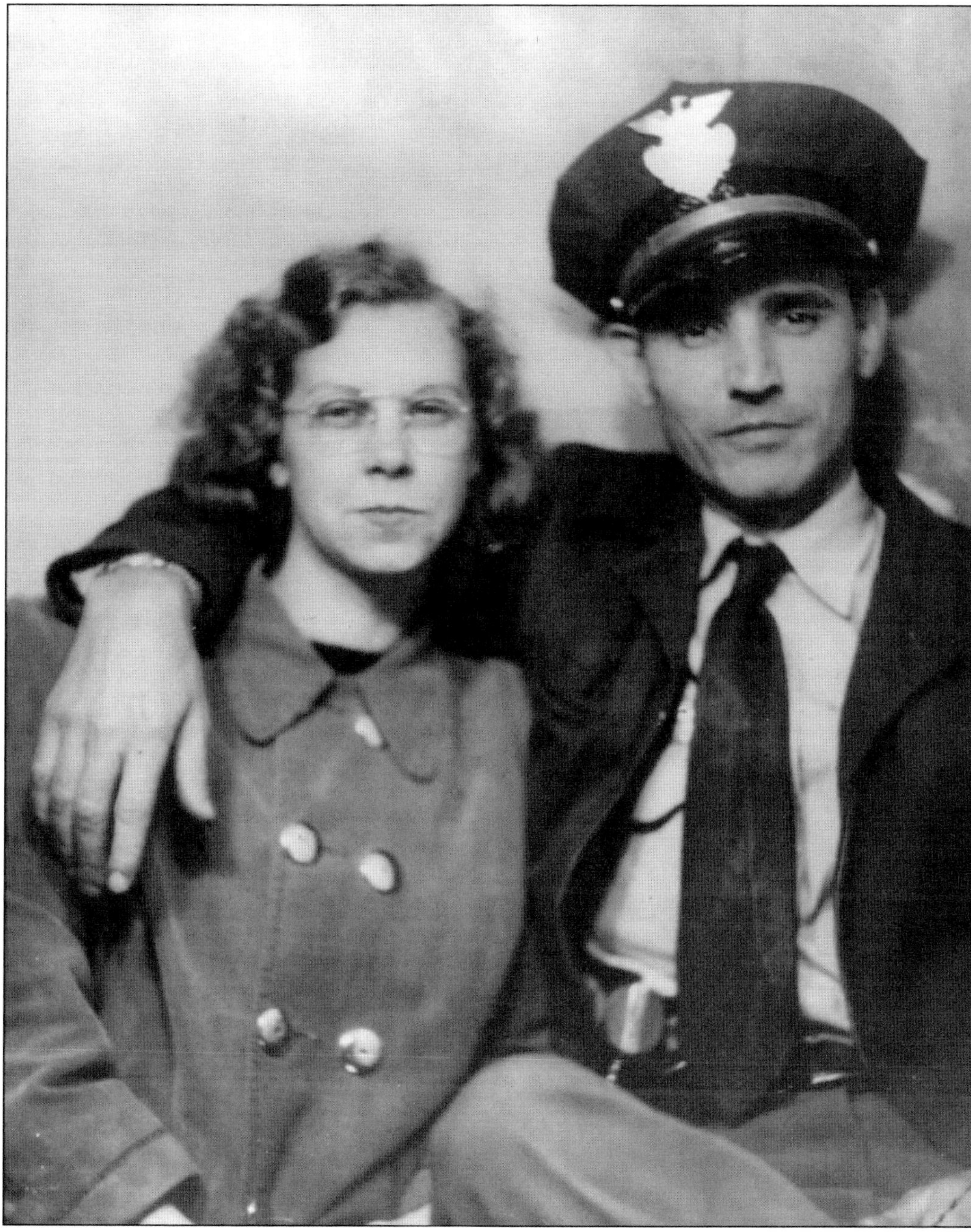

This photograph of Hazel Marie Isaac and Tom C. Chafin was taken in the 1940s. At the time, Tom was a constable in the Magnolia District of Mingo County. He was elected to that office in November 1944. It was the first of many elected offices that he would hold during his 36-plus years of public service to the citizens of Mingo County. Tom was the first sheriff in Mingo County to ever succeed himself due to a change in the law. Tom and Hazel were married on June 29, 1936. Tom was 25 years of age and Hazel was 19 years of age. They had three sons—Andrew, Don, and Truman—and two daughters, Georgia Ann and Jeanne. (Courtesy of Hazel M. Chafin.)

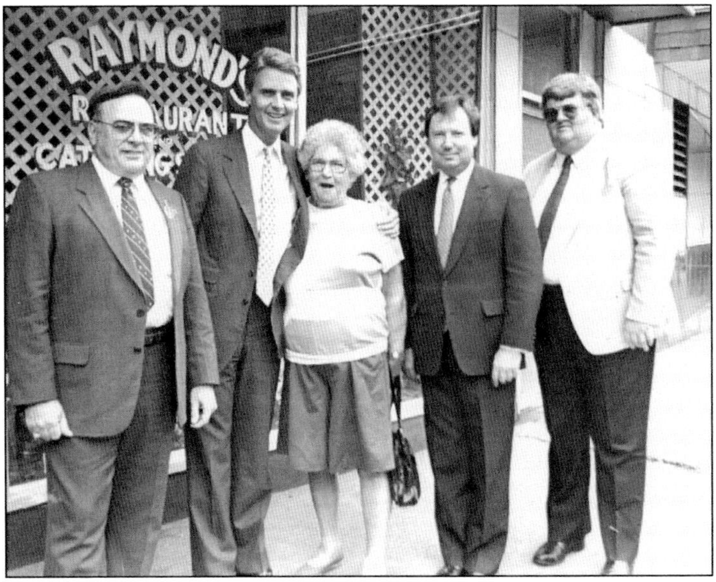

In this 1990s photograph, local Mingo County Democratic leaders are pictured. Second from the left is Gov. Caston Caperton, who served as governor of West Virginia from 1989 until 1997. Fourth from left is Sen. H. Truman Chafin. Senator Chafin has served in the West Virginia Senate for the past 28 years. He served as Senate majority leader. He is the son of Hazel M. Chafin and Tom C. Chafin. (Courtesy of Hazel M. Chafin.)

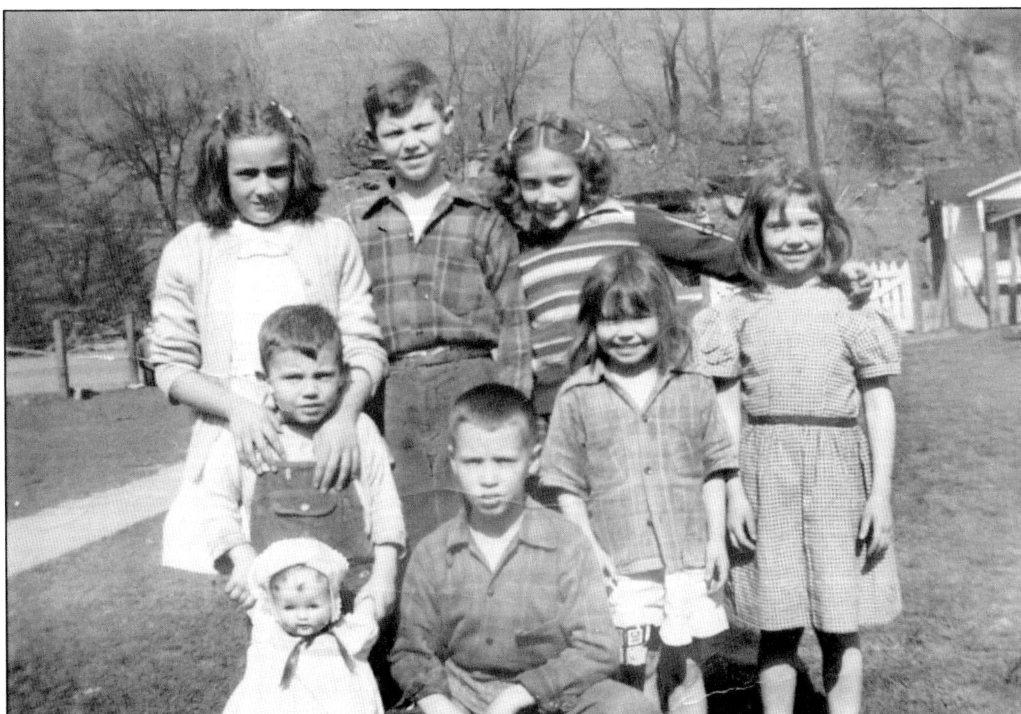

This photograph of New Town kids was taken in the late 1940s.From left to right are (first row) Truman Chafin, Donald Ray Chafin, and Jeanne Chafin; (second row) Brenda Mitchell, Andy Chafin, Tinkey Barrett, and Georgia Ann Chafin. This photograph was taken in the front yard of the Tom C. Chafin house, which was often used as a gathering place for neighborhood children. (Courtesy of Hazel M. Chafin.)

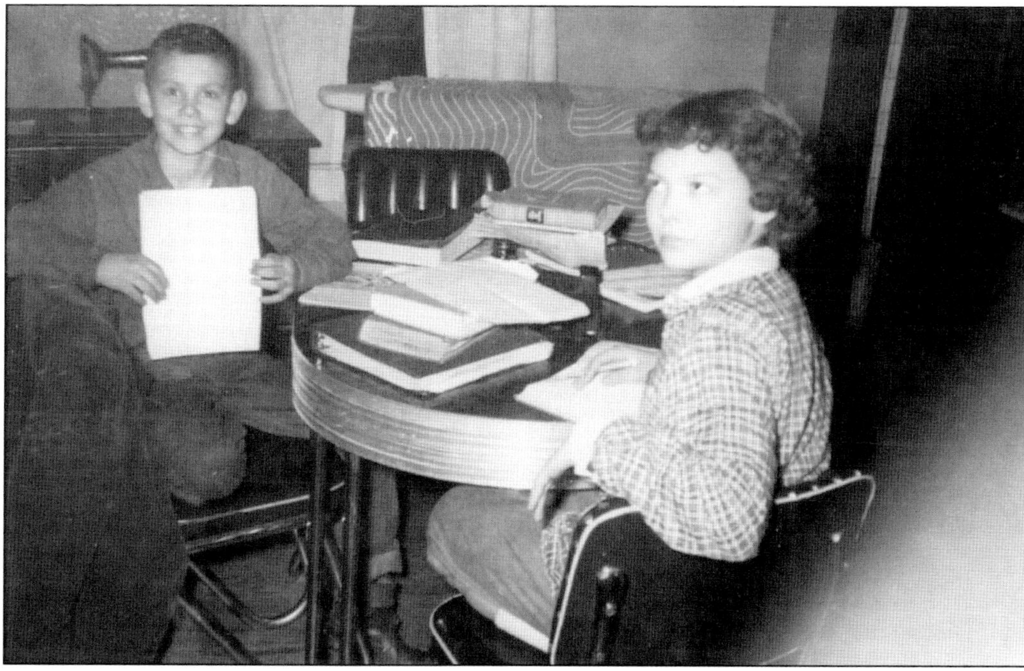

Truman and Jeanne Chafin do their homework in this early-1950s photograph. They were the children of Tom and Hazel Chafin. Note Hazel's sewing machine in the background. Most women made many of the clothes their children wore in the 1940s and 1950s. (Courtesy of Hazel M. Chafin.)

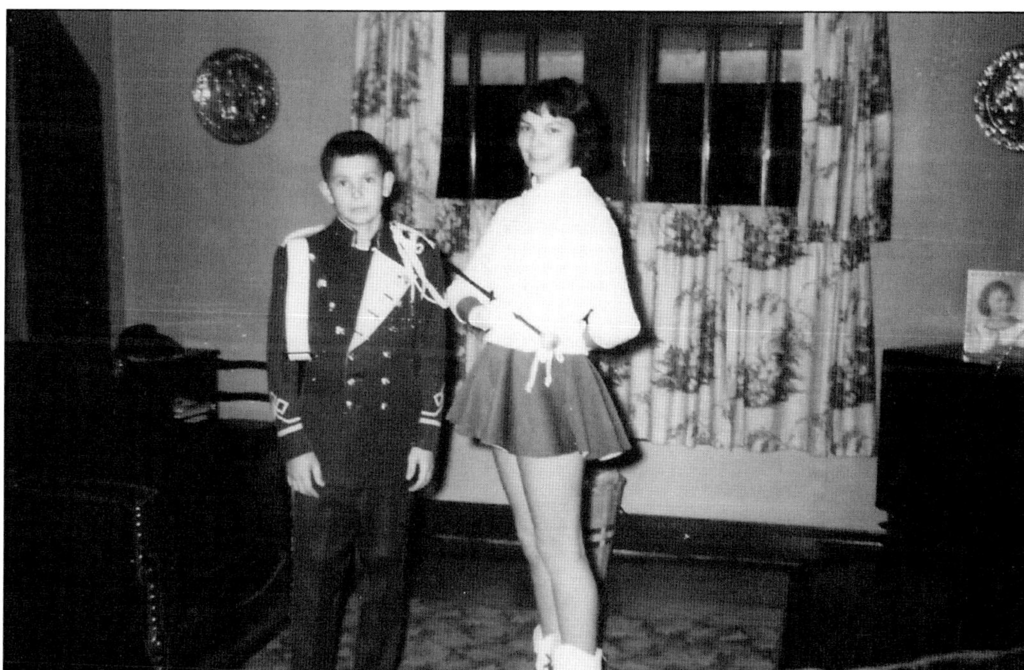

H. Truman and Jeanne Chafin's Matewan Tigers' support shows in this 1958 photograph. (Courtesy of Hazel M. Chafin.)

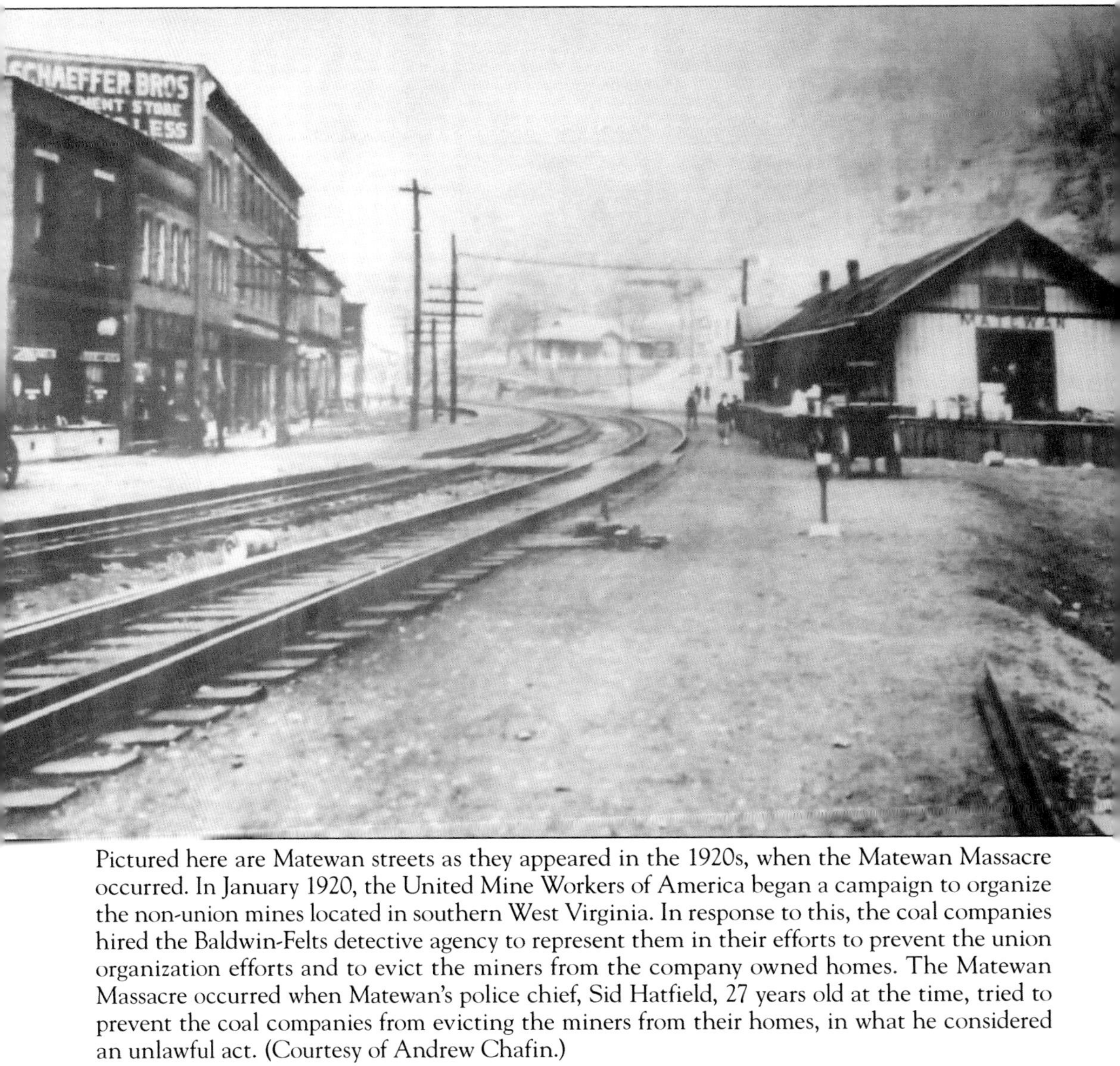

Pictured here are Matewan streets as they appeared in the 1920s, when the Matewan Massacre occurred. In January 1920, the United Mine Workers of America began a campaign to organize the non-union mines located in southern West Virginia. In response to this, the coal companies hired the Baldwin-Felts detective agency to represent them in their efforts to prevent the union organization efforts and to evict the miners from the company owned homes. The Matewan Massacre occurred when Matewan's police chief, Sid Hatfield, 27 years old at the time, tried to prevent the coal companies from evicting the miners from their homes, in what he considered an unlawful act. (Courtesy of Andrew Chafin.)

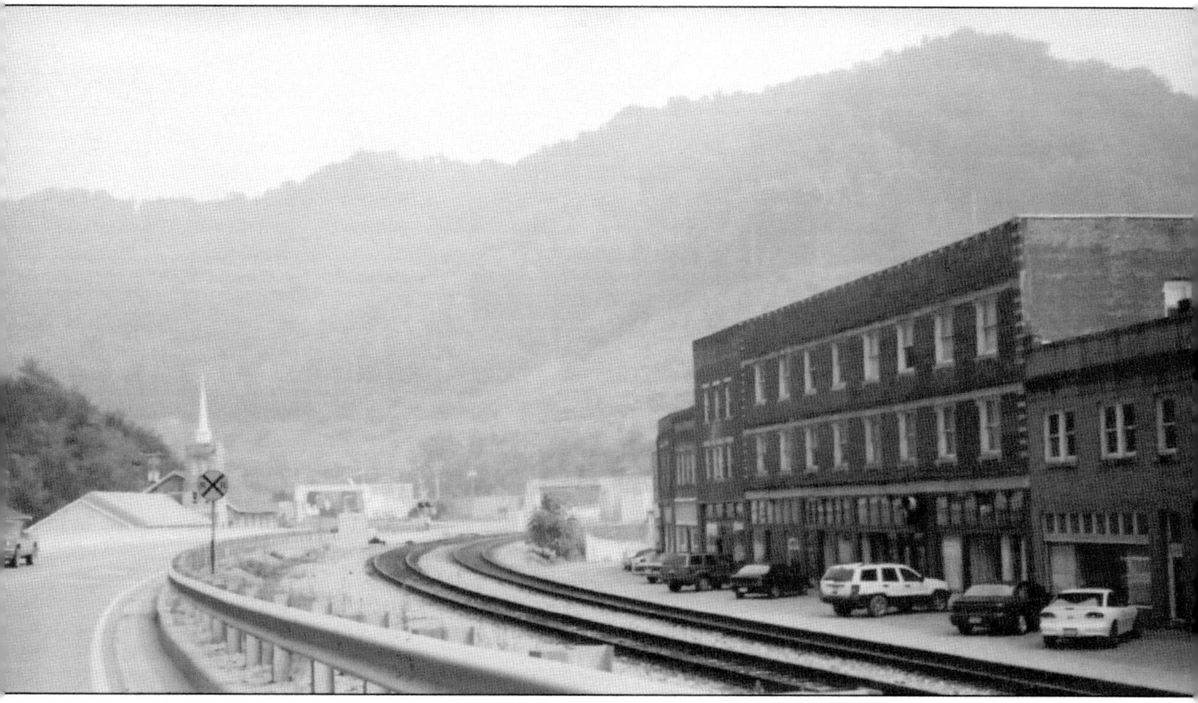

Pictured here are the Matewan streets as they appear today. This photograph was taken from the opposite direction of the previous image. This little town remains to a large degree the same as it did in the 1920s and is one of the most historical towns in America. Many of the events which took place here affected the history of the United States. The Matewan Massacre, as it came to be known, was the beginning of the coal wars and the eventual Battle at Blair Mountain, which pitted Americans against Americans as 3,000 armed miners battled for the their rights against the coal operators. During what was considered the largest labor uprising in US history, the US Army was called in to restore control, by presidential order. (Courtesy of Andrew Chafin.)

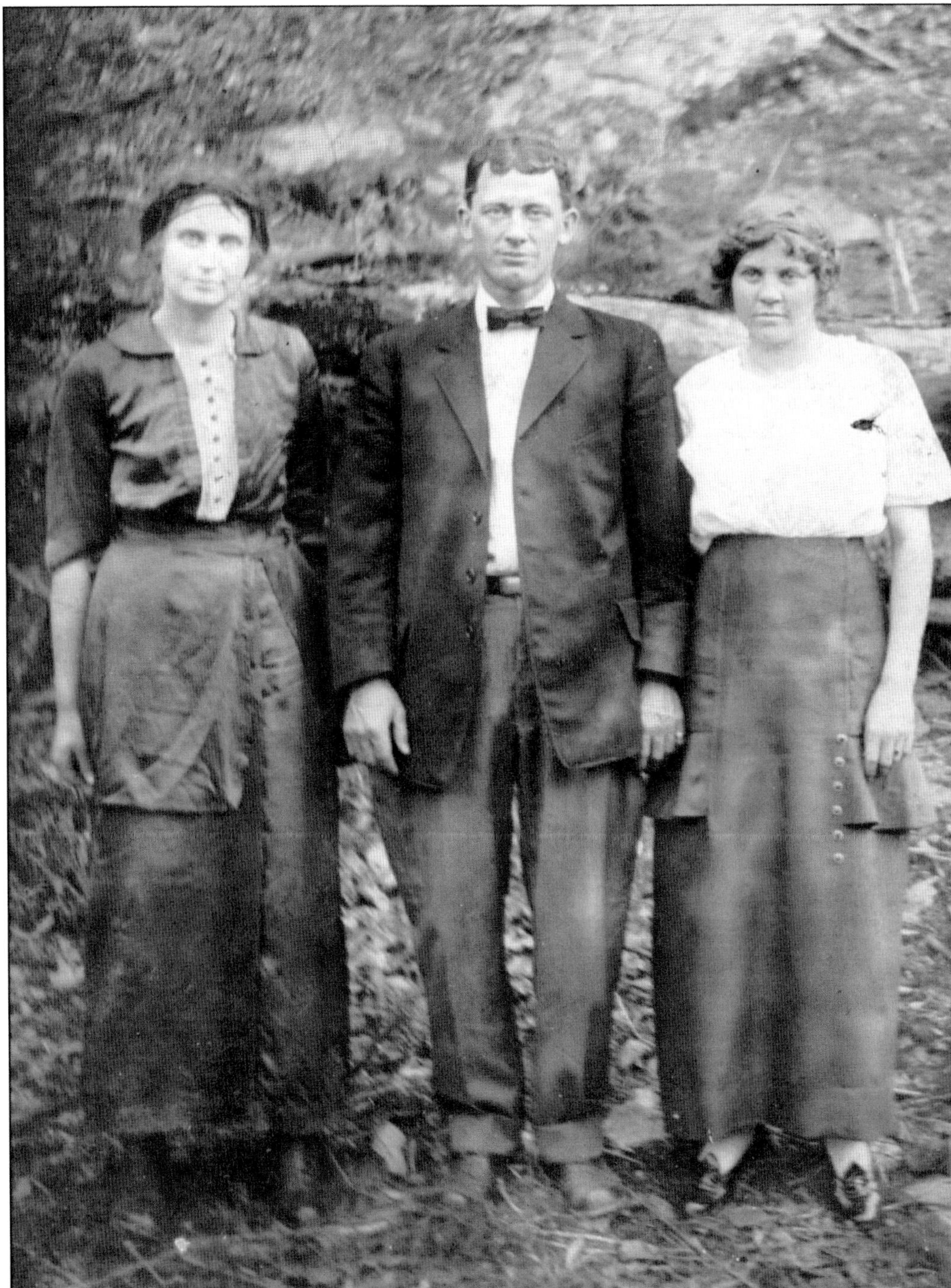

Pictured from left to right are an unidentified woman, Charles Isaac, and Georgia Ann Isaac. They exhibit the dress of the day in the early 1920s. It was common to name children after family, thereby resulting in a number of individuals in a family with the same name. It was a source of pride to pass down the name and insure a continuation of that name into the future generations. (Courtesy of Hazel M. Chafin.)

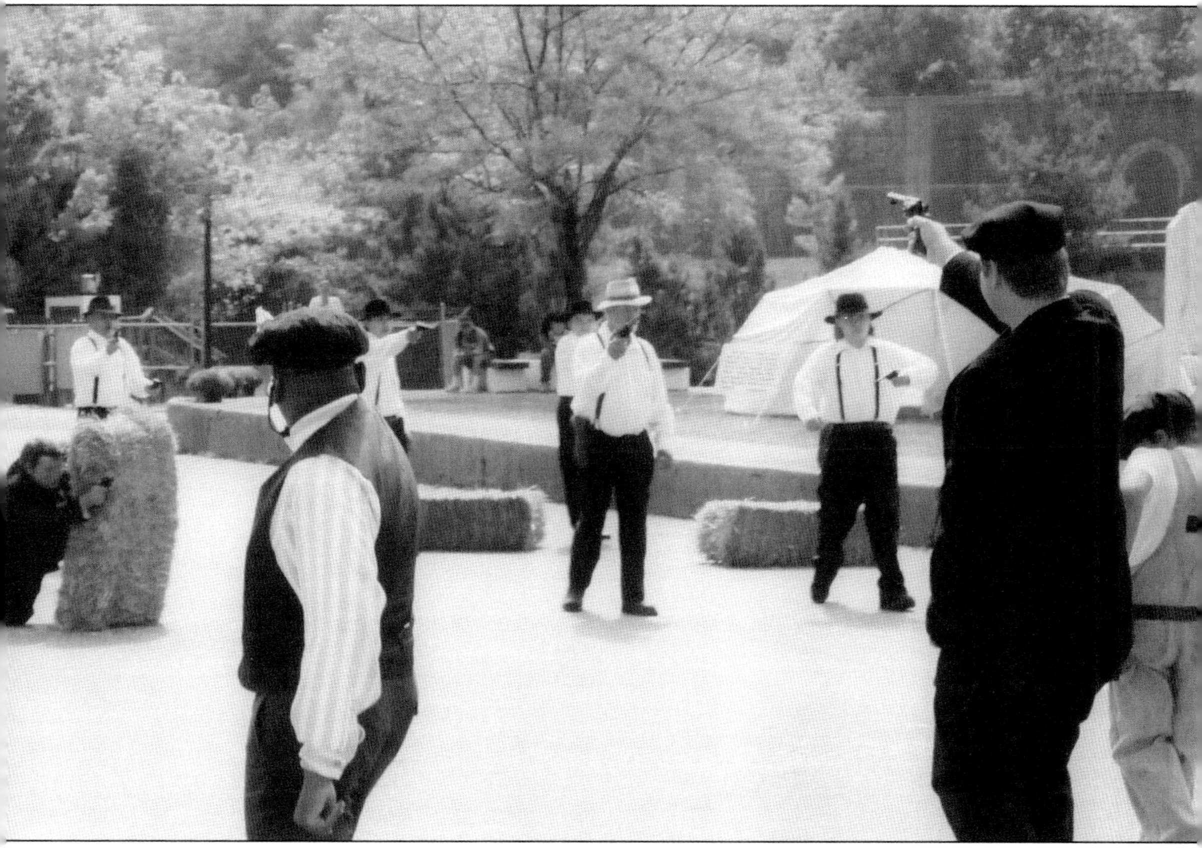

The bloody battle between the striking miners and the Baldwin Felts detectives seen here portrays the actual gunfight as captured in this reenactment, held on the streets of Matewan each summer. The Baldwin-Felts detectives were unaware they had been surrounded by armed miners. The miners were watching from windows, doorways, and other hiding places along the street. While Chief of Police Sid Hatfield, Mayor Cabell Testerman, and Albert Felts of the Baldwin-Felts detective agency were arguing, a single gunshot was heard. At this sound, gunfire erupted from all directions. The spray of gunfire only lasted for about two minutes, but when it was over, 10 people were dead: seven Baldwin-Felts detectives, two miners, and Mayor Cabell Testerman. (Courtesy of Andrew Chafin.)

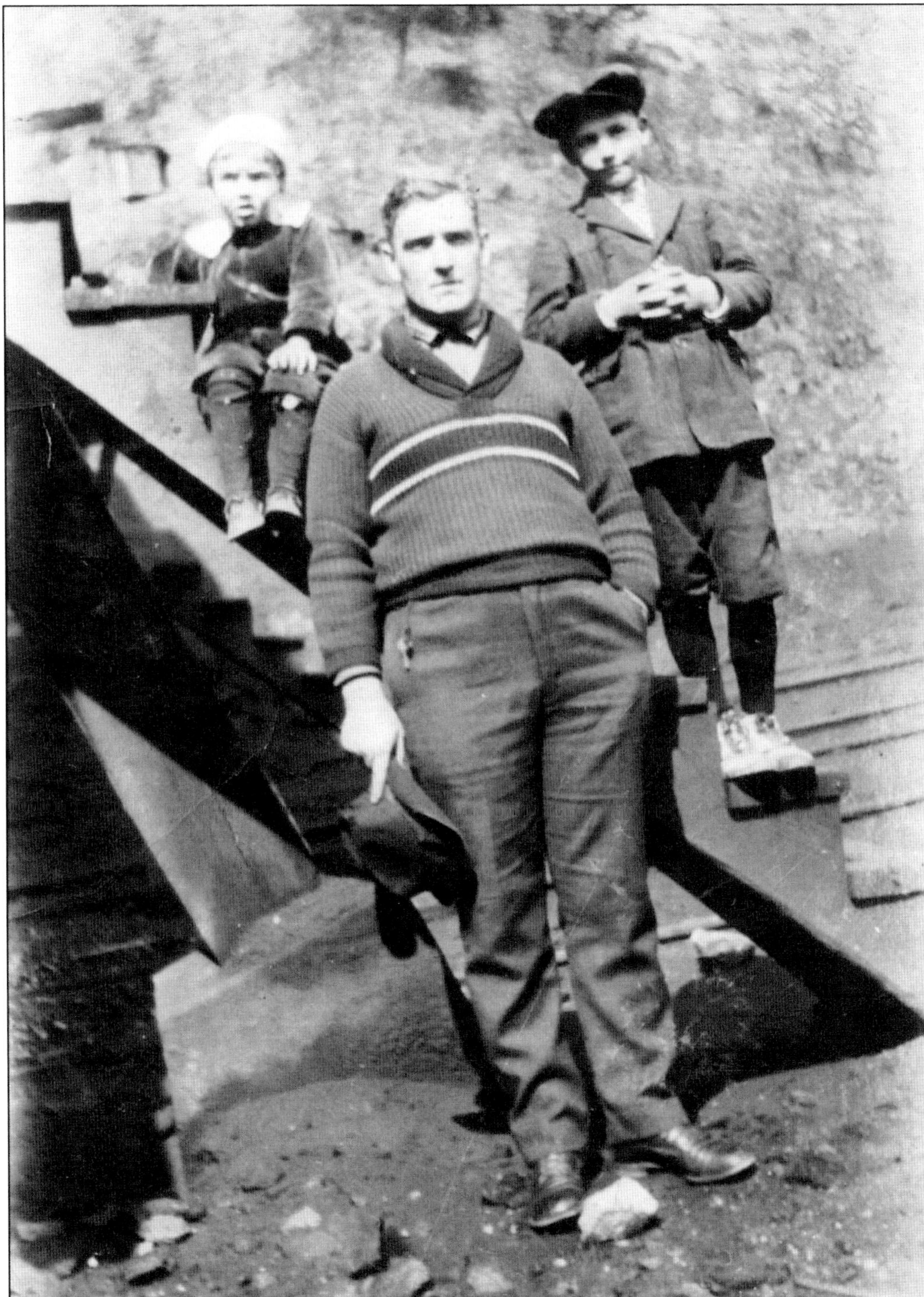

This early-1930s photograph of Tom Chafin was made at New Town. Tom was married to Maude Chafin and their children included Paul, Peaky, Don, Sue, and Georgia. Tom was a pioneer of Mingo County and raised his large family on Mate Creek. (Courtesy of Hazel M. Chafin.)

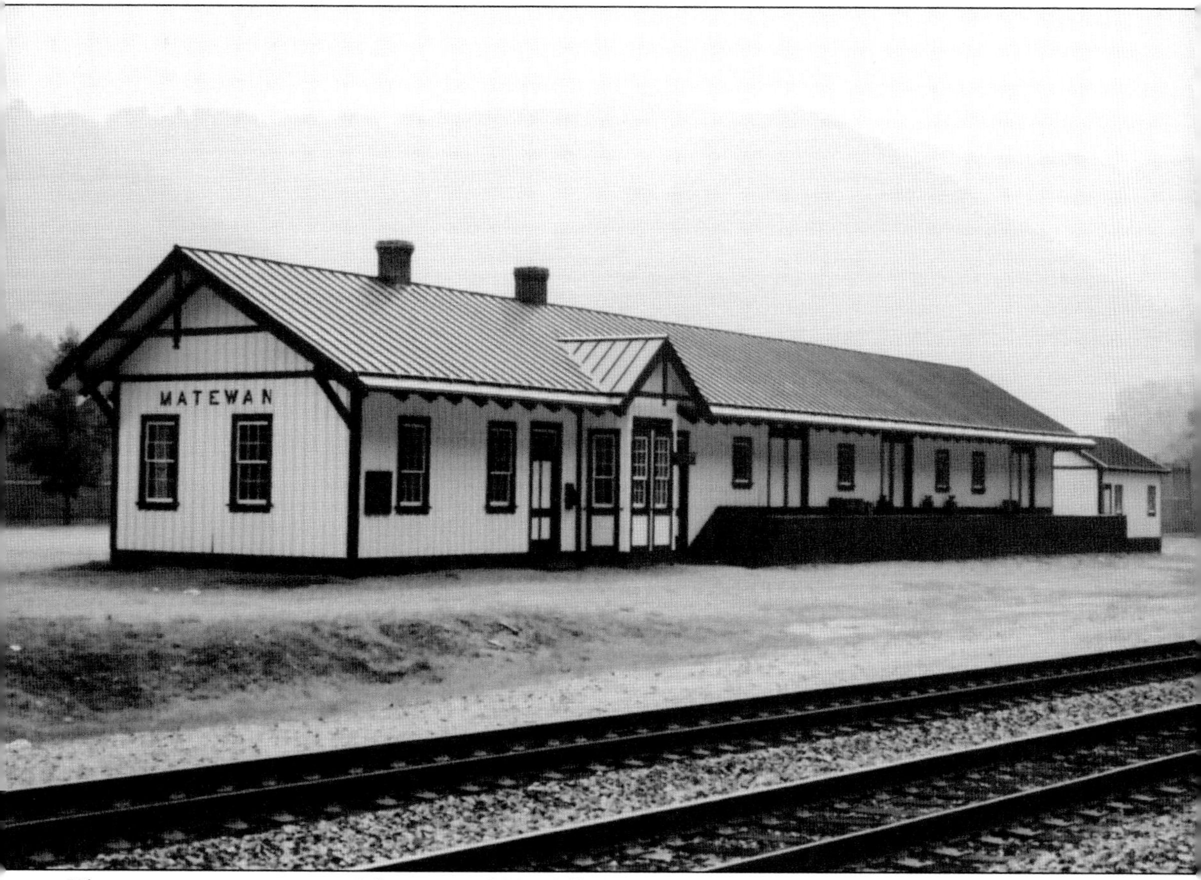

This is a reconstruction of the original Norfolk & Western Railway Depot in Matewan, West Virginia. This replica of the old Matewan Depot is now a museum and is open to the public. Great effort and support have combined to create a trip back in time for those visitors and the families of the region who visit the Matewan Depot. (Courtesy of Andrew Chafin.)

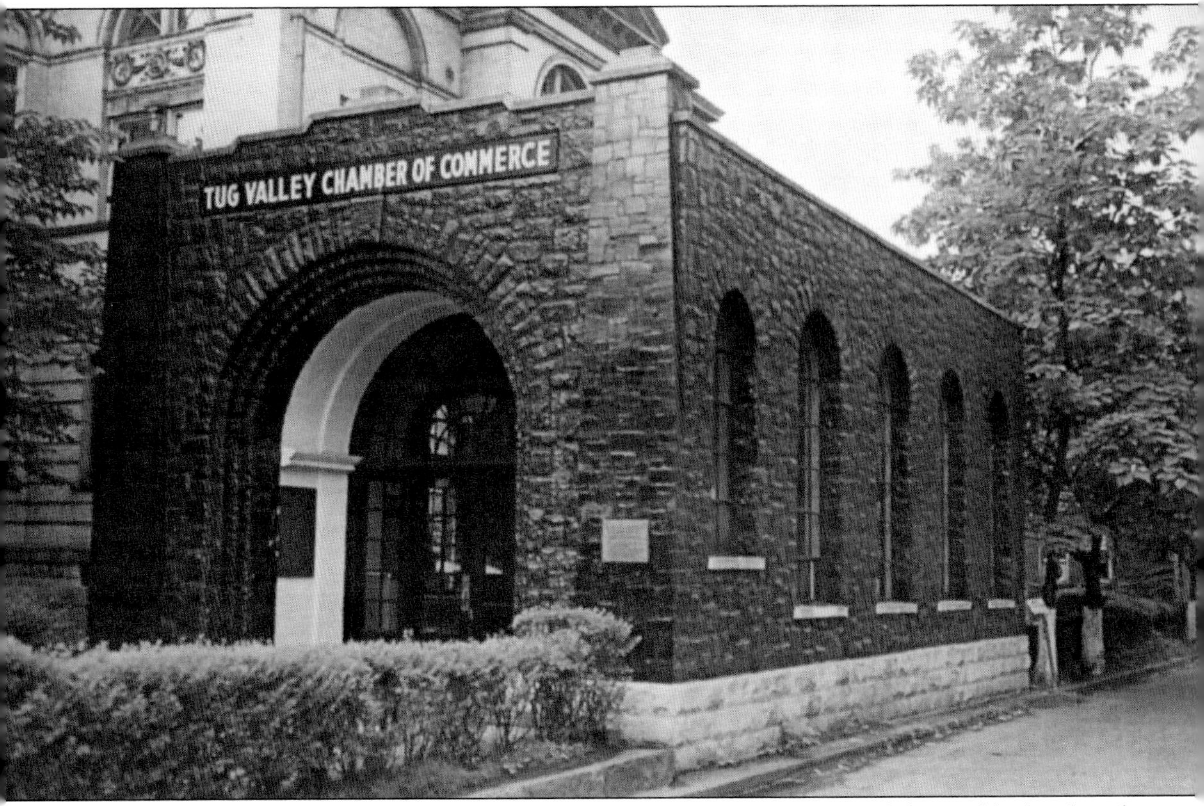

The Coal House was constructed in 1933 with 65 tons of bituminous coal donated by local coal companies. It sits beside the Mingo County Court House in Williamson and for many years has housed the Tug Valley Chamber of Commerce. The Coal House was the idea of O.W. Evans, who was the general superintendent of the fuel mines of the Norfolk & Western Railway. H.T. Hicks, an architect from Welch, designed the coal house. Local businesses and community people contributed materials and labor. The Coal House is listed in the National Register of Historic Places. On October 11, 2010, it was severely damaged on the inside; however, through the determination and efforts of many groups and local residents, it was once again reopened on September 26, 2011. (Courtesy of Andrew Chafin.)

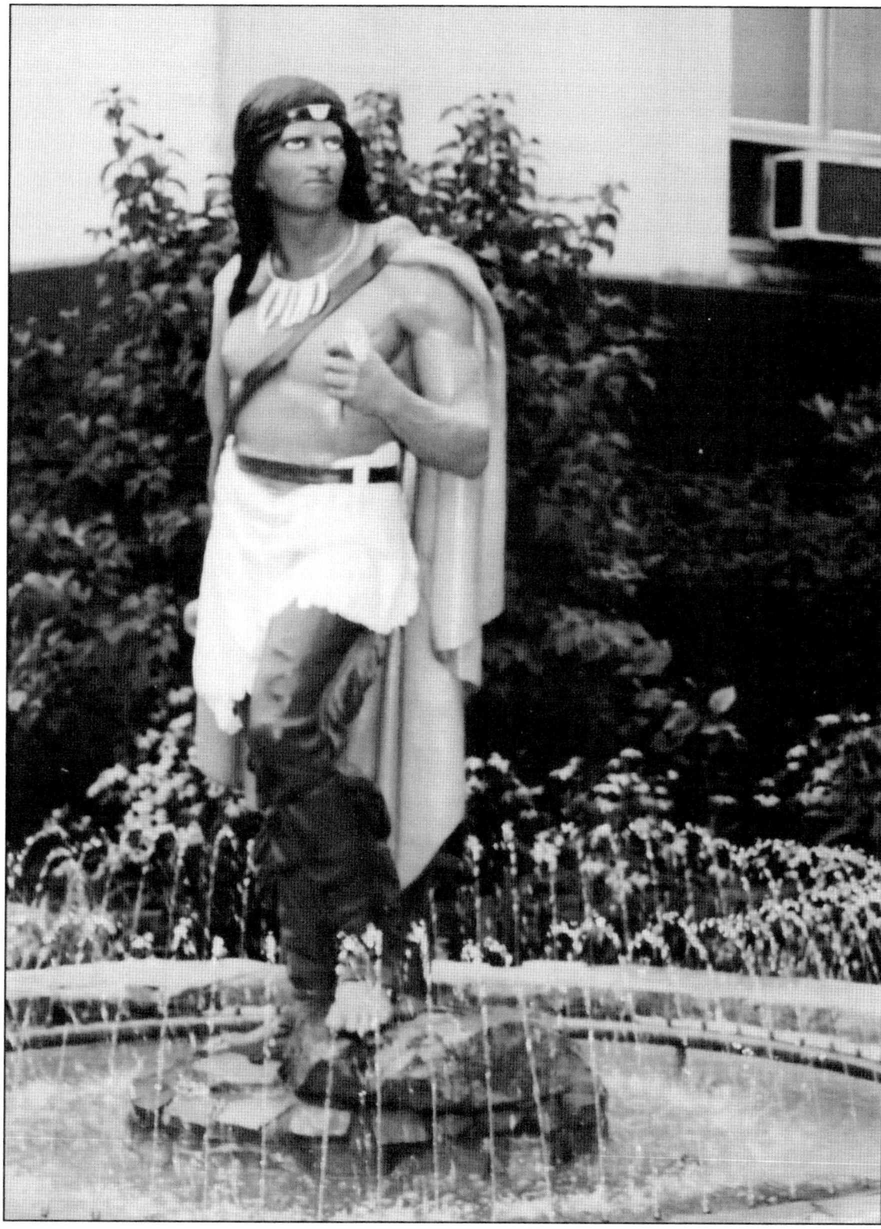

The statue of Chief Logan of the Mingo tribe stands in front of Mingo County Courthouse in Williamson. He was befriended by a Quaker named James Logan and was educated. Due to his bravery, education, and ability to get along with others, he was named chief of the Mingoes. Chief Logan's father, brother, and sister were murdered by a group of white men. Following the massacre, Logan turned from a friend of the whites to a relentless avenger. When Colonel Cresap, whom Chief Logan believed had killed his family, was found innocent, Logan discontinued his attacks on white settlers. When Logan was not present for the peace party held between the governor of Virginia and the chiefs of the tribes, the governor sent for him. He was found in the woods seated on a log with tears rolling down his cheeks. It was said that Logan burst into a beautiful speech: "Such was my love for the whites that my countrymen pointed at me as they passed and said, 'Logan is the friend of the white man.'" (Courtesy of Andrew Chafin.)

Consistent with our mission to preserve history on a local level, this book was printed in South Carolina on American-made paper and manufactured entirely in the United States. Products carrying the accredited Forest Stewardship Council (FSC) label are printed on 100 percent FSC-certified paper.